DAVID OBSERVED

Hebrew Bible Monographs, 5

Series Editors
David J.A. Clines, J. Cheryl Exum, Keith W. Whitelam

Editorial Board
A. Graeme Auld, Marc Brettler, Francis Landy, Hugh S. Pyper,
Stuart D.E. Weeks

DAVID OBSERVED

A KING IN THE EYES OF HIS COURT

Keith Bodner

SHEFFIELD PHOENIX PRESS

2008

Copyright © 2005, 2008 Sheffield Phoenix Press
First published in hardback 2005
First published in paperback 2008

Published by Sheffield Phoenix Press
Department of Biblical Studies, University of Sheffield
Sheffield S10 2TN

www.sheffieldphoenix.com

All rights reserved.
No part of this publication may be reproduced or transmitted in any form or by any means, electronic or mechanical, including photocopying, recording or any information storage or retrieval system, without the publishers' permission in writing.

A CIP catalogue record for this book
is available from the British Library

Typeset by Forthcoming Publications
Printed by Lightning Source

ISBN 978-1-905048-23-6 (hardback)
ISBN 978-1-906055-11-0 (paperback)

CONTENTS

Abbreviations	ix
Acknowledgments	xi

Chapter 1
A SHORT INTRODUCTION 1

Chapter 2
ELIAB AND THE DEUTERONOMIST 10
   1. Scene One: 1 Samuel 16.1-13 13
   2. Scene Two: 1 Samuel 17.23-29 16
   3. Conclusion 22

Chapter 3
REVISITING THE 'COLLUSION AT NOB' IN 1 SAMUEL 21–22 25
   1. Delayed Exposition 1: The Presence of Doeg
   on That Day in Nob (1 Samuel 21.8) 28
   2. Delayed Exposition 2: The Consciousness of Doeg
   on That Day in Nob (1 Samuel 22.9-10) 31
   3. Delayed Exposition 3: The Consciousness of David
   on That Day in Nob (1 Samuel 22.22-23) 35
   4. Conclusion 36

Chapter 4
BAKHTIN'S *PSEUDO-OBJECTIVE MOTIVATION*
AND THE DEMISE OF ABNER 38
   1. A Brief Outline of Bakhtin's Theory 38
   2. The Unleashing of Abner in the House of Saul 42
   3. House Work 44
   4. Who Let the Dog Out? 46
   5. Canine Teeth 47
   6. Reservoir Dogs 52
   7. A Perfect Murder? 56
   8. The Usual Suspects 58
   9. The Latest Opinion Polls 61
   10. Conclusion 62

Chapter 5
NATHAN: PROPHET, POLITICIAN, AND PLAYWRIGHT — 67
  1. Episode 1: 2 Samuel 7.1-17 — 68
  2. Episode 2: 2 Samuel 12.1-15, 24-25 — 70
  3. Episode 3: 1 Kings 1.1-31 — 72
  4. Conclusions — 76

Chapter 6
LAYERS OF AMBIGUITY IN 2 SAMUEL 11.1 — 77
  1. 2 Samuel 11.1: The Overture to a Narrative 'Fraught with Ambiguity' — 78
  2. Do Kings or Messengers 'Go Forth' in 2 Samuel 11.1a? — 80
  3. Why Does David Remain in Jerusalem? — 84
  4. Conclusion — 87

Chapter 7
THE ROYAL CONSCIENCE ACCORDING TO 4QSAM^A — 89
  1. Introduction — 89
  2. A Roof with a View — 90
  3. A Sovereign Soliloquy? — 94
  4. Conclusion — 96

Chapter 8
JOAB AND THE RISKS OF READER-RESPONSE CRITICISM — 98
  1. The Epistle of David (2 Samuel 11.14-15) — 99
  2. Joab as a Reader-Response Critic of the Epistle of David (2 Samuel 11.16-17) — 101
  3. Retrospective: Joab's 'Hermeneutic of Suspicion' in the Abner Affair — 103
  4. Joab's Reply, and his Reading of the Abimelech Narrative (2 Samuel 11.18-22) — 105
  5. David's Interpretation of Joab's Messenger (2 Samuel 11.23-25) — 108
  6. Conclusion — 110

Chapter 9
TWICE-TOLD TALES: ANGER MANAGEMENT AND THE MESSENGER(S) IN 2 SAMUEL 11.22-25 — 112
  1. Introduction — 112
  2. Example A: Elkanah's Caution — 114
  3. Example B: The Gate of Hebron — 115
  4. A Hebrew and a Hellenist: Tales of Two Messengers — 116

Chapter 10
MOTIVES FOR DEFECTION: AHITHOPHEL'S AGENDA IN 2 SAMUEL 15–17   124
1. Introduction   124
2. Conspiracy Theory   125
3. Extreme Measures   127
4. Spy Games   133
5. Suspended Sentence   135
6. Conclusion   137

Chapter 11
SOLOMON'S SUCCESSION AND JACOB'S KNAVERY:
CONNECTIONS BETWEEN GENESIS 27 AND 1 KINGS 1   140
1. Introduction   140
2. Aged Husbands   142
3. Enterprising Mothers   144
4. Younger Sons   146
5. The Sacred Name   147
6. Conclusions   148

Chapter 12
THE SWEARING ISSUE: A CURSORY SURVEY OF OATHS IN 1 KINGS 1–2   153
1. Oath 1: Nathan's 'Reminder' to Bathsheba
   of David's (Purported) Oath Regarding the Succession
   of Solomon (1 Kings 1.5-10)   154
2. Oath 2: Bathsheba's 'Quotation' of David's (Supposed)
   Oath Regarding the Succession of her 'Issue', Solomon
   (1 Kings 1.17-18)   156
3. Oath 3: David's Oath Concerning Solomon,
   Which Includes a 'Self-Quotation' of his (Apparent)
   Earlier Oath (1 Kings 1.29-31)   158
4. Oath 4: Adonijah's Request for an Oath of Amnesty
   and Solomon's Noncompliance (1 Kings 1.50-53)   160
5. Oath 5: David's 'Self-Quotation' of his Oath
   concerning Shimei to Solomon (1 Kings 2.8-9)   162
6. Oath 6: Solomon's Vitriolic and Oath-laden Reaction
   to Adonijah's Bridal Request (through Bathsheba)
   for Abishag (1 Kings 2.23-25)   166
7. Oath 7: Circumlocutions around David's Awkward Oath
   to Shimei, and the Resolution of This 'Cursed' Affair
   (1 Kings 2.42-43)   169
8. Conclusions   173

Bibliography   177
Index of References   191
Index of Authors   196

ABBREVIATIONS

AB	Anchor Bible
ABD	David Noel Freedman (ed.), *The Anchor Bible Dictionary* (New York: Doubleday, 1992)
BDB	Francis Brown, S.R. Driver and Charles A. Briggs, *A Hebrew and English Lexicon of the Old Testament* (Oxford: Clarendon Press, 1907)
Bib	*Biblica*
BibInt	*Biblical Interpretation: A Journal of Contemporary Approaches*
BZAW	Beihefte zur *ZAW*
CBQ	*Catholic Biblical Quarterly*
DJD	Discoveries in the Judaean Desert
ET	English translation
FOTL	The Forms of the Old Testament Literature
GKC	*Gesenius' Hebrew Grammar* (ed. E. Kautzsch, revised and trans. A.E. Cowley; Oxford: Clarendon Press, 1910)
HCOT	Historical Commentary on the Old Testament
HS	*Hebrew Studies*
HSM	Harvard Semitic Monographs
ICC	International Critical Commentary
Int	*Interpretation*
JANES	*Journal of the Ancient Near Eastern Society of Columbia University*
JBL	*Journal of Biblical Literature*
JETS	*Journal of the Evangelical Theological Society*
JNSL	*Journal of Northwest Semitic Languages*
JR	*Journal of Religion*
JSNTSup	*Journal for the Study of the New Testament*, Supplement Series
JSOT	*Journal for the Study of the Old Testament*
JSOTSup	*Journal for the Study of the Old Testament*, Supplement Series
JTS	*Journal of Theological Studies*
KAT	Kommentar zum Alten Testament
KB	Ludwig Koehler and Walter Baumgartner (eds.), *Lexicon in Veteris Testamenti libros* (Leiden: E.J. Brill, 1953)
LXX	Septuagint
MT	Massoretic text
NAB	*New American Bible*
NAC	The New American Commentary
NASB	*New American Standard Bible*
NCB	New Century Bible
NCBC	New Century Bible Commentary
NEB	*New English Bible*
NIB	*The New Interpreter's Bible* (12 vols.; Nashville: Abingdon Press, 1994–98)
NIBC	New International Biblical Commentary
NICOT	New International Commentary on the Old Testament
NIV	New International Version
NIVAC	New International Version Application Commentary

NJB	*New Jerusalem Bible*
NJPS	*Tanakh: The Holy Scriptures: The New JPS Translation according to the Traditional Hebrew Text*
NKJV	New King James Version
NRSV	New Revised Standard Version
OBO	Orbis biblicus et orientalis
OTE	*Old Testament Essays*
OTL	Old Testament Library
OTS	Oudtestamentische Studiën
RSV	Revised Standard Version
SJOT	*Scandinavian Journal of the Old Testament*
TynBul	*Tyndale Bulletin*
VT	*Vetus Testamentum*
VTSup	*Vetus Testamentum*, Supplements
WBC	Word Biblical Commentary
ZAW	*Zeitschrift für die alttestamentliche Wissenschaft*

ACKNOWLEDGMENTS

Just as the Deuteronomistic History has a cast of thousands, it seems that an equally sprawling and diverse number of characters have assisted in the making of this book. Tim Larsen and Duncan Burns were early redactors of the *Ur*-text, and I would like to thank the hall-of-fame triumvirate—Professors Cheryl Exum, David Clines, and Keith Whitelam—for accepting the final form. Some of these chapters previously have been published as articles, so I would extend a word of gratitude to the editors and publishers of the *Journal for the Study of the Old Testament*, *Studies in Religion*, *Ephemerides theologicae lovanienses*, and *Dead Sea Discoveries* for kind permission to use earlier material.

Of the many scholars whose work I draw on, I would like to thank Robert Alter, Lyle Eslinger, Gary Knoppers, Barbara Green, Scott Hahn, John Bergsma, and Robert Polzin—who have read my work or patiently discussed various issues with me. A number of these chapters originated as papers read to the venerable Canadian Society of Biblical Studies, and I would like to express appreciation to various session chairs and generous interlocutors: Ehud Ben Zvi, David Vanderhooft, John Kessler, Glen Taylor, John McLaughlin, Christine Mitchell, Stanley Porter, Rebecca Idestrom, Ellen White, Mark Boda, Tyler Williams, Daniel Miller, Ken Ristau, and Richard Middleton. My church and community have offered encouragement along the way, and included in this great cloud of witnesses are: Jim Dell, David E. Smith, Brian Althouse, Bob McKay, Mike Kwong, Scott Masson, Steve Dempster, Brock Angle, George Sweetman, Jason Lee, Paul Johansen, Seth Crowell, Kelly Bury, Greg and Jen Maillet, and the original Canadian/American Idol, Stanley D. Walters.

My students have been indefatigable in listening to these stories (and my behind-the-times anecdotes!) over and over again—I am grateful for the lively exchange of ideas and reflection on the marvelous intersection of the LORD's grace with our lives. I have been amazed at the spiritual relevance they find, and the messianic anticipations that fill the plot (despite the often scandalous and carnivorous behavior from high and low alike). In new ways my students have shown me that this story is extraordinary, and that we all are players in the drama.

The working title for this book was 'The King and his Court', as a modest tribute to Eddie Feigner, the greatest fastball pitcher who ever lived (sort of like a Shane Warne bowler in cricket). When I was eight years old my father took me to see this four-man team, and on the way home we discussed the possibility of excellence through application and creativity. Still on the familial note, my own wife and kids have journeyed with me from Dan to Beersheba. So, while I would like to give this book to my little clan—Coreen, Evelyn, Victoria, and young Jeff—they have actually given it to me. The least I can do is invoke David's prayer in 2 Sam 7.29a:

וְעַתָּה הוֹאֵל וּבָרֵךְ אֶת־בֵּית עַבְדְּךָ

So now, be pleased and bless the house of your servant.

1

A Short Introduction

The story of David is probably the greatest single narrative representation in antiquity of a human life evolving by slow stages through time, shaped and altered by the pressures of political life, public institutions, family, the impulses of body and spirit, the eventual sad decay of the flesh.[1]

Robert Alter

David lives for us much more immediately, much more fully, than figures far better attested to by history: Caesar, Napoleon...[2]

Gabriel Josipovici

David's personality is complex, elusive, and impenetrable...[3]

Cheryl Exum

Now what have I done?[4]

David

A plethora of scholars, artists, writers, theologians, and other interested readers have pointed to King David as perhaps the most fully-drawn of biblical figures. From his clandestine anointing in 1 Samuel 16 to his deathbed speech in 1 Kings 2, David emerges as a surprising and enigmatic character, richly presented through a legion of narrative situations where the literary resources of dialogue and narrational exposition are memorably exploited. The sheer range of behavior and variety of situations in the David story are impressive. David is by turn: pious, funny, dissembling, feigning madness, attracting women, repelling Saul, captivating the crowd, alone in prayer, seeking oracles, interacting with foreign dignitaries, escaping through a

---

1. R. Alter, *The David Story: A Translation with Commentary of 1 and 2 Samuel* (New York: Norton, 1999), p. ix.
2. G. Josipovici, *The Book of God: A Response to the Bible* (New Haven: Yale University Press, 1988), p. 209.
3. J.C. Exum, *Tragedy and Biblical Narrative: Arrows of the Almighty* (Cambridge: Cambridge University Press, 1992), p. 142.
4. 1 Samuel 17.29: מֶה עָשִׂיתִי עָתָּה. Unless otherwise indicated, translations from the Hebrew text in this book are my own.

window, leaping before the ark, rebuking his servants, hiding in a cave, writing letters, visited by a prophet, violent, dealing with troubled offspring, having dirt thrown on him by an unsympathetic Benjaminite, sneaking into a camp by night, melancholic, fighting giants, writing songs, and monosyllabically lamenting the death of his handsome son. Such variety is augmented by a rich supporting cast in Samuel–Kings, a troupe of characters that have extraordinary breadth and diversity. There are a number of factors, therefore, that contribute to the Davidic complexity: major players in the supporting cast, minor characters at every juncture of the narrative, and even text-critical issues that provide angles to view this biblical king. Such matters are the central interest in this book, as I explore various characters and texts that serve to enrich the narrative and illuminate the personality of David through a host of narrative configurations.

Before the formal introduction of David himself, the reader has a fleeting acquaintance with his older brother and Jesse's firstborn son, Eliab. One guesses that Eliab is tall, handsome, and 'not elected' based on God's words to Samuel: 'Do not gaze toward his appearance or the height of his stature, for I have rejected him' (1 Sam. 16.7). In Chapter 2 I trace the characterization of Eliab over his two appearances in the narrative. I suggest that the two scenes where Eliab appears (1 Sam. 16 and 17) need to be read together, as Eliab's *character zone* contains a pair of 'double-voiced' utterances as defined by Bakhtin: in the first scene of 1 Samuel 16, Eliab is used as an instrument of correction for the prophet Samuel; in the second scene of 1 Samuel 17, Eliab is used as an instrument of correction for the young David. Eliab's words to David in 17.28 seem scathing: 'Why is this you've come down? With whom have you left that little flock in the wilderness? *I'm someone who knows your insolence and the evil in your heart.* Indeed, you've come down in order to see the battle!' A brief survey of secondary literature reveals that most scholars take the words of Eliab at face value, and feel that surely Eliab is wrong in his assessment of David's 'evil heart'. My study of Eliab in Chapter 2 takes a different approach. It is argued in that chapter that Eliab's words are used to sound a warning about the heart of David, a highly nuanced literary figure who will be developed over a long narrative stretch. Moreover, since Eliab is used at a very early point in the narrative to inject a note of caution and a foreshadowing of potential flaws surrounding the heart of David, it is presumably not coincidental that Eliab's speech accents reverberate later in 2 Samuel 11 and 12, the story of David and Bathsheba and the subsequent exposé by Nathan the prophet. I conclude this chapter by suggesting that in the Deuteronomist's grand scheme of things, Eliab plays a role—easily overlooked but nonetheless important—in the overall strategy for characterizing King David.

1. A Short Introduction

After his national triumph over Goliath, sundry military promotions, and acquisition of Saul's daughter Michal, David grows in stature and public acclaim. Such triumphs, however, are somewhat offset as David spends a considerable amount of time avoiding the javelin of his brooding father-in-law and employer, King Saul. For a number of reasons David is successful in eluding Saul, not least because several key allies come to his aid at integral moments during this 'fugitive' period. Included among such allies is Ahimelech, the priest at Nob, to whom David comes in 1 Samuel 21. Traditionally, most commentators have argued that David inveigles Ahimelech, and concocts his story in order to acquire various commodities from the naïve priest. However, Pamela Reis has proffered an alternative hypothesis, and considers the possibility that David and the priest are partners in 'collusion', and extemporaneously formulate a plan for deceiving Doeg the Edomite—Saul's henchman who is lurking in the sanctuary shadows 'on that day'. The strange dialogue between David and the priest has the covert utility of warding Doeg off the scent, and it thus allows David to continue on his journey away from Saul.

In Chapter 3 I suggest that Reis's thesis can be enhanced in a number of ways. First, a key literary technique used by the Deuteronomist in this episode is *delayed exposition*, and much of the plot is developed by means of this technique. A second way in which the 'collusion' idea can be furthered is by seeing Ahimelech's actions unfold within the larger *motif of deceptive alliances* that can be seen to operate within 1 Samuel 19–22, as Ahimelech's conduct is measured beside other characters (e.g. Jonathan and Michal) who contribute to David's escapes from Saul. A third way that the 'collusion' proposal can be enhanced is through the genealogical data of Ahimelech: by means of *delayed exposition* the reader discovers that Ahimelech is part of the doomed line of Eli. As discussed by Gerhard von Rad, there is a 'proclamation and fulfillment' *schema* inherent in the Deuteronomistic History. Ironically, through his pro-David conduct, Ahimelech the priest becomes an instrument in the fulfillment of the prophetic word spoken against his *own house* in 1 Sam. 2.27-36.

A number of chapters in this book draw on the literary criticism of Mikhail Bakhtin, a theorist whose work is becoming increasingly popular as a conversation partner in biblical studies. There is a growing body of commentaries and studies that utilize Bakhtin, and a new section of the Society of Biblical Literature's Annual Meeting is entitled 'Bakhtin and the Biblical Imagination'. In *The Dialogic Imagination*,[5] Bakhtin outlines his notion of *pseudo-objective motivation* by drawing on, among other works, Charles Dickens's *Little Dorrit*. Bakhtin illustrates that *pseudo-objective motivation*

---

5. M.M. Bakhtin, *The Dialogic Imagination: Four Essays* (ed. M. Holquist; Austin: University of Texas Press, 1981).

is a literary technique whereby there is a certain stylization of the narrator's speech: what may look like a typical utterance of the narrator in fact contains the view of 'the crowd', and not the posited 'author's' view at all. Dickens adopts this technique for the purposes of satire and parody, and uses 'official' language to undermine the credibility of the character(s) in question.

After discussing Bakhtin's notion of *pseudo-objective motivation* and surveying his examples from *Little Dorrit*, I suggest that the idea of *pseudo-objective motivation* may help elucidate certain aspects of 2 Samuel 3, an episode that features the assassination of Abner (commander-in-chief of Israel's 'northern alliance') and King David's apparent innocence. Abner, one recalls, is introduced quite early in the narrative, and his future prominence is perhaps anticipated when Saul's uncle (probably Abner's father) implores him, 'Tell me what Samuel said to you' (1 Sam. 10.15). Saul himself questions Abner in 1 Sam. 17.55 by asking, 'Whose son is this, O Abner?' Such a mode of inquiry must serve to foreground David and Abner as rivals, and indeed, later in the story Abner is the recipient of a Davidic catcall in 1 Sam. 26.15: 'Aren't you a man? Who is like you in Israel? Why then have you not kept watch over your lord the king?' Despite this uncomfortable public rebuke of Abner, during Abner's funeral David refers to him in majestic terms: 'Don't you know that a prince and a great one has fallen today?' It is hard to know how to hear such words in light of the previous rivalry, and a number of commentators understand David to be spinning some public relations work here. Especially challenging to interpret is 2 Sam. 3.36-37: 'All the people noticed this, and it was good in their eyes; indeed, everything the king did was good in the eyes of the people. Hence all the people knew, even all Israel, on that day that it was not from the king to cause the death of Abner son of Ner.' Is this the 'author's' opinion of the matter, or, like Dickens, does the Deuteronomist adopt 'official' language to refract the opinion of the crowd 'on that day'? In Chapter 4 I suggest that *pseudo-objective motivation* is a heuristic critical category that is useful to consider while reading 2 Samuel 3.

The dynamic between prophet and king is a significant issue in the larger Deuteronomistic History stretching from Joshua to 2 Kings. As seen in the relationship between Samuel and Saul, there are personal and ideological tensions between the two that surely contribute to Saul's increasing despair and eventual madness. It is an extreme contrast, therefore, when David has barely any contact with Samuel, considering that Saul was so intensely involved with the prophet. There is no decisive evidence to suggest that David takes steps to distance himself from Samuel, but the lack of contact with this principal prophet is telling. David's career, though, is not without prophetic involvement. At several pivotal moments in the story Nathan the prophet appears in the king's presence (invited or otherwise). Chapter 5 examines three episodes where Nathan and David interact: 2 Samuel 7,

2 Samuel 12, and 1 Kings 1. An analysis of Nathan's conduct indicates that he possesses both a political resourcefulness and a literary creativity. The suggestion is made that all three of the 'Nathan narratives' are subtly linked, and when they are read together, a coherent portrait of the prophet emerges. The conclusion is that Nathan is a complex character who is incrementally developed between his initial appearance to deliver the 'dynastic oracle' in 2 Samuel 7 and his final appearance in the narrative of Solomon's accession in 1 Kings 1.

2 Samuel 11 is a momentous chapter in the David narrative, and it is often referred to as the 'turning point' of the whole story. Notably, there are some interesting and reasonably important text-critical issues that emerge from a careful study of the Hebrew text of 2 Samuel 11. Chapters 6 and 7 of this book address a different textual issue in 2 Samuel 11. Chapter 6 is concerned with the opening line of 2 Sam. 11.1, and exploring the layers of ambiguity that surface: 'At the spring of the year, the time when messengers/kings go out, David sent Joab with his officers and all Israel with him, and they ravaged the Ammonites, and besieged Rabbah, but David sat in Jerusalem'. In my analysis, a key issue is: Do messengers (המלאכים) or kings (המלכים) go forth at the turn of the year? As with many text-critical issues, there are plausible arguments either way. But as it stands, I argue that the latent ambiguity of the Hebrew text is a pointed introduction to the layers of *intentional* ambiguity that occupy this very important episode in David's life.

In the same vein, Chapter 7 analyzes another important line early in this episode, 2 Sam. 11.3: 'And David sent and inquired about the woman, and he said, "Is this not Bathsheba, the daughter of Eliam, the wife of Uriah the Hittite?"' By any measure, this query would sting the royal conscience. Yet the subject of this utterance remains unclear: Is it an unspecified messenger who delivers this bold string of questions, or is this the king's own conscience engaging in some 'self-talk'? Further, in this chapter I explore a small variant of 2 Sam. 11.3 attested in 4QSam\u1d43. The MT reads as I have quoted it above, but at the end of the sentence the Qumran text also includes the phrase '…Uriah the Hittite *armor-bearer of Joab*?' Josephus (*Ant.* 7.7.1) also includes the phrase. The additional phrase raises several interpretive issues for the characters of Joab and Uriah in this narrative, as well as 'David's troubled conscience' that emerges. In this chapter, I suggest that 2 Sam. 11.3 merits consideration since so many conflicts in the forthcoming narrative are hinted at here in this genealogical data about Bathsheba.

Throughout the David story, Joab is a far-from-simple character. It is somewhat fitting that Joab does not formally appear on the scene until after David is crowned king in Hebron, but quickly gains a position of narrative prominence during the protracted struggle with the house of Saul. During this transition period and certainly beyond, Joab is a key power-broker in the

Davidic court. Joab frequently disregards or undermines the king's instructions, yet it is possible to argue that his actions are crucial for David's hold on power to continue. Indeed, a conspicuous pattern of 'interpretive license' emerges when Joab's conduct is analyzed through the numerous vicissitudes in the course of the narrative. Such interpretive license is acutely seen in 2 Samuel 11, where Joab receives David's letter outlining the manner in which Uriah is to be killed, yet he proceeds to implement his own exegesis of the king's plan. This act of 'reader-response criticism', as the term is rather playfully appropriated in Chapter 8, is consistent with a number of Joab's other (mis)deeds in the narrative. Joab's reader-response criticism of David's letter concerning Uriah is ultimately motivated by political interests. Commentators have mentioned that he is a man of action rather than words —but he is also an acute 'reader' of the king. While Joab's interpretive license arguably benefits his employer, in the end it would appear that this kind of hermeneutical creativity has lethal consequences for Joab once Solomon enters the scene. After a career spent keeping David in power, Joab's contract is terminated once the new king is on the throne: 'and he was buried in his own house, in the wilderness' (1 Kgs 2.34).

It is a truth universally acknowledged that the text of Samuel presents the scholar with a plethora of textual problems. In my discussion of Joab I footnote an issue at 2 Sam. 11.22-25, where there is a divergence between the MT and the LXX. Joab—having modified the king's orders in the letter—instructs his messenger to deliver the news of Uriah's death to David in Jerusalem. Chapter 9 explores the issue in greater detail. While the messenger certainly appears before the king in both the Hebrew and Greek readings, there are nonetheless substantial differences between the MT and the LXX at this point in the story. The LXX unfolds David's reaction in a manner that is more or less consistent with what Joab suggests might happen: the king's anger will be aroused, and he will invoke the lesson of Abimelech in his wrath. By contrast, the MT contains a virtually opposite delivery of the message and unfolding of events in the royal court. In Chapter 9 I am not concerned with making an attempt to 'recover' a putative original text. As Greenberg has already noted, there can be other advantages to a close reading of divergent texts: '...although there is no logical basis for choosing one version over another when they both make sense, a comparison of the divergences, each read in its own context, provides a powerful heuristic resource that can alert us to the particular focus of each version'.[6] Along such lines, Chapter 9 is a comparison of what I view as two rather different

---

6. M. Greenberg, 'The Use of Ancient Versions for Interpreting the Hebrew Text', in *Congress Volume: Göttingen, 1977* (VTSup, 29; Leiden: E.J. Brill, 1978), pp. 131-48; cited by L. Eslinger, *Kingship of God in Crisis: A Close Reading of 1 Samuel 1–12* (Bible and Literature Series, 10; Sheffield: Almond Press, 1985), p. 437.

texts. Hence, I focus on some of the key differences between the MT and the LXX in this passage, and highlight some of the literary implications that emerge when these textual trajectories are compared. In placing the MT and the LXX side by side, I am primarily interested in the various characterizations that emerge of the messenger, Joab, and David.

Chapter 10 turns to the narrative of 2 Samuel 15–17, where the hirsute Absalom conspires against his father and attempts to seize the throne of Israel. In 2 Samuel 15 Absalom's rebellion gains a key ally when Ahithophel, designated as one of David's senior advisors, joins the forces of Absalom. The reasons behind this defection are obscure in the narrative, and there is no explicit motive stated in the text explaining why Ahithophel would act in this manner toward David. However, Gerhard von Rad has drawn attention to an interesting connection between Bathsheba (with whom David has an affair in 2 Sam. 11) and Ahithophel. As noted above, in 2 Sam. 11.3 Bathsheba is identified as 'the daughter of Eliam'. In 2 Sam. 23.34, Eliam is identified as 'the son of Ahithophel', hence Bathsheba and Ahithophel seem to be close relatives. Chapter 10 surveys the major scenes where Ahithophel appears in 2 Samuel 15–17, and explores this genealogical connection as a possible motive for Ahithophel's defection: he is angry and disillusioned with David after the Bathsheba affair and subsequent murder by proxy of her husband, Uriah the Hittite. David of course marries Bathsheba and brings her to his house at the end of 2 Samuel 11. In the next episode (2 Sam. 12.10), Nathan the prophet declares: 'So now, the sword will never depart from your house'. Consequently, the Ahithophel and Bathsheba connection is explored in light of this prophetic declaration.

Numerous scholars have pointed out connections between the Genesis material and the life of David in the Deuteronomistic History. Chapter 11 explores a further link between these texts, one that surrounds the accession of Solomon. The opening episodes of 1 Kings abound with conspiracy and intrigue, as a variety of agendas intersect in a power struggle for the Davidic kingdom. The aged King David himself is the object of several competing interest groups hoping to fill the vacuum created by his lack of virility and impending death. At the end of 1 Kings 1, Solomon is the candidate placed on the throne of Israel, yet he himself is entirely passive until *after* his coronation. Chapter 11 investigates the manner in which Solomon accedes to his father's throne, and argues that a careful study of various *intertextual allusions* can help the reader to make sense of the curious circumstances that eventually result in Solomon being proclaimed as the king of Israel in 1 Kings 1. In particular, I argue that the accession of Solomon has a number of shared motifs with the 'stolen blessing' of Jacob in Genesis 27. The chapter then concludes with a discussion of the literary and theological significance of this intertextual connection.

The final chapter of the book picks up several themes discussed in the preceding discussion of Solomon's accession. The initial idea for this chapter was inspired by the speech-act theory of language philosopher J.L. Austin, 'How to Do Things with Words'. Among other things, speech-act theory 'treats an utterance as an act performed by a speaker in a context with respect to an addressee'. A speaker's communicative competence is evaluated by a set of 'appropriateness conditions', depending on the circumstances of the address, the nature and attitudes of the participants, and whether the terms can be fulfilled by the speaker. Moreover, Austin makes a primary distinction between two broad types of locutions: *constatives* ('sentences that assert something about a fact or state of affairs and are adjudged to be true or false') and *performatives* ('sentences that are actions that accomplish something, such as questioning, promising, praising and so on'). Thus, in terms of biblical narrative, an oath would be classified as a performative utterance. For Chapter 12, the relevance of this kind of inquiry is that it serves to introduce a parameter of appraisal for a character's speech. This brief consideration of Austin's work is relevant for the opening episodes of 1 Kings, a stretch of narrative that the Deuteronomist could have subtitled, 'How to Do Things with Oaths'. In these scenes there are a wide variety of oaths, all of which somehow involve Solomon: Nathan's instructions to Bathsheba surrounding an alleged oath about her son's prospects for the throne (1.13), Bathsheba's subsequent declaration to David about this same purported oath (1.17), David's 'oath within an oath' concerning the accession of Solomon (1.29), Adonijah's request for an oath and Solomon's noncompliance (1.51-52), David's oath involving Shimei the Benjaminite (2.8) and its sequel (2.42), and the rare instance of a 'double oath' sworn by Solomon with respect to Adonijah (2.23-24). Chapter 12 underscores the point that the *character zone* of Solomon is encompassed by the language of oaths, and argues that attention to the manner in which various personages 'do things with oaths' has implications for issues of characterization in this narrative stretch. Moreover, this final chapter explores the use of oaths as part of the larger story of the transition from the reign of David to the era of Solomon.

Each of these chapters began as lectures in my classes, and most were subsequently presented at professional meetings. Several of the chapters have been published as articles in scholarly journals. The chapters are designed as stand-alone pieces, and my primary audience is students and interested readers wanting a literary angle on various texts in the David story. Only a small percentage of the longer narrative is covered here. There is some overlap among the chapters, but multiple coverage is what I consider a strength of this book. For instance, 1 Kgs 1.11-18 is examined in three chapters. Yet in each of these chapters there is a different perspective: Chapter 5 views the events of 1 Kgs 1.11-18 from the vantage point of Nathan the prophet,

Chapter 11 analyzes the same section in light of Genesis 27, while Chapter 12 focuses on the 'oath' as it relates to the unfolding characterization of Solomon. I am obviously interested in the major moments of David's story—the king *in* his court, as it were—such as 2 Samuel 11 and 1 Kings 1, and that is why these chapters command a fair bit of attention in this book. Likewise, Abner's assassination in 2 Samuel 3 is examined in two separate chapters. In Chapter 4 the emphasis falls on David's perspective, while in Chapter 8 the interest is Joab's involvement. Thus, the same event is observed through different lenses. Such a move is appropriate, I think, since the Deuteronomistic History—the great narrative that spans Joshua to 2 Kings and tells of Israel's experience in the land from outside (Moab) to outside (Babylon)—is a brilliant theological work that rewards much rereading.

2

ELIAB AND THE DEUTERONOMIST

Eliab, the firstborn son of Jesse and David's older brother, formally appears in two scenes within 1 Samuel 16 and 17. The first scene includes 1 Sam. 16.6-7, when Samuel is divinely commanded to anoint one of Jesse's sons. The prophet Samuel erroneously considers Eliab 'the LORD's anointed', and receives a divine commentary on his misperception. The second scene featuring Eliab is situated on the battlefield of 17.23-30, where he engages in a brief dialogue with his brother David.[1] This chapter is a study in the literary representation of Eliab, and an exploration of this character's function within the broader narrative of 1 and 2 Samuel. In both popular exegesis and scholarly commentaries the interpretation of Eliab's words to David in 1 Sam. 17.28 has been somewhat uniform.[2] The most frequent interpretation

---

1. Debate surrounding the compositional history of this stretch of text has been extensive. Overviews can be found in E. Tov, 'The Composition of 1 Samuel 16–18 in the Light of the Septuagint Version', in J.H. Tigay (ed.), *Empirical Modes for Biblical Criticism* (Philadelphia: University of Pennsylvania Press, 1985), pp. 97-130, and J. Lust, 'The Story of David and Goliath in Hebrew and Greek', *ETL* 59 (1983), pp. 5-25. Cf. some of the standard commentaries: H.P. Smith, *A Critical and Exegetical Commentary on the Books of Samuel* (ICC; Edinburgh: T. & T. Clark, 1899), pp. 143-59; J. Mauchline, *First and Second Samuel* (NCB; London: Oliphants, 1971), pp. 128-34; H.W. Hertzberg, *1 and 2 Samuel* (trans. J.S. Bowden; OTL; Philadelphia: Westminster Press, 1964), pp. 135-51. See also A.G. Auld and C.Y.S. Ho, 'The Making of David and Goliath', *JSOT* 56 (1992), pp. 19-39; D. Barthélemy, D.W. Gooding, J. Lust, and E. Tov (eds.), *The Story of David and Goliath: Textual and Literary Criticism* (OBO, 73; Freiburg: Editions Universitaires Fribourg; Göttingen: Vandenhoeck & Ruprecht, 1986).

2. See, e.g., J.P. Fokkelman, *Narrative Art and Poetry in the Books of Samuel*. II. *The Crossing Fates* (Assen: Van Gorcum, 1986), p. 163: 'This attack [Eliab's speech of 17.28], however, reveals that he is already on the defensive; he really feels inferior. No wonder he cannot tolerate the idea that this kid should see the general paralysis and, particularly, the failure of his three "big" brothers. Eliab is in fact really afraid of David's "seeing the war" and he really does not know what else to do than shout down his own feelings of anxiety and impotence vis-à-vis Goliath and his shame at his own failings.' Cf. B.C. Birch, 'The First and Second Books of Samuel', in *NIB*, II, pp. 947-1383 (1111):

of his speech is that it represents an older brother's embarrassment and jealousy at a younger brother's show of courage in the midst of military hostility. Moreover, the older brother's envy is correspondingly heightened because he was passed over in the anointing, and the younger was chosen. Although this interpretation has an obvious plausibility, bearing in mind the sophistication of the Deuteronomist's narrative enterprise in Samuel–Kings, perhaps there are other alternatives.[3]

This chapter will analyze Eliab's two appearances in the narratives of 1 Samuel 16 and 17 and argue several main points. First, from a literary perspective, Eliab has an important role in terms of the indirect characterizations of Samuel and David. Utilizing the theoretical work of Mikhail Bakhtin, I would contend that Eliab's character zone contains a pair of double-voiced utterances.[4] Hence, Eliab's representation in the narrative

---

'In what almost seems a distraction from the main story, Eliab, the oldest son of Jesse, overhears his young brother quizzing soldiers about royal rewards, and his reaction seems typical of older brothers to kid brothers (v. 28). He is angry; he overreacts; he accuses David of abandoning his responsibilities with the sheep; he labels David as presumptuous and evil-hearted; he accuses David of boyish voyeurism, just showing up to gawk at the battle.' See M. Garsiel, *The First Book of Samuel: A Literary Study of Comparative Structures, Analogies and Parallels* (Ramat-Gan: Revivim, 1985), p. 109: 'The incident of Eliab's rebuke of David also constitutes a difficulty. Eliab, his eldest brother, berates him for leaving his flock in order to view the battle (17.28-29). This attitude to David seems incomprehensible if he has been anointed as king in front of his brothers (16.13).'

3. The final form of the MT is assumed here, and the conventional term 'Deuteronomist' is employed as a synonym for 'author'. The interest here is not on the putative sources or theories of redaction, but rather on how the Deuteronomist uses Eliab as a narrative device. Notwithstanding the present debate surrounding Noth's articulation of the 'Deuteronomistic History' (as evidenced in recent works such as L.S. Schearing and S.L. McKenzie [eds.], *Those Elusive Deuteronomists: The Phenomenon of Pan-Deuteronomism* [JSOTSup, 268; Sheffield: Sheffield Academic Press, 1999]; R.F. Person, *The Deuteronomic School: History, Social Setting, and Literature* [Studies in Biblical Literature, 2; Atlanta: Scholars Press, 2002]), retaining the term 'Deuteronomist' for the implied author is heuristically used 'to designate that imagined personification of a combination of literary features that seem to constitute the literary composition of the Deuteronomic History' (R. Polzin, *Moses and the Deuteronomist: A Literary Study of the Deuteronomic History*. I. *Deuteronomy, Joshua, Judges* [Bloomington: Indiana University Press, repr., 1993 (1980)], p. 18).

4. Both 'double-voiced discourse' and 'character zone' are terms from Bakhtin. Double-voiced discourse is discussed below; for a definition of character zone, see Bakhtin, *The Dialogic Imagination*, p. 434, where a character zone is described as both the narrative territory occupied by a character and also the sphere of influence which surrounds any given figure. The character of Eli in 1 Sam. 1 provides an example, as Polzin describes: 'When the story begins in verse 9, we are immediately introduced to Eli, who is "sitting on the seat" in the temple. The narrator uses words here that are "double-voiced", and give us our first indication of the character zone surrounding Eli: he is

affords a useful opportunity to probe the double-voiced capabilities of direct discourse in Hebrew prose.[5] Furthermore, the contention of this chapter is that Eliab's presence in 1 Samuel 17 has to be read in terms of *dialogue* with David. Eliab's indictment in 17.28 is serious: he is accusing David of having an 'evil heart'. Many commentators, it would appear, suspect Eliab of holding a grudge against his younger brother, and hence this arraignment stems from resentfulness of David's anointing, David's audacity on the battlefield, or both. However, the question in this chapter involves the particular speech accents of Eliab's accusation, and whether Eliab's description of David has any literary effect later in the narrative. What if, in other words, Eliab is being used by the Deuteronomist to reveal another side of David at this very early point in his career? David is a multifaceted character, and Eliab, I would suggest, is an underrated element in the framing of David's narrative complexity. David's rejoinder to Eliab in 1 Sam. 17.29, 'What have I done now…?', is a phrase that David uses repeatedly in the story. Thus, Eliab's question and David's answer have a role in the larger narrative consecution. As Polzin notes, 'The Deuteronomist surrounded the *character zone* of David in 1 Samuel with a series of questions that follow him throughout his career'.[6] I am arguing that Eliab is an important element in the configuration of David, foreshadowing a host of ambiguities and inherent divisions within David's personal and political lives. It is all the more significant that Eliab's two scenes both involve 'matters of the heart', as Eliab is used by the Deuteronomist to signal a warning sign about David's problematic heart.

presented as a *royal figure* as well as a priest' (R. Polzin, *Samuel and the Deuteronomist: A Literary Study of the Deuteronomic History*. II. *1 Samuel* [Bloomington: Indiana University Press, repr., 1993 (1989)], p. 23).

5. While this article is not a Bakhtinian study as such, it is argued here that applying some of Bakhtin's insights is useful for making sense of how the Deuteronomist configures Eliab as a character in this narrative. Moreover, this chapter attempts to build on the work of R. Polzin and others in terms of using Bakhtin within biblical studies. Among the numerous recent examples of such an enterprise, in addition to other works cited below, see C.A. Newsom, 'Bakhtin, the Bible, and Dialogic Truth', *JR* 76 (1996), pp. 290-306, and 'The Book of Job as Polyphonic Text', *JSOT* 26.3 (2002), pp. 87-108; H.C. White, 'The Trace of the Author in the Text', *Semeia* 71 (1995), pp. 45-64; S. Sykes, 'Time and Space in Haggai–Zechariah 1–8: A Bakhtinian Analysis of a Prophetic Chronicle', *JSOT* 76 (1997), pp. 97-124; D.T. Olson, 'Biblical Theology as Provisional Monologization: A Dialogue with Childs, Brueggemann, and Bakhtin', *BibInt* 6 (1998), pp. 162-80; L.J.M. Claassens, 'Biblical Theology as Dialogue: Continuing the Conversation on Mikhail Bakhtin and Biblical Theology', *JBL* 122 (2003), pp. 127-44. For a study that includes discussion of Bakhtin's notion of intertextuality, see P. Tull, 'Intertextuality and the Hebrew Scriptures', *Currents in Research: Biblical Studies* 8 (2000), pp. 59-90.

6. R. Polzin, *David and the Deuteronomist: A Literary Study of the Deuteronomic History*. III. *2 Samuel* (Bloomington: Indiana University Press, 1993), p. 85 (italics in original).

1. *Scene One: 1 Samuel 16.1-13*

One of the more comprehensive treatments of Eliab's characterization in 1 Samuel 16 is undertaken by J.P. Fokkelman.[7] Fokkelman points out that the key figure in vv. 1-11 is the prophet Samuel himself, and in line with a number of recent studies of the prophet's characterization,[8] argues that these narrative moments do not present Samuel in the most flattering light. The narrative of 1 Samuel 16 commences with the divine imperative to the prophet, 'Fill your horn with oil, and go; I am sending you to Jesse the Bethlehemite, for I have seen among his sons a king for me' (16.1). Samuel is hesitant, though, and seemingly unwilling to carry out the divine directive. The LORD then designs a pretext for Samuel, commanding him to assemble a sacrificial meal where he is to invite Jesse, 'and you will anoint for me the one whom I say to you' (16.3). As the narrative unfolds, the prophet is not only somewhat disobedient, but also presumptuous.[9] He invites Jesse and his sons to the sacrifice, 'and when they came, he saw Eliab, and said (ויאמר), "Surely, before the LORD is his anointed one!"' (16.6).[10] This presumption is not aligned with the previous divine imperative, 'and you will anoint for me the one whom I say to you', and consequently occasions an intriguing divine oration. The prophet receives a lengthy tutorial, worded as yet another imperative, as the LORD says to Samuel: 'Do not gaze upon his appearance or the height of his stature, for I have rejected him. Indeed, not as humanity

---

7. Fokkelman, *The Crossing Fates*, pp. 117-33.

8. For example, D.M. Gunn, *The Fate of King Saul* (JSOTSup, 14; Sheffield: Almond Press, 1985); Eslinger, *Kingship of God in Crisis*; *idem*, 'A Change of Heart: 1 Samuel 16', in L. Eslinger and G. Taylor (eds.), *Ascribe to the Lord: Biblical and Other Studies in Memory of Peter C. Craigie* (JSOTSup, 67; Sheffield: JSOT Press, 1988), pp. 341-61; W. Brueggemann, *First and Second Samuel* (Interpretation; Louisville, KY: John Knox Press, 1990); Polzin, *Samuel and the Deuteronomist*; Alter, *The David Story*. Alternatively, see V.P. Long, *The Reign and Rejection of King Saul: A Case for Literary and Theological Coherence* (Atlanta, GA: Scholars Press, 1989); R. Rendtorff, 'Samuel the Prophet: A Link between Moses and the Kings', in C.A. Evans and S. Talmon (eds.), *The Quest for Context and Meaning: Studies in Biblical Intertextuality in Honor of James A. Sanders* (Leiden: E.J. Brill, 1997), pp. 27-36.

9. Cf. M. Kessler, 'Narrative Technique in 1 Sm 16, 1-13', *CBQ* 32 (1970), pp. 543-54. See also P.D. Miscall (*1 Samuel: A Literary Reading* [Bloomington: Indiana University Press, 1988], p. 115), who refers to this scene as 'the call narrative of Samuel'. Polzin (*Samuel and the Deuteronomist*, p. 153) notes that this scene 'constitutes the second element of a kind of authorial *inclusio* bracketing the prophetic career of Samuel', as there are a host of intriguing connections with 1 Sam. 3—the first 'call narrative of Samuel'.

10. Cf. M. Sternberg, *The Poetics of Biblical Narrative: Ideological Literature and the Drama of Reading* (Bloomington: Indiana University Press, 1985), p. 97: 'Considering the ambiguity of the biblical "said" [אמר] between thought and speech, he [Samuel] may well have announced his verdict, only to retract it the next moment'.

sees—for humanity sees according to the eyes, but the LORD sees according to the heart'.[11] It should be stressed that this comment needs to be read as an open-ended critique, certainly directed toward the prophet himself, but it is also, as is suggested below, a double-voiced utterance that carries considerable thematic weight. Notably, Samuel is not presented as speaking immediately after this. The narrator simply records Jesse as 'passing' his sons before the prophet, who says 'not chosen' at various intervals, until finally the youngest son is retrieved from tending the flock, and anointed 'in the midst of his brothers' (16.13).

In this passage, the inevitable comparisons between Eliab and Saul (height, good looks, and divine rejection) make it tempting for exegetes to understand Eliab as a second Saul.[12] Indeed, Samuel himself makes this mistake, and equates a handsome appearance and imposing physical stature as the necessary prerequisites for a king. The feelings of Eliab, though, are not presented in the narrative; his interior life is opaque at this point. While one can speculate that he might have been embittered by Samuel's rejection (and by extension, God's), there is no narrative anchor for this supposition. Antithetically, one could argue (based on the Saul model) that Eliab may have not desired the kingship, just as Saul did his best to avoid it. Saul is pictured as hesitant to disclose to his uncle 'the matter of the kingship', and is 'hiding among the baggage' when the lots are cast in 1 Samuel 10. So, simply because a young man is tall and handsome, it does not necessarily follow that he harbors royal ambitions. The point here is that the text is entirely silent on the matter of Eliab's feelings, and, like the prophet, readers should be cautious about being led astray by appearances.[13]

---

11. The MT of 1 Sam. 16.7 (כי לא אשר יראה האדם כי האדם יראה לעינים ויהוה יראה ללבב) has generated considerable scholarly discussion, and some textual critics have contended that a proper noun appears to have been omitted. See, e.g., NRSV: '...for the LORD does not see as mortals see; they look on the outward appearance, but the LORD looks on the heart'; cf. Mauchline, *First and Second Samuel*, p. 129: 'In 7b the longer text preserved by LXX and indicated by the line space available in 4QSam^b should be accepted: "for not as man sees does God see; man looks on the outward appearance while the LORD looks on the heart"'. C.R. Fontaine (*Traditional Sayings in the Old Testament: A Contextual Study* [Bible and Literature Series, 5; Sheffield: Almond Press, 1982], pp. 95-108) has analyzed this utterance as a 'proverbial saying', which in its context serves 'to suggest that there is more to David's election than meets the human eye' (p. 108). Given Polzin's observations on the various 'surface adulations' of David by a host of members of the *dramatis personae*, one could argue that there is more to David's characterization than meets the public eye as well (cf. *David and the Deuteronomist*, p. 127).

12. Cf. Eslinger, 'A Change of Heart', pp. 346-47.

13. The irony of David being described as 'beautiful-eyed and good of appearance' (יפה עינים וטוב ראי) is acute. Sternberg (*The Poetics of Biblical Narrative*, pp. 354-64) discusses at length the motif of 'good looks' in the books of Samuel, and the complex theme of wariness in terms of both outward appearance and matters of the heart.

2. Eliab and the Deuteronomist

For this chapter, there are two issues that emerge from the 1 Samuel 16 narrative. First, as a literary character, Eliab is primarily used as an instrument of correction. In the overall narrative design, the Eliab incident functions as an occasion whereby God can castigate his prophet and provide an alternative to Samuel's immediate horizon of understanding.[14] A predominant feature of Eliab's role, therefore, is the indirect characterization of another figure, in this case the prophet Samuel. A second key point which emerges pertains to the quality of the divine remonstrance ('for humanity sees according to the eyes, but the LORD sees according to the heart'), direct speech which is profoundly 'double-voiced'. As a definition of a double-voiced word or statement, Robert Polzin provides this quotation from literary theorist Mikhail Bakhtin:

> an utterance that belongs, by its grammatical (syntactic) and compositional markers, to a single speaker, but that actually contains mixed within it two utterances, two speech manners, two styles, two 'languages', two semantic and axiological belief systems... There is no formal—compositional and syntactic—boundary between these utterances, styles, languages, belief systems; the division of voices and languages takes place within the limits of a single syntactic whole, often within the limits of a single sentence. It frequently happens that even one and the same word will belong simultaneously to two languages, two belief-systems that intersect in a hybrid construction—and consequently the word has two contradictory meanings, two accents.[15]

For direct discourse to be double-voiced, then, there are at least two levels of meaning: one meaning in the immediate context that the speakers and hearers readily understand, and a second meaning that is directed toward a larger theme or ideological component of the author's literary work: 'The speech of a character within a text always represents the overlay of (at least) two different dialogic situations in the form of words—the dialogue between characters and the dialogue between author and reader. In Bakhtin's terminology, these words are "double-voiced".'[16] In a recent monograph on the

---

14. As Fokkelman persuasively intones, 'The man who in Saul's hearing had so hammered home the theme "listen to the voice of God" has forgotten this auditory guideline and allows himself to be dragged along by the force of visual impressions, and by the conditioning of the mind, which has to assimilate the sensorial details' (*The Crossing Fates*, p. 120). In my view, this is part of the theme advanced by the divine *double-voiced* utterance of 1 Sam. 16.7.

15. Polzin, *Samuel and the Deuteronomist*, p. 117, quoting Bakhtin, *The Dialogic Imagination*, p. 305. This present chapter is less interested in psychological assessments of Eliab, and more interested in how Eliab is used by the Deuteronomist as a literary device. Hence, Bakhtin provides a useful methodological angle since he argues for an analysis of *representation*, rather than a purely mimetic appraisal of character.

16. H.S. Pyper, *David as Reader: 2 Samuel 12.1-15 and the Poetics of Fatherhood* (Biblical Interpretation Series, 23; Leiden: E.J. Brill, 1996), p. 69.

implications for Bakhtin's work within the discipline of biblical studies, Barbara Green explains that according to Bakhtin, double-voicedness involves 'a specific engagement of two voices in a single utterance'.[17] Both Green and Polzin would opine that biblical narrative in general and 1 Samuel in particular contain numerous instances of double-voiced discourse. In light of this, one could argue that 1 Sam. 16.7 ('for humanity sees according to the eyes, but the LORD sees according to the heart') is a prime example of a double-voiced utterance. On the one hand, this divine statement intimates that a person's inner nature is more important than the normal human signs of success and means of victory. On the other hand (or rather, at the same time), it could be suggested that God's words have an 'authorial' accent—they become a thematic vehicle in the narrative, and serve to undermine or destabilize the notion of Samuel as an impartial prophet and kingmaker in a reader's mind.[18] To summarize, 'We find here in God's words a *hybrid construction*, in which two accents sound—one God's and another the author's. Even as we hear the LORD contrasting Eliab's physical stature with the reality of divine rejection, we also hear the author contrasting Samuel's prophetic reputation with the reality of divine evaluation.'[19] My contention is that just as Eliab is used by the Deuteronomist to show a problematic side to Samuel the prophet, by extension he is the means of illustrating another side of David at the outset of the young leader's career and his first instance of direct speech in the narrative.[20] If, therefore, the character zone of Eliab in 1 Samuel 16 is used both as an instrument of correction, and to provide an occasion for a 'double-voiced' utterance in the narrative, then a reader may anticipate this trend to continue in Eliab's next appearance in ch. 17.

2. *Scene Two: 1 Samuel 17.23-29*

Eliab's next and final scene in the narrative occurs in 1 Samuel 17. The context is the battle with the Philistines, where three of Jesse's sons (including Eliab) are fighting. The irony, of course, is they are not fighting, but rather

---

17. B. Green, *Mikhail Bakhtin and Biblical Scholarship: An Introduction* (Atlanta: Society of Biblical Literature, 2000), p. 35.

18. In this instance, the rebuke is readily apparent in the language itself: the prophet is disciplined for not operating according to God's instruction, and placing his own (intrinsically human) perceptions above the divine.

19. Polzin, *Samuel and the Deuteronomist*, p. 155.

20. For example, L.G. Perdue ('"Is there Anyone Left of the House of Saul...?" Ambiguity and the Characterization of David in the Succession Narrative', *JSOT* 30 [1984], pp. 67-84) has earlier discussed the latent ambiguities in David's narrative presentation. My suggestion here is that such ambiguities are unfolded at the earliest points in the future king's career.

2. Eliab and the Deuteronomist

are immobilized by the image and words of the Philistine champion. David has also been sent by Jesse to deliver provisions to his brothers and their captain, and is instructed by his father to see if there is 'peace' with them and to bring back a pledge of their safety.[21] David duly inquires if there is 'peace' to his brothers, and as he continues speaking with them, Goliath emerges:

> As he talked with them, the champion, the Philistine of Gath, Goliath by name, came up out of the ranks of the Philistines, and spoke the same words as before. And David heard him. All the Israelites, when they saw the man, fled from him and were very much afraid. The Israelites said, 'Have you seen this man who has come up? Surely he has come up to defy Israel. The king will greatly enrich the man who kills him, and will give him his daughter and make his family free in Israel'. David said to the men who stood by him, 'What shall be done for the man who kills this Philistine, and takes away the reproach from Israel? For who is this uncircumcised Philistine that he should defy the armies of the living God?' The people answered him in the same way, 'So shall it be done for the man who kills him'. (1 Sam. 17.23-27 NRSV)

In 17.26, David's first moment of direct speech in the narrative occurs. According to a basic principle of Hebrew narrative, a character's first words often can provide 'a defining moment of characterization'.[22] Since David is one of the central personalities of the Hebrew Bible, this rule-of-thumb would surely apply. The context of David's first words, as the otherwise redundant narration of 17.25 makes clear, is the context of reward, and the delineation of dividends that will be heaped upon the successful soldier is unequivocal. David's first words, though, reiterate this reward theme that he has just heard moments earlier, as he asks, 'What will be done for the man who kills this Philistine...?' (v. 26). There are two halves to this opening

---

21. Cf. the discussion of this episode by M. George, 'Constructing Identity in 1 Sam. 17', *BibInt* 7 (1998), pp. 389-412.

22. Alter, *The David Story*, p. 105: '"And David said..., 'What will be done for the man?'" These are David's first recorded words in the narrative—usually, in biblical narrative convention, a defining moment of characterization. His first words express his wanting to know what will be gained—implicitly in political terms—by the man who defeats Goliath. The inquiry about personal profit is then immediately balanced (or covered up) by the patriotic pronouncement "who is this uncircumcised Philistine that he should insult the battle lines of the living God?" David has, of course, just heard one of the troops stipulate the reward for vanquishing the Philistine, but he wants to be perfectly sure before he makes his move, and so he asks for the details to be repeated.' In contrast to this final question about why David wants the details repeated, I would argue that it is for two reasons. First, from David's point of view, to guarantee publicly the terms and substance of the reward. Second, from the author's point of view, to underscore that reward and political advantage are a very tangible aspect of David's willingness to enter into hand-to-hand combat.

speech of David: the first half addresses the human sphere of reward and political advantage, while the second half emphasizes the theological and patriotic side of the equation.[23] Since at the end of his speech the people answer him 'in the same way, "So shall it be done to the man who kills him"', it is evident that they interpret his words according to the reward scheme that they have previously outlined. It may be that David already is aware of the compensation package on offer, but seeks to have it publicly emphasized 'for the record'. Notably, this kind of posturing occurs later in the betrothal scenes with King Saul (1 Sam. 18.17-29). So, while David's speech has a certain theological freight in contrast to the army's paralysis in battle, the issue of the reward is equally pointed. It is at this crucial narrative moment that David's brother Eliab is strategically afforded his first (and only) portion of direct speech:

> His eldest brother Eliab heard him talking to the men; and Eliab's anger was kindled against David. He said, 'Why have you come down? With whom have you left those few sheep in the wilderness? I know your presumption and the evil of your heart; for you have come down just to see the battle'. David said, 'What have I done now? It was only a question'. He turned away from him toward another and spoke in the same way; and the people answered him again as before. (17.28-30 NRSV)

Eliab's words have several rhetorical dimensions.[24] He commences by asking two questions, the answers to which, presumably, he knows since David has

---

23. Cf. Polzin, *David and the Deuteronomist*, p. 91: 'From the moment David enters the picture, he comes across as someone who is as much self-serving as God-fearing. The very first words we hear from him immediately establish this feature of his character.' These two sides of David—the political and military leader, and the one who has an uncommon theological vision—remain in tension throughout his narrative life, even to his final speech at the end of his life to his son Solomon. In that speech (1 Kgs 2.2-9), these two poles of political and religious life are chiastically inverted: he commences with a long theological discourse to Solomon, and concludes with the most pragmatic of political advice. Garsiel (*The First Book of Samuel*, p. 116) observes that 'this duality' in David is also apparent in his dialogue with Saul in 1 Sam. 17.32-37.

24. Polzin (*Samuel and the Deuteronomist*, p. 168) comments on the dialogue between Eliab and David in relation to the surrounding context: 'Between these two sides of the dialogue occurs the middle ground of David's conversation with Eliab, and it too is constructed along a question–answer pattern, but one even more complex than those surrounding it. First Eliab asks David two questions (v. 28), and then David answers him with two questions (v. 29). But the stylization goes deeper: just as Eliab's discourse itself contains the answer to one of his questions ("Why have you come down?... You have come down to see the battle", v. 28), so also David's response equivalently contains the answer to one of his own questions ("Is it not [הֲלוֹא] a word?" means "Is it not a word? Yes, it is").' Cf. Garsiel's discussion (*The First Book of Samuel*, p. 115) on Eliab and Saul's physical statures, which would make them more likely candidates for battling Goliath. Garsiel comments, 'The reader must necessarily wonder why the "big" and "tall"

already been conversing with his brothers (17.22-23). This indicates that the opening questions are 'public' and act as an overture to a lecture of correction. Since he does not wait for a reply, they are framed in such a way as to create a sense of occasion. Again, traditional exegesis states that these are the words of a jealous older brother, as maintained by Fokkelman: 'Eliab's intervention is an obstacle to the sub-plot (David on his way to Saul) and in the composition of the scene-part it is the negative counterpart of v. 23a, David's interest in his brothers' welfare as a positive pole at the beginning'.[25] From a literary standpoint, given that they follow closely behind David's first direct speech, these words are significant for David's characterization. Eliab claims to 'know' David intimately, reinforced by the assertive Hebrew syntax 'I *myself* know (אני ידעתי) your conceit', where an independent personal pronoun is used with a first common singular verb.[26] As Alter notes, 'The relative clause here reflects the special emphasis on the Hebrew first-person pronoun *'ani*, which ordinarily would not be used because the verb that follows it, *yada'ti*, has a first-person ending'—hence his translation, 'I'm the one who knows...'[27] As an older brother, the possibility exists that he does have a measure of insight into David's personality. There is clearly a measure of hyperbole in the words, as the reference to 'those few sheep' reveals. While this indicates that not everything in his speech is to be taken at face value, it also enhances the point about the need for caution. David is on the threshold of entering the national stage of Israel, and his brother is warning him to pay close attention to matters of the heart. The note of caution is intensified as Eliab's words occur immediately after David's inquiry about rewards and political advancement. On the one hand, it may be that he fully supports his brother's anointed claim to the throne of Israel, and thus Eliab proclaims a public warning. Rather than a jealous older brother, he may well have David's best interests in mind, and offers what he

---

Eliab (see 16.7) does not accept the challenge himself'. This is a natural question, and it is entirely possible that Eliab is angry at David for reasons of jealousy that Garsiel and others posit. Nonetheless, in this chapter I am suggesting that Eliab's words have a dramatic irony that transcends the present context, and hence they need to be left unfinalized at this moment in the story.

25. Fokkelman, *The Crossing Fates*, p. 161. In P.D. Miscall's study of this passage (*The Workings of Old Testament Narrative* [Semeia Studies; Philadelphia: Fortress Press; Chico, CA: Scholars Press, 1983], pp. 62-67), he notes the broader themes of 'knowledge' and 'heart' and how Eliab's words provide an intriguing point of intersection.

26. Cf. the translations of various commentators, such as P.K. McCarter, *I Samuel: A New Translation with Introduction, Notes, and Commentary* (AB, 8; Garden City, NY: Doubleday, 1980), p. 300, '*I* know your impudence and your naughty scheme', and R.W. Klein, *1 Samuel* (WBC, 10; Waco, TX: Word Books, 1983), p. 169, 'I know your arrogance and your bad intentions'.

27. Alter, *The David Story*, p. 106.

deems wise counsel.²⁸ On the other hand, I am not advocating that Eliab's words be read sympathetically or with a positive spin; rather, in this chapter I am stressing that Eliab's divine rejection in 1 Samuel 16 for the office of kingship should not automatically be deemed the reason for his anger toward David in 1 Samuel 17. Eliab may well be angry, jealous and embarrassed, but his mood or feelings, it seems to me, are far less important than the *content of his speech*, the echoes of which are heard beyond the context of 1 Samuel 17.

Thus, I would suggest that Eliab's speech is a double-voiced utterance, meaning that in these words the distinctive accent of the Deuteronomist can be heard. The narrative timing of this double-voiced speech is precise: directly following David's opening words in the narrative the author allows a voice of warning, implying that while this character (David) may be a hero, even a hero with a 'heart after God', the ensuing portrait is going to be intricate, rich in tension, and even paradox. Through the words of Eliab, the reader receives a signal that the characterization of David will not be entirely straightforward, and that his personality will be subject to rigorous scrutiny. This speech, then, operates as a larger *voice of conscience*, the accents of which will be heard again as the narrative of David continues.²⁹ Indeed, recent literary treatments of 1 and 2 Samuel have evaluated the portrait of David as artfully complex. For example, M.J. Steussy's study certainly outlines the traditional notion of David's heroic innocence as a man 'after God's own heart': yet her study also discusses at length a number of more troubling episodes in David's life which illustrate that there is more to this oft-quoted phrase than meets the eye.³⁰ At this early moment in David's public

28. The Chronicler (1 Chron 27.18) seems to regard 'Elihu' as a leader in Judah. Since the LXX reads Ελιαβ at this point, many commentators view this as a reference to Eliab. Note the discussions of S. Japhet, *I and II Chronicles* (OTL; Louisville, KY: Westminster/John Knox Press, 1993), p. 477, and W. Johnstone, *1 and 2 Chronicles*. I. *1 Chronicles–2 Chronicles 9: Israel's Place Among the Nations* (JSOTSup, 253; Sheffield: Sheffield Academic Press, 1997), p. 269. Elsewhere in 1 Samuel (e.g. 22.1-4) there are no hints of fraternal hostility.

29. As the succinct discussion of the issue by Smith (*A Critical and Exegetical Commentary on the Books of Samuel*, p. 159) illustrates, David's response to Eliab's speech (מה עשיתי עתה הלוא דבר הוא) has elicited a variety of translations. It is possible that David is intentionally ambivalent here. If David is responding in a somewhat cavalier manner, it may indicate that he is not taking this advice of his older brother with a great deal of seriousness. This is of great consequence, since later in the narrative he receives other warnings that he treats in a similar way, perhaps pre-eminently in 2 Sam. 11.3.

30. M.J. Steussy, *David: Biblical Portraits of Power* (Columbia: University of South Carolina Press, 1999). As a sample of the burgeoning examples of studies that address David's literary complexity, in addition to others cited in this article, see D.M. Gunn, *The Story of King David: Genre and Interpretation* (JSOTSup, 6; Sheffield: JSOT Press, 1978); *idem*, 'In Security: The David of Biblical Narrative', in J.C. Exum (ed.), *Signs and*

life, the narrative seems to emphasize that Eliab's comments are words of warning, and hence David's rejoinder is worth considering. Eliab's speech serves to introduce an identifiable pattern in David's responses, as he answers, 'What have I done?' David uses the same declamation a number of times in 1 Samuel (e.g. before Jonathan in 1 Sam. 20.1, publicly before Saul in 26.18, and before Achish king of Gath in 29.8). In each of these cases one could argue that there is a measure of political calculation.[31] This objection to Eliab, thus, is the first in a chain of strategically similar protestations, and serves to construct a significant (if ambiguous) aspect of David's character zone. Consequently, for larger studies of David's representation in this narrative material, I would propose that the words of Eliab add a valuable edge, and should be attended to with heightened awareness of their double-voiced endowment.[32] The contention here is that Eliab's 'reading' of David

---

Wonders: Biblical Texts in Literary Focus (Semeia Studies; Atlanta: Scholars Press, 1988), pp. 133-51; *idem*, 'Reflections on David', in A. Brenner and C. Fontaine (eds.), *A Feminist Companion to Reading the Bible: Approaches, Methods, and Strategies* (The Feminist Companion to the Bible, 11; Sheffield: Sheffield Academic Press, 1997), pp. 548-66; R.C. Bailey, *David in Love and War: The Pursuit of Power in 2 Samuel 10–12* (JSOTSup, 75; Sheffield: Sheffield Academic Press, 1990); D. Marcus, 'David the Deceiver and David the Dupe', *Prooftexts* 6 (1986), pp. 163-71; F. Polak, 'David's Kingship—A Precarious Equilibrium', in H.G. Reventlow, Y. Hoffman, and B. Uffenheimer (eds.), *Politics and Theopolitics in the Bible and Postbiblical Literature* (JSOTSup, 171; Sheffield: Sheffield Academic Press, 1994), pp. 119-47; J.W. Whedbee, 'On Divine and Human Bonds: The Tragedy of the House of David', in G.M. Tucker, D.L. Petersen, and R.R. Wilson (eds.), *Canon, Theology, and Old Testament Interpretation: Essays in Honor of Brevard S. Childs* (Philadelphia: Fortress Press, 1988), pp. 147-65.

31. Cf. K.R.R. Gros Louis, 'The Difficulty of Ruling Well: King David of Israel', *Semeia* 8 (1977), pp. 15-33 (23), but contrast J. Rosenberg, *King and Kin: Political Allegory in the Hebrew Bible* (Bloomington: Indiana University Press, 1986), p. 178: 'As if by reflex against the voice of his domineering and belittling older brother ("...that little herd..."), who, like Jesse, is blind to matters of the heart (cf. 16.7), David adopts a familiar and no doubt habitual defensive posture, and, notably, the gesture is one of bad faith: a retreat and self-exculpation, appealing to the empty and inconsequential ways of small talk, as a cover for the idea coming to birth within'. Gros Louis (p. 22) perceptively notes that Eliab, as David's 'own brother', may recognize an ambiguity in David's motives.

32. For example, in a provocative recent study of the David traditions from a literary and historical perspective, Baruch Halpern (*David's Secret Demons: Messiah, Murderer, Traitor, King* [Grand Rapids: Eerdmans, 2001], p. 38) notes the host of 'contradictions in David's character' which the books of Samuel present to the reader. Although Eliab does not receive much attention in Halpern's analysis, it strikes me that this present chapter merges nicely with a number of Halpern's observations of the implicit *criticisms* of David readily apparent in 1 and 2 Samuel. Cf. Perdue, '"Is there Anyone Left of the House of Saul...?"'. Further, the question of this present study is: In light of ambiguities and complexities of David's character, how should the words of Eliab be heard? A reading which is guided strictly by a kind of 'mimetic formalism' usually produces a

needs to be kept open and unfinalized, as these words have a larger purpose in the Deuteronomist's presentation of the king.

3. Conclusion

To conclude, there are two main points which have been argued in this chapter. First, from a literary perspective, Eliab has an important function. Fokkelman is surely right to insist that these two scenes where Eliab appears (1 Sam. 16.6-7 and 17.23-30) must be read together.[33] A principal reason for doing so, however, is because Eliab's primary function in the narrative is as a means of *indirectly characterizing others*. In his first scene (16.6-7), Eliab is used as a means of correction for Samuel. In his second scene (17.23-30), Eliab is used as a means of specific correction for David. Moreover, the sibling's words can be understood not simply as a jealous older brother, but rather as a concerned one.[34] Traditional exegesis has read in these words an Eliab who is fundamentally preoccupied with himself. This is certainly a defensible position, but it is nonetheless possible that Eliab's dialogue with David has an altogether different utility.[35] At the very least, I am suggesting that Eliab's discourse potentially yields a moment of insight into David's

rather one-dimensional angle, such as a view of Eliab as simply a ranting older brother. The theoretical work of Bakhtin, in my view, is more helpful, as it points to how Eliab as a character is used in the larger program of the Deuteronomist.

33. Fokkelman, *The Crossing Fates*, p. 163: 'Forming this link with 16.1-13 is not only attractive in a semiotic reading of the given text, but is also essential'. From a reader's standpoint, I would concur that intertextually aligning Eliab's two scenes is a necessary step in understanding the narrative design.

34. In contrast to, again for example, R.D. Bergen, *1, 2 Samuel* (Nashville: Broadman & Holman, 1996), pp. 192-93: 'David's interest in this matter proved irritating to Eliab, perhaps because of his fear of Goliath, and he caustically accused David of having a haughty and wicked heart that motivated him to abandon his duty to the family's livestock for the sake of watching others die in battle. Of course, Eliab's accusation was false.' While the present study is outlining alternative ways of reading Eliab's words, the issue of Eliab's (plausible) anger is less of an issue. See further Eslinger, 'A Change of Heart', p. 357: 'David's heart is not mentioned again until 17.28. There Eliab says that David is proud and has a naughty heart [רֹעַ לְבָבֶךָ]. Though Eliab's opinion is that of an involved character caught in the ubiquitous web of the elder/younger son motif (cf. Fokkelman 1986 [= *The Crossing Fates*]: 129), the aspersion seems to fit the role that David plays here, following as he does in the footsteps of Joseph in Egypt. As the many perceptive studies of the story of David have recently shown, David will continue throughout his career to act out of a heart that seems very black indeed (e.g. 2 Sam. 11; 1 Kgs 1).'

35. As W. Brueggemann might suggest, David's older brother may not be acting out of inherent self-interest, but rather is *attentive to the other*. See Brueggemann's *The Covenanted Self: Explorations in Law and Covenant* (Minneapolis: Fortress Press, 1999).

character that will be important as the narrative unfolds. The issue here is not whether Eliab's words should be read sympathetically, but rather the argument here is that Eliab's questions of the heart constitute an intentional aspect of the Deuteronomist's larger strategy in the configuration of David.

Second, from a broader theoretical perspective, Eliab appears in two scenes where a double-voiced utterance occurs. In the first scene (1 Sam. 16.6-7), it is the divine speech to Samuel surrounding Eliab's character zone which is double-voiced. As well as being a means of delivering a specific correction for the prophet, it functions as a broader means of evaluation of Samuel's involvement in kingship, and a subsequent destabilization of his words in 1 Sam. 16.6 ('and when they came, he saw Eliab, and said [ויאמר], "Surely, before the Lord is his anointed one!"'). This function is purposeful, and integral to the narrative design. In the second scene (1 Sam. 17.23-30), I would argue that Eliab's speech itself is double-voiced. In addition to being used as an occasion for specific correction of David, Eliab's words carry an authorial accent. The author is providing a narrative signpost about the complexity of David's characterization that will unfold in the ensuing narrative. It is not incidental that Eliab's double-voiced speech occurs in the same cluster of dialogue as David's first words in the story. Furthermore, a number of terms that Eliab uses are intimately connected with 2 Samuel 11 and 12—the affair of David, Bathsheba and Uriah the Hittite and its aftershock, the parable of Nathan the prophet. The fact that words such as 'few' (מעט, 2 Sam. 12.8), 'flock' (צאן, 12.2, 4), 'evil' (רע, 12.9, 11), 'see' (ראה, 11.2), and 'battle' (מלחמה, e.g. 11.7, 25) are used, makes this an intriguing intertext, and intimates that this character has a broader thematic purpose in the books of Samuel.[36] In addition, it is striking that just as Eliab's 'wrath is kindled against David' (ויחר־אף אליאב בדוד), so David's 'wrath is kindled against the man' (ויחר־אף דוד באיש) of Nathan's parable—and, of course, that 'man' is David himself. If the speech of Eliab is heard in light of the affair of Uriah the Hittite, the words of David's older brother sound rather different. If Eliab's speech in its present context of 1 Samuel 17 is viewed proleptically, the accent of warning is surely discernible. It may be that the Deuteronomist's literary strategy encourages the reader not simply to make a series of psychological pronouncements on Eliab as merely a jealous older sibling on the rampage. Rather, in light of the broader narrative, the reader is obliged to leave Eliab's disturbing words *unfinalized* (to use Bakhtin's

---

36. See, e.g., J.S. Ackerman, 'Knowing Good and Evil: A Literary Analysis of the Court History in 2 Samuel 9–20 and 1 Kings 1–2', *JBL* 109 (1990), pp. 41-60. Ackerman discusses the persistent theme of 'good and evil' in the Succession Narrative, and also the king's often ambivalent motives that are apparent through the many epistemological gaps in the story. In particular, the notion of discernment that Ackerman discusses strikes me as especially germane to the function of Eliab's character in the broader narrative.

terminology), and to keep them open-ended as a potential point of insight into David's complex personality. Even though Eliab is a minor character, his presentation in 1 Samuel provides an instructive example of the double-voiced sophistication of this narrative material, and the overall portrait of David is correspondingly enriched by careful attention to Eliab's literary function in the Deuteronomist's enterprise.

3

REVISITING THE 'COLLUSION AT NOB' IN 1 SAMUEL 21–22

After some narrow escapes and deft evasions of Saul's spear, in 1 Samuel 21 David comes to Ahimelech the priest at Nob. Most commentary on this episode assumes that David acts deceptively toward Ahimelech, and thus procures food and weaponry from the oblivious priest. However, in an intriguing study of 1 Samuel 21–22 that was published as a *JSOT* article in 1994, Pamela Reis unfolds a reading of this material that, to my mind, deserves further consideration.[1] Reis begins her study by observing that there has been a considerable (and somewhat surprising) degree of unanimity in the interpretation surrounding David and his encounter at Nob. As far as the main plot of the story is understood among a legion of interpreters, there may be some 'variation in detail and emphasis, but the overall consensus is that David deceived Ahimelech at Nob and that the priest therefore replied in innocence to Saul's interrogation and went guiltlessly to his death'.[2] Antithetically, Reis argues that David and Ahimelech together are in 'collusion' against Doeg the Edomite (and by extension, King Saul), and therefore Ahimelech the priest is an *accomplice in deception* with David. When this assumption is made, David and Ahimelech's transaction of dialogue throughout 21.1-10 can be viewed as an attempt by both Ahimelech and David to beguile Doeg the Edomite, an ally of Saul detained in Nob on that

---

1. P.T. Reis, 'Collusion at Nob: A New Reading of 1 Samuel 21–22', *JSOT* 61 (1994), pp. 59-73 (59). Reis reissued this study in her collection, *Reading the Lines: A Fresh Look at the Hebrew Bible* (Peabody, MA: Hendrickson, 2002), pp. 131-47.

2. Reis, 'Collusion at Nob', p. 59. Cf. the recent views of A.F. Campbell, *1 Samuel* (FOTL, 7; Grand Rapids: Eerdmans, 2003), p. 226: 'Ahimelech is afraid; whether for David or for himself we are not told. What are the options at this point? The tradition knows of Ahimelech's death, so it is not possible for him here either to refuse David or to join David. Either he dies a martyr or he dies innocent. Equally, David either tells the truth and makes Ahimelech a martyr, or David tells a lie and makes Ahimelech his innocent unwitting accomplice. The narrative opts for Ahimelech as the innocent accomplice.' See also V.P. Hamilton, *Handbook on the Historical Books* (Grand Rapids: Baker Book House, 2001), p. 270; Halpern, *David's Secret Demons*, p. 285; B.T. Arnold, *1 & 2 Samuel* (NIVAC; Grand Rapids: Zondervan, 2003), p. 310; B. Green, *King Saul's Asking* (Interfaces; Collegeville, MN: Liturgical Press, 2003), p. 83.

day. Utilizing this line of exposition, as Reis maintains, results in a more cohesive story line: David and the priest are partners in intrigue, and their discourse in the sanctuary is fraught with equivocation. In this chapter I would like to suggest that Reis's thesis can be enhanced in three ways: first, by attending to the literary technique of *delayed exposition*; second, by viewing Ahimelech's actions as part of the larger *motif of deceptive alliance* that can be seen to operate within 1 Samuel 19–22; and third, I would like to make a case that Ahimelech the priest is used by the Deuteronomist as an instrument in the prophecy/fulfillment *schema* as articulated some years ago by Gerhard von Rad.[3]

In terms of background, when David enters Nob in 1 Samuel 21 he has been eluding the lethal schemes of King Saul since ch. 18. Saul, acting alone with his javelin as well as through his attendants, has made a number of attempts on David's life. These assassination attempts have, of course, been unsuccessful thus far, in large part because David receives support from a number of key allies who have aided him over and against the king. Such assistance from 'important figures' is a key element within chs. 19–22, as Michal, Jonathan, Samuel, Gad, and the king of Moab—individuals of high standing in Saul's court or elsewhere—facilitate in one way or another the Davidic dodging of Saul and his partisans.[4] Most recently, Jonathan has warned David that his father's designs on him are emphatically negative, and urged him to flee. With this appeal, Jonathan proceeds on his way, and David on his, and the narrative in ch. 21 commences with David's entry into Nob. Consider, then, the opening moments of 1 Sam. 21.2-4:

> David came to Nob, to Ahimelech the priest. Ahimelech trembled to meet David, and said to him, 'Why are you alone, and no one is with you?' David said to Ahimelech the priest, 'The king has charged me with something, and he said to me, "No one is to know anything about where I'm sending you or what I've charged you". As for the young lads, I've let them know about such-and-such a place. So now, what have you got? Give me five loaves of bread, or whatever can be found.'

For several reasons, it is plausible to assume that David and Ahimelech have an established relationship. To start with, it seems unlikely that David would flee to a place where he does not have a trustworthy ally. There is also the

---

3. G. von Rad, *Studies in Deuteronomy* (trans. D. Stalker; SBT, 9; London: SCM Press, 1953). Cf. also his *Old Testament Theology*. I. *The Theology of Israel's Historical Traditions* (trans. D.M.G. Stalker; Louisville, KY: Westminster/John Knox Press, 2001 [originally published 1962]), p. 340: 'It can actually be said that the Deuteronomist gave the historical course of events which he describes its inner rhythm and its theological proof precisely by means of a whole structure of constantly promulgated prophetic predictions and their corresponding fulfillments, of which exact note is generally made.' See also Polzin, *Moses and the Deuteronomist*, pp. 19-20.

4. Birch, 'The First and Second Books of Samuel', p. 1138.

tantalizing though tenuous detail about Goliath's weaponry: in 1 Sam. 17.54, 'David took the Philistine's head and brought it to Jerusalem, but he put his weapons in his tent'.[5] Since the reader will shortly discover that the 'sword of Goliath' is hidden behind the ephod at Nob, one may be inclined to think that David has visited the sanctuary before. At any rate, in Ahimelech's speech to Saul in 22.14-15 the priest denotes an intimacy with David and a thorough knowledge of his position in the court of Saul. Furthermore, the manner in which the priest initiates the dialogue between them implies that they not only have a relationship, but are allies as well.

The initial action of Ahimelech is that he 'hurries' or 'comes anxiously (חרד) to meet David'. John Mauchline opines, 'Ahimelech's nervousness at David's approach was probably due to the fact that David, the victor at Elah over Goliath was now a son-in-law of the king and a member of the royal court'.[6] While Mauchline raises a useful point, an alternative conclusion is that Ahimelech's nervousness derives from a different source: it is not the arrival of David that arouses his fear, but rather *the arrival of David while Doeg, Saul's servant, is there*. Although Doeg is formally introduced in the narrative through *delayed exposition* in 21.8, his presence is felt beforehand.[7] It is notable that the verb 'to tremble' (חרד) also occurs in 1 Sam. 16.4, as the elders of Bethlehem 'come trembling' to meet Samuel,[8] and they inquire, 'Have you come in peace?' One might expect the same kind of query from Ahimelech here, a terse statement congruent with his 'trembling'. Instead, he provides this more 'poetic' interrogative, or even an upbraiding, one that is quite different from the question of the Bethlehem elders to Samuel. Therefore it seems that the verb חרד is a reflection of the priest's inner state, whereas his words have a more authoritative tone. As Reis argues, Ahimelech's poetic verse has the subversive purpose of warning David that he is *not* alone.[9]

---

5. Cf. J.W. Wesselius, 'Collapsing the Narrative Bridge', in J.W. Dyk *et al.* (eds.), *Unless Some One Guide Me: Festschrift for Karel A. Deurloo* (Amsterdamse cahiers voor exegese van de Bijbel en zijn tradities, Supplement Series, 2; Maastricht: Shaker, 2001), pp. 247-55 (248-49).

6. Mauchline, *First and Second Samuel*, p. 150.

7. For this reason, the priest's opening words are highly significant, as is the fact that Ahimelech himself opens the dialogue. In 19.18, when David escapes to Samuel, he arrives and tells Samuel 'all which Saul did to him'. As well, in 20.1, David flees again and comes before Jonathan, saying, 'What have I done, what is my guilt, and what is my sin before your father that he is seeking my life?' With this pattern, it is most important that David does not arrive in Nob trumpeting his innocence and telling of 'all that Saul has done to him', for then Doeg would be alerted that David is fleeing. Therefore, before David has an opportunity to speak, Ahimelech gets the first words in.

8. Compare ויחרדו זקני העיר לקראתו in 1 Sam. 16.4 with ויחרד אחימלך לקראת דוד in 21.2.

9. Reis, 'Collusion at Nob', pp. 64-65.

For his part, David commences his rejoinder to Ahimelech by focusing on a supposed instruction from Saul: 'The king commanded me with something, and he said to me, "No man is to know anything concerning the matter on which I am sending you or what I have commanded you".' David emphasizes solidarity with the king, and surrounds this task commissioned by Saul with an atmosphere of weightiness. He is careful to stress the *covertness* of the operation. There is considerable effectiveness in supplying an alleged quotation from Saul's direct speech, lending an air of authenticity to the discourse. David's opening words both respond to the priest's question and continue the chicanery toward Doeg.

Further, David explains that he is alone because he has instructed his men to rendezvous at 'such and such a place' (פלני אלמוני). This is an expression in Hebrew prose that can serve to designate an arbitrary or intentionally ambiguous person or location.[10] As Robert Alter notes, this phrase is 'a clear signal of authorial abstraction', and 'what the writer seems to have in mind is David's manifest desire to fabricate a story that will allay Ahimelech's suspicions'.[11] While agreeing with the basic sense of this observation, Reis proposes an inversion of its efficacy: namely, it is to neutralize Doeg's suspicions.[12] I would further contend that rather than inventing a real place name, David uses this ambiguous designation to discourage Doeg from potentially *going* to the place to verify the story. David then continues the stratagem with a request for food, strengthening the deception to make it appear as though this visit to Nob is a refueling stop. David's 'and now' (ועתה) in v. 4 explains to Doeg why he came here, and he effectively turns the priest's query into a pretense for his visit: to obtain food (לחם).

1. *Delayed Exposition 1: The Presence of Doeg on That Day in Nob (1 Samuel 21.8)*

> Now one of Saul's servants was there on that day, detained before the LORD. His name was Doeg the Edomite, head of Saul's shepherds. (1 Sam. 21.8)

In 21.8 the formal introduction of Doeg the Edomite is given, and the narrator provides this introduction by means of *delayed exposition*. In terms of definition, one literary theoretician explains *delayed exposition* or 'analepsis' as a form of dischronologizing 'by which some of the events of a story are

---

10. Cf. other uses of the expression in Ruth 4.1, where it is ironically used to highlight the 'namelessness' of the one who refuses to act as a kinsman-redeemer; and 2 Kgs 6.8, where it is used to ironically underscore the frustration of the king of Aram by the prophet Elisha.

11. R. Alter, *The Art of Biblical Narrative* (New York: Basic Books, 1981), p. 71.

12. Reis, 'Collusion at Nob', p. 66. This may also be a clandestine signal to Ahimelech that he is aware of the 'such and such a one' (פלני אלמוני) in the sanctuary.

related at a point in the narrative after later story-events have already been recounted. Commonly referred to as retrospection or flashback', such a device 'enables a storyteller to fill in background information about characters and events'.[13] By using this technique of *delayed exposition*, the narrator is able to characterize Doeg *before* he has been formally introduced to the reader, or is even reported as performing an action or is involved in dialogue. Even though the reader has not been aware that Doeg is in the sanctuary, Doeg's presence now pervades the entire scene and causes a reappraisal of the dialogue of Ahimelech and David. Doeg does not say or do anything in this scene, yet he is characterized as *being* there in a most portentous way through this dislocation of normal chronology.[14]

By delaying the introduction of Doeg, there is now an ambiance of foreboding that envelops this shadowy figure. As *delayed exposition* causes an analeptic flashback in the narrative, the re-vision of events now takes a more sinister tone with the epithet of 'Edomite'. As H.W. Hertzberg notes, such nomenclature 'would certainly have made the listener prick up his ears and think "This means no good"'.[15] Moreover, Doeg is initially defined in

13. C. Baldick, *The Concise Dictionary of Literary Terms* (Oxford: Oxford University Press, 1990), p. 9. A lengthier treatment from the perspective of general literary theory is found in G. Genette, *Narrative Discourse: An Essay in Method* (trans. J.E. Lewin; Ithaca, NY: Cornell University Press, 1980), and S. Rimmon-Kenan, *Narrative Fiction: Contemporary Poetics* (London: Routledge, 1983), pp. 43-58. For an application of the theory of 'flashback' to biblical studies, see M.A. Powell, *What is Narrative Criticism?* (London: SPCK, 1993), pp. 36-38, and Sternberg, *The Poetics of Biblical Narrative*, pp. 264-320. Sternberg refers to this kind of feature as a 'retrospection'. As defined here, *delayed exposition* deals with a new divulgence of a past action in the narrative sequencing, *after* it has happened in the story. Despite its displacement in the structure of the narrative, *delayed exposition* is the report of something which happens previously in the narrative, but reported at a later juncture. Moreover, *delayed exposition* can be divulged by the narrator or through the direct speech of a member of the *dramatis personae*. The implication is that this analeptic disclosure now causes the audience to review the narrative in light of this new detail, which has been known to the other characters but withheld from the reader until this moment.

14. P. Brooks, *Reading for the Plot: Design and Intention in Narrative* (Cambridge, MA: Harvard University Press, 1984), p. 13. The remark about Doeg's presence in Nob also provides an instance of foreshadowing or *prolepsis*. The latter term is helpfully defined by M. Riffaterre (*Fictional Truth* [Baltimore: The Johns Hopkins University Press, 1990], p. 129) as 'any segment of a narrative that either explicitly announces a future event or is remembered when this event takes place as having foretold it or figuratively anticipated it. The narrative segment that triggers this memory is the *analepsis*. An implicit or figurative prolepsis therefore has two functions: diegetic when first encountered in its own context and proleptic when reread retrospectively as an analogon of the analepsis.'

15. Hertzberg, *1 & 2 Samuel*, p. 181. R.P. Gordon (*1 & 2 Samuel: A Commentary* [Grand Rapids: Zondervan, 1986], p. 170) notes that Doeg is one of the few of Saul's

relation to Saul. This implies that Doeg's interests are tied to Saul, something which increases with the further epithet of vocation: 'mightiest of [Saul's] shepherds' (אֲבִיר הָרֹעִים). Commentators are unsure of the exact nature of Doeg's employment, but his appearance in the next chapter with the other servants of Saul indicates that he has a prominent position, and therefore should have a high degree of loyalty to the king.[16] Shawn Aster has recently argued that based on comparisons with analogous ancient Near Eastern appellations, Doeg could well be understood as a military figure responsible for dealing with treasonous individuals.[17] This fits well with the overall contours of the passage since, as Alter mentions, there is a word-play on the name of דֹּאֵג in this episode.[18] The root דאג has appeared before in connection with Saul (1 Sam. 9.5; 10.2), with a clear meaning of 'worry'. This word-play provides a situational irony since Doeg ('worry') is in the dark about the anxiety of the other two, while the reader can now observe the real cause of their *worry* due to the *delayed exposition* that introduces the Edomite. Ahimelech the priest is 'worried' because Doeg ('worry') is lurking in the sanctuary confines on that day.

The deferment of Doeg's formal introduction becomes even more pronounced in light of the next portion of direct speech in 1 Sam. 21.9, as David now asks Ahimelech for a weapon: 'Is there not here under your hand a spear or sword? For my sword and my weapons I have not taken in my hand because the king's mission was urgent.' Several commentators note that Doeg's introduction is immediately followed by David's request for a weapon, and that this is an ominous portent.[19] The narrator seems to be inviting the inference that David's request for a weapon is triggered by the reality of Doeg's menacing presence. As implied above, it is plausible that David *does* know that there is a weapon on hand, and distrust of Doeg compels him to ask for it. Thus the *antagonist* of the story is strategically

---

officials to be named. In 14.52 the text reads, 'And if Saul saw any brave or valiant man he brought him to himself'.

16. McCarter, *I Samuel*, p. 350, translates אֲבִיר הָרֹעִים as 'the chief of Saul's runners'. Cf. Klein, *1 Samuel*, p. 213.

17. S.Z. Aster, 'What was Doeg the Edomite's Title? Textual Emendation versus a Comparative Approach to 1 Samuel 21:8', *JBL* 122 (2003), pp. 353-61. See also the study of J.M.M. Roberts, 'The Legal Basis for Saul's Slaughter of the Priests at Nob (1 Samuel 21–22)', *JNSL* 25 (1999), pp. 21-29.

18. Alter, *The Art of Biblical Narrative*, p. 66. He also notes, 'Do'eg is not the subject here of any proper narrated action—indeed in the Hebrew no verb is attached to him, for the verb "to be" has no present or participial form, and the report of Do'eg's being in the sanctuary is cast in the present in what would be the equivalent of a long noun phrase. In this way, attention is focused on the man rather than on anything he might have done.'

19. Alter, *The Art of Biblical Narrative*, p. 66. Reis ('Collusion at Nob', pp. 68-69) also discusses the opportune mention of a weapon.

introduced directly preceding the mention of the sword, compounding the sense of danger and characterizing Doeg as a threatening figure in the narrative. The scene concludes (1 Sam. 21.10-11a) as follows:

> The priest said, 'The sword of Goliath, the Philistine, whom you struck down in the valley of Elah, behold, it is wrapped up in some clothes behind the ephod. If you want to take it, go ahead, for there's nothing else here except that one.' David said, 'There's none like it! Let me have it.' And David arose and on that day he fled from the presence of Saul, and he came to Achish king of Gath.

There are at least two significant aspects of Ahimelech's final speech in ch. 21. First, the reference to the 'sword' is framed with rhetorical intent. There is an emphatic, deliberative delivery of all the details: 'The sword of Goliath, the Philistine, whom you slew in the valley of Elah, behold...' If this careful enunciation of all the details of David's triumph is to intimidate Doeg, it must be quite effective. In the context of the deception, this occasion for mentioning the infamous Philistine serves as a reminder to Doeg of David's fierce loyalty and bravery on behalf of King Saul. Recalling David's past triumph also enhances the credibility of the king sending David on the 'secret mission' which is the cornerstone of the deception.

Second, the priest's confession that the sword is hidden 'behind the ephod' (הָאֵפוֹד) functions as a foreshadowing device. Not only does the sword of Goliath come into David's possession for a second time, but later in the narrative the ephod will also be delivered to him. David's final action in v. 11 merits consideration: 'And David arose on that day and fled from the presence of Saul'. While this could signify his departure from Israelite territory and entry into the land of the Philistines, it seems more likely that 'from the presence of Saul' (מִפְּנֵי שָׁאוּל) here alludes to the danger represented by the person of Doeg. It is quite a bizarre moment as David then proceeds to Gath, the hometown of Goliath, presumably armed with nothing less than the sword of Goliath himself, with which David had killed the large man in ch. 17.[20]

2. *Delayed Exposition 2: The Consciousness of Doeg on That Day in Nob (1 Samuel 22.9-10)*

> Now Saul was sitting in Gibeah, under the tamarisk tree on the hill. His spear was in his hand, and members of his staff were standing around him. Saul said to his staff standing around him, 'Listen to me, men of Benjamin! Will the son of Jesse give to every one of *you* fields and vineyards? Will every one

---

20. See Birch, 'The First and Second Books of Samuel', p. 1142: 'This brief story serves to introduce Achish, who plays a larger role later in the story', and it also serves to illustrate that David is 'resourceful when in danger'.

of *you* be appointed as captains of thousands or hundreds? For you've all conspired against me! None of you have revealed to my ear that my son cut a deal with the son of Jesse, and none of you has pity on me and reveals to my ear that my son has incited my servant against me to lie in ambush as he does today!' Then Doeg the Edomite spoke up (he was standing among the servants of Saul), and he said, 'I saw the son of Jesse come to Nob, to Ahimelech son of Ahitub. He inquired of the LORD for him, gave him provisions, and gave him the sword of Goliath the Philistine.' (1 Sam. 22.6b-10)

While Doeg is silent in Nob, in the presence of Saul and his retinue the Edomite suddenly becomes rather loquacious, and his words provide a second instance of *delayed exposition* in the narrative. Peter Miscall notes that 'Doeg said nothing of having seen David at Nob until Saul rebuked his servants; perhaps he thought there was nothing amiss with David's presence at the sanctuary'.[21] There are grounds for arguing that Doeg now speaks because he has been successfully duped until this moment, and also because he is made aware that his personal interests and position in the court of Saul are threatened by the rise of David. Consequently, 'he comes forward with a more lethal case than the narrative supports'.[22] Doeg provides an 'eye-witness' testimony to the arrival of David: 'I saw the son of Jesse come to Nob, to Ahimelech son of Ahitub'. This admission, furnished by means of *delayed exposition* reveals that Doeg is fully aware of the transaction between David and the priest.[23]

Doeg's deposition before Saul contains two startling expansions with respect to the narrative of ch. 21. First, Doeg reports that the priest 'inquired of the LORD for him'. This raises an issue over which commentators are divided.[24] Nothing of the sort has been reported to have occurred by the

---

21. Miscall, *1 Samuel*, p. 135. McCarter (*I Samuel*, p. 251) notes that the priest 'seems to anticipate' that this encounter at Nob will have a grim sequel. This is a perceptive comment, and could bolster the argument that there is more to the characterization of Ahimelech in this narrative than simply a maladroit old priest who is hoodwinked by David.

22. Reis, 'Collusion at Nob', p. 70.

23. The *delayed exposition* in 1 Sam. 22.9 provides a retrospective view of Doeg's cognitive state during the transaction at Nob, and provides an interior view of what he has seen and heard. This connects with the narrator's *delayed exposition* in 1 Sam. 21.8, and confirms that Doeg is a very animated presence on that day, and his mind is highly active. Moreover, Doeg uses the epithet 'son of Jesse' with what seems to be a measure of contempt, an echo of Saul's use of it in 1 Sam. 22.7. J.P. Fokkelman (*The Crossing Fates*, p. 388) notes, 'We soon find that Doeg's speech is remarkably selective', and this suggests that Doeg is a rhetorical manipulator.

24. Reis ('Collusion at Nob', p. 70) summarizes the discussions: 'Is Doeg lying? Interpreters disagree. Ralbag, in support of Doeg's account, says that general terms rather than specific questions were used to consult the oracle in order to maintain the fiction that David was acting on Saul's behalf. Brueggemann flatly rejects Doeg's assertion, calling it false. Peter Miscall accepts it readily, for he considers it confirmed by Ahimelech's

narrator, and so the decision of whether this is a reliable observation rests in large measure with one's appraisal of the personality of Doeg: whether he is deemed trustworthy. It seems ill-advised to trust Doeg on the matter of the divine inquiry: since the narrator has presented a situation where the consultation of the oracle is not reported, and seems unlikely to have occurred, on balance it appears that this is Doeg's fabrication. But why does he bring it up? Fokkelman proposes that this 'consultation of an oracle on behalf of the rival must particularly rile Saul, because he himself in the presence of Ahijah of the house of Eli had received no further answer from God (14.37)'.[25] The implication is that Doeg concocts the oracle business to kindle further Saul's wrath toward the priest. Bruce Birch notes, 'As we have seen before in 1 Samuel, there is an ironic play on words here, since the verb שאל ("to ask, inquire") is the root of Saul's own name. While Saul was seeking David, David was seeking a שאל from Ahimelech.'[26] There is a further irony here: Doeg, having been deceived by David and Ahimelech, now becomes a deceiver himself.[27]

Furthermore, Doeg refers to Ahimelech as 'the son of Ahitub' in his opening sentence. Notwithstanding the rather caustic tone this epithet seems to be spoken with, it interposes a new dimension into the narrative. Ahimelech is now associated with the doomed house of Eli, and it is rather haunting that the one who is subsequently commanded by Saul to destroy 'the house of priests'—Doeg the Edomite—is the one who first reveals to the reader that Ahimelech is connected with Eli's ill-fated lineage. Assuming Doeg is unaware of this charged significance, he is being caricatured as a conduit for purposes that certainly transcend himself, and while his vengeance on the

---

response to Saul's accusation. Fokkelman provides an extensive evaluation of both options and finally decides to leave the dilemma indeterminate. On this question of whether or not Ahimelech actually did act as oracle-giver for David, I come down firmly in the negative.' No doubt the problematic statement of Ahimelech in 22.15a (היום החלתי לשאול־לו באלהים חלילה לי) serves to complicate the matter. Cf. Green, *King Saul's Asking*, pp. 86-87.

25. Fokkelman, *The Crossing Fates*, p. 392.
26. Birch, 'The First and Second Books of Samuel', p. 1148.
27. This accusation deeply incriminates David for seeking divine guidance from the priest, which Saul probably equates with David's 'waiting in ambush'. The fact that Saul mentions this with pointed clarity in his charges against Ahimelech indicates that Doeg is a shrewd perjurer. Doeg's malediction climaxes with the specifying of the weapon Ahimelech gives to David: 'the sword of Goliath the Philistine'. It may be that he views this as equally incriminating evidence, but Saul does not mention it specifically—what seems to matter to him is the divine inquiry. Notably absent from Doeg's report is any mention of 'the men' who are supposedly with David, or 'the mission' which David alleged he was on. Doeg's speech appears to confirm that he now realizes he was deceived.

city of priests may be motivated by personal reasons, at the same time he unwittingly participates in the fulfillment of the prophetic word of 1 Sam. 2.27-36.[28] Here is where von Rad is helpful, since he points out that such a pattern is woven into the fabric of the larger narrative: 'that system', he says, 'of prophetic predications and exactly noted fulfillments which runs through the Deuteronomist's work. With it we may speak of a theological *schema*, no less than in the case of the "framework *schema*", even if it is used more freely and with greater elasticity, corresponding to the nature of the subject'.[29] When commenting on the early chapters of 1 Samuel, Polzin observes that in 1 Sam. 4.11 the Benjaminite messenger is described as one who brings 'good news' (הַמְבַשֵּׂר), and notes that almost invariably when this root occurs in the Deuteronomic History, it is in the context of someone bringing news that is ultimately *beneficial for the house of David*. For instance, several other messengers bring 'good news' that usually involves the demise of someone threatening the Davidic or Solomonic kingship (e.g. Saul, Absalom, and Adonijah) and hence the root בשׂר carries with it a larger thematic significance. Polzin further contends that the figure of Eli has royal overtones and is intricately 'tied into the coming account of kingship in the books of Samuel and beyond'.[30] The fall of Eli's house thus intersects with the rise of David. In 1 Samuel 21–22, Ahimelech, a member of the doomed priestly line, is acting in a manner that promotes the interests of the Davidic house over and against other rejected dynastic alternatives, namely: Eli and Saul. Lest this reading be criticized as overly subtle, Helga Weippert provides a welcome refuge, since she argues that such subtlety is a central characteristic

---

28. See also the discussion of McCarter, *I Samuel*, p. 366. Despite the objection by J. Van Seters (*In Search of History: Historiography in the Ancient World and the Origins of Biblical History* [New Haven: Yale University Press, 1983], p. 351 n. 104), who argues 'The connection of Abiathar with the house of Eli is a weak one and may be entirely artificial and of late polemical interest', there are reasonable grounds for inferring otherwise. Cf. E.T. Mullen, Jr, *Narrative History and Ethnic Boundaries: The Deuteronomistic Historian and the Creation of Israelite National Identity* (Atlanta: Scholars Press,1993), p. 238; D. Jobling, *1 Samuel* (Berit Olam; Collegeville, MN: Liturgical Press, 1998), p. 285; Arnold, *1 & 2 Samuel*, p. 74. On a more ambivalent note, A.F. Campbell and M.A. O'Brien (*Unfolding the Deuteronomistic History: Origins, Upgrades, Present Text* [Minneapolis: Fortress Press, 2000], pp. 224-25, 335) opine that 1 Kgs 2.27b 'may be from the Dtr...but it is by no means certain'. For a helpful overview of the denouement of the 'Abiathar' episode in 1 Kgs 2.27, see R.D. Nelson, *First and Second Kings* (Interpretation; Atlanta: John Knox Press, 1987), p. 27: 'The reference to the oracle against the house of Eli (I Sam. 2.27-36) reminds the reader for a moment of the greater story, of which Solomon's kingdom is just a part, the saga of Yahweh's dealings with Israel from exodus to exile'.

29. Von Rad, *Studies in Deuteronomy*, p. 78.
30. Polzin, *Samuel and the Deuteronomist*, p. 62.

of the Deuteronomist's narrative; after all, 'if a promise and fulfillment follow [too] closely together within a narrative, then the symmetry between the two elements can be boring'.[31]

3. *Delayed Exposition 3: The Consciousness of David on That Day in Nob (1 Samuel 22.22-23)*

Acting on the Edomite's affidavit, Saul summons Ahimelech and Nob is consumed by the sword of Doeg. Yet, as Birch observes, 'the judgment against the house of Eli speaks of one who would escape to weep and grieve (1 Sam. 2.33). This prediction is fulfilled when Abiathar, the son of Ahimelech, escapes the massacre and flees to David (v. 20) and reports the news of this tragedy to David (v. 21).'[32] The stage is now set for a third instance of *delayed exposition*, this time from David himself in 22.20-23:

> But a single son of Ahimelech son of Ahitub was able to slip away. His name was Abiathar, and he fled after David. Abiathar reported to David that Saul killed the priests of the LORD. David said to Abiathar, 'I knew on that day that Doeg the Edomite was there, and that he'd be sure to tell Saul. I'm the one who has turned around against the life of your father's house! Stay here with me. Don't be afraid, for the one who seeks your life also is seeking my life. Indeed, you'll be under guard with me.'

In David's speech that concludes the 'Nob narrative', there is another example of *delayed exposition*, as David confesses to Abiathar, '*I knew* on that day that Doeg the Edomite was there'. David thus reveals his own cognizance about the inherent danger signified by the presence of Doeg at Nob. Moreover, it indicates that while David is with Ahimelech, Doeg occupies a central place in his thinking and, as has been suggested above, motivates his action of deception. Further, David realizes that simply being aware of this threat was insufficient, and the guilt that he confesses to Abiathar is not that he deceives Ahimelech, but rather that the collusion is unsuccessful, and he is as much to blame for that as anyone. As Graeme Auld points out: 'David had been aware when he noted the presence of Doeg at Nob that he was putting Ahimelech at risk. It is said, though it is not always true, that my enemy's enemy is my friend. Abiathar, the sole surviving member of the

---

31. H. Weippert, ' "Histories and "History": Promise and Fulfillment in the Deuteronomistic Historical Work', in G.N. Knoppers and J.G. McConville (eds.), *Reconsidering Israel and Judah: Recent Studies on the Deuteronomistic History* (trans. P.T. Daniels; Winona Lake, IN: Eisenbrauns, 2000), p. 47-61 (47). (Weippert's article was originally published as 'Geschichten und Geschichte: Verheissung und Erfüllung im deuteronomistischen Geschichtswerk', in J.A. Emerton [ed.], *Congress Volume: Leuven, 1989* [VTSup, 43; Leiden: E.J. Brill, 1991], pp. 116-31.)

32. Birch, 'The First and Second Books of Samuel', p. 1148.

priestly clan, is persuaded to commit his security to David.'[33] Of course, through yet another instance of *delayed exposition* the reader will discover in the next chapter (23.6) that Abiathar has not arrived to David empty-handed. Abiathar comes to David with a piece of oracle software in his hand: the ephod (behind which the sword of Goliath was hidden?) which will prove to be a vital implement for David the fugitive in the ensuing narrative.

4. *Conclusion*

In summary, I have suggested that the notion of a 'collusion at Nob' is enhanced by attending to the literary technique of *delayed exposition*, and by viewing the actions of Ahimelech the priest as part of the larger matrix of actions that I am calling the *motif of deceptive alliance*. The various instances of *delayed exposition* ultimately serve to redirect the reader's attention to the antecedent prophetic word regarding the house of Eli. The introduction of Doeg by the narrator in 21.8 makes him a suspenseful figure in the shadows, a disruptive 'intrusion' that is 'perhaps merely puzzling, perhaps a bit ominous'.[34] However, once this intrusion is understood as a piece of *delayed exposition*, the narrative of 21.1-10 is re-read in light of this new information. The presence of Doeg now becomes a toxic fume pervading the episode. The next *delayed exposition*, Doeg's own eye-witness account, indicates that he is fully alert during David's sojourn in Nob. It is clear that he observes everything, and thus is able both to report what happened to Saul and to modify his account for his own self-serving purposes. A third *delayed exposition* occurs in David's acknowledgment to Abiathar that he was fully aware of Doeg's presence in Nob. In 21.1-10, Doeg performs no action nor is given any direct speech, he is only presented as being in Nob on that day 'restrained before the LORD'.[35] Through the literary technique of *delayed exposition* the Deuteronomist underscores that Doeg the Edomite is being

---

33. A.G. Auld, '1 and 2 Samuel', in J.D.G. Dunn and J.W. Rogerson (eds.), *Eerdmans Commentary on the Bible* (Grand Rapids: Eerdmans, 2003), p. 225.

34. Alter, *The Art of Biblical Narrative*, p. 66.

35. See B. Green, *How Are the Mighty Fallen? A Dialogical Study of King Saul in 1 Samuel* (JSOTSup, 365; Sheffield: Sheffield Academic Press, 2003), p. 350: 'The connotation of "constrained" [נֶעְצָר] is not obvious, but the word is used three times in the Saul narrative. Besides Doeg's constrained situation at the shrine and that of the hypothetical young men whom David has just assured the priest are held in a condition of purity to eat the consecrated bread, Saul was also charged by God into the ear of Samuel (9.17) to constrain the people.' I would add that the verb 'constrain' (עצר) contributes to the fulfillment of the prophetic word: it is indeed unclear how and why Doeg is 'constrained', and hence the point seems to be that Doeg is an unconscious agent for the realization of the prophetic word against the house of Eli.

used as an instrument in the gradual fulfillment of the prophetic word spoken against the house of Eli in 1 Samuel 2 (and reiterated in 1 Sam. 3).

Ahimelech himself has a role to play in the fulfillment of the prophetic word spoken against his own house by virtue of his participation in the *motif of deceptive alliances* that accompany David and his various escapes from King Saul. Michal protects David and hoodwinks her father in ch. 19, while Jonathan is involved in devising an intricate plan both to discover Saul's attitude toward David and subsequently to inform David of the result in ch. 20. In light of such actions, the reader is not surprised at a similar unfolding of events in ch. 21 as the priest acts deceptively to protect David from Saul and his allies. If one of the purposes of a motif in a literary work is to draw a correlation between two or more events, Ahimelech can now be compared with Michal and Jonathan, who act in a manner that is beneficial to David over and against Saul.[36] With Jonathan and Michal, the audience is explicitly told that they 'love' David (18.1 and 18.20), and one infers that this provides the motivation for assisting David, even against their father. With Ahimelech, though, no such qualifier is given, and his motivation is more difficult to ascertain.[37] Ahimelech's 'deceptive alliance' plausibly derives from a desire to protect David, knowing full well that such action risks the wrath of Saul, and in accepting this risk he marches toward a fateful destiny rather than trying to avoid it. Fokkelman asks: 'Where does this altruism come from in the face of death?'[38] The answer, I would submit, lies in von Rad's prophecy/fulfillment *schema* that is a central component of the Deuteronomist's enterprise. When David enters the sanctuary at Nob, two figures with contrasting destinies enter into dialogue: David, the future monarch, and Ahimelech of the condemned house of Eli. The priest defends David rather than himself before the Saulide inquisition, and thus makes the journey toward fulfillment of the prophetic word anything but 'boring'.[39]

---

36. Saul has an uncanny knack for uncovering deceptive alliances. Saul discovers that Michal has acted fraudulently, and interrogates her in 19.17: 'Why have you deceived me like this? You have sent my enemy and he has escaped!' He also upbraids Jonathan. In the 'Nob narratives', therefore, both the collusion and the subsequent interrogation of Saul are imbued with the same foreboding atmosphere: since Saul has discovered 'deceptive alliances' before, one might expect him to do so again.

37. Cf. Birch, 'The First and Second Books of Samuel', p. 1139: 'The king's own son and daughter had already helped David escape from Saul. This episode adds the aid of Ahimelech, the head of the surviving Elide priesthood that once served the ark in Shiloh.'

38. Fokkelman, *The Crossing Fates*, p. 398.

39. In terms of the Deuteronomistic History, note the use of von Rad's theory in the study of 1 Kgs 11–12 by G.N. Knoppers, 'Rehoboam in Chronicles: Villain or Victim?', *JBL* 109 (1990), pp. 423-40 (427-28). For an application of promise-and-fulfillment within a wider biblical theology, see C.R. Seitz, *Word without End: The Old Testament as Abiding Theological Witness* (Grand Rapids: Eerdmans, 1998), p. 149.

4

BAKHTIN'S *PSEUDO-OBJECTIVE MOTIVATION* AND THE DEMISE OF ABNER

1. *A Brief Outline of Bakhtin's Theory*

In other portions of this book I note that the work of literary theorist Mikhail Bakhtin has been helpfully applied to study of the Hebrew Bible.[1] A number of Bakhtin's concepts—such as carnivalesque, double-voiced utterance, hidden polemical discourse, and chronotope—have been applied to biblical narrative, particularly in the wake of Robert Polzin's discussions of the Deuteronomistic History.[2] In light of such promising forays, it seems that there is ample scope for further applying Bakhtin's insights to biblical narrative. In this chapter I would like to argue that there is a suggestive correspondence between Bakhtin's notion of *pseudo-objective motivation* and the 'Abner narrative' of 2 Samuel 3.

---

1. See especially Polzin, *Moses and the Deuteronomist*; idem, *Samuel and the Deuteronomist*; idem, *David and the Deuteronomist*; D.T. Olson, 'The Book of Judges', in *NIB*, II, pp. 721-888; Green, *Mikhail Bakhtin and Biblical Scholarship*; eadem, *King Saul's Asking*; eadem, 'Enacting Imaginatively the Unthinkable: 1 Samuel 25 and the Story of Saul', *BibInt* 11 (2004), pp. 1-23; C. Mandolfo, *God in the Dock: Dialogic Tension in Psalms of Lament* (JSOTSup, 357; Sheffield: Sheffield Academic Press, 2001); C. Mitchell, 'The Dialogism of Chronicles', in M.P. Graham and S.L. McKenzie (eds.), *The Chronicler as Author: Studies in Text and Texture* (JSOTSup, 263; Sheffield: Sheffield Academic Press, 1999), pp. 311-26.

2. Convenient summaries and bibliographies can be found in B. Green, *How Are the Mighty Fallen? A Dialogical Study of King Saul in 1 Samuel* (JSOTSup, 365; Sheffield: Sheffield Academic Press, 2003); C.A. Newsom, *The Book of Job: A Contest of Moral Imaginations* (New York: Oxford University Press, 2003); J.A. Barnet, *Not the Righteous But Sinners: M.M. Bakhtin's Theory of Aesthetics and Problem of Reader–Character Interaction in Matthew's Gospel* (JSNTSup, 246; London/New York: T. & T. Clark, 2003); M.P. Knowles, 'What Was the Victim Wearing? Literary, Economic, and Social Contexts for the Parable of the Good Samaritan', *BibInt* 12 (2004), pp. 145-74; M.M. Caspi, 'Forgotten Meaning: Dialogized Hermeneutics and the Aqedah Narrative', *SJOT* 18 (2004), pp. 93-107; C. Mandolfo, '"You Meant Evil Against Me": Dialogic Truth and the Character of Jacob in Joseph's Story', *JSOT* 28 (2004), pp. 449-65.

4. *Bakhtin's* Pseudo-Objective Motivation

In the fourth essay of *The Dialogic Imagination*, Bakhtin explores the theory of 'hybrid constructions' and *pseudo-objective motivation* by drawing on, among other works, *Little Dorrit* by Charles Dickens.[3] In conceptual terms, *pseudo-objective motivation* is a literary technique that an author uses for representing the 'common view' in a work of narrative; that is, what appears to be an authorial utterance in narration is actually the presentation of a commonly held opinion by a given general population. On the surface, such an utterance looks like a comment by the narrator (and thus looks like the implied author's opinion), but in fact it is the opposite: the viewpoint of the collective citizens. Instead of an authoritative utterance, there is actually a tension between the 'belief' as stated and the author's actual opinion of the matter at hand. 'To one degree or another', Bakhtin writes, 'the author distances himself from this common language, he steps back and objectifies it, forcing his own intentions to refract and diffuse themselves through the medium of the common view that has become embodied in language (a view that is always superficial and frequently hypocritical)'.[4] Of course, detecting *pseudo-objective motivation* requires discernment on the part of the reader, so as an illustration Bakhtin turns to Book 2, Chapter 12 of *Little Dorrit*:

> Mr. Tite Barnacle's view of the business was of a less airy character. He took it ill that Mr. Dorrit had troubled the Department by wanting to pay the money, and considered it a grossly informal thing to do after so many years. But Mr. Tite Barnacle was a buttoned-up man, and *consequently* a weighty one. All buttoned-up men are weighty. All buttoned-up men are believed in. Whether or no the reserved and never-exercised power of unbuttoning fascinates mankind; whether or no wisdom is supposed to condense and augment when buttoned up, and to evaporate when unbuttoned; it is certain that the man to whom importance is accorded is the buttoned-up man. Mr. Tite Barnacle never would have passed for half his current value, unless his coat had been always buttoned-up to his white cravat.

The context of this quotation from *Little Dorrit* is a grand dinner party at the home of the redoubtable financier, Mr Merdle, a party that includes a number of very important members of the ineffable 'Circumlocution Office'. In general, one gets the sense that Dickens is not overly fond of the likes of Mr Merdle and Tite Barnacle. The line that Bakhtin isolates in this paragraph is, 'But Mr. Tite Barnacle was a buttoned-up man, and *consequently* a weighty one'. Bakhtin places the adverb *consequently* in italics, and notes that this is an example of *pseudo-objective motivation*, 'one of the forms for concealing another's speech—in this example, the discourse of "current opinion"'.[5] He

---

3. Bakhtin, *The Dialogic Imagination*, pp. 301-422.
4. Bakhtin, *The Dialogic Imagination*, p. 302.
5. Bakhtin, *The Dialogic Imagination*, p. 305. Even a surface reading of *Little Dorrit* reveals the possibilities of *pseudo-objective motivation* for satirically undermining the houses of Merdle and Barnacle.

continues, 'If judged by the formal markers above, the logic motivating the sentence seems to belong to the author, i.e., he is formally at one with it; but in actual fact, the motivation lies within the subjective belief system of his characters, or of general opinion'.[6] Bakhtin's next example from *Little Dorrit* (Book 2, Chapter 13) features the 'collective voice' contained in narrational speech:

> As a vast fire will fill the air to a great distance with its roar, so the sacred flame which the mighty Barnacles had fanned caused the air to resound more and more with the name of Merdle. It was deposited on every lip, and carried into every ear. There never was, there never had been, there never again should be, such a man as Mr. Merdle. Nobody, as aforesaid, knew what he had done; *but everybody knew him to be the greatest that had appeared.*

Again, Bakhtin places the final words of this paragraph in italics, and notes that this is an example of 'an epic, "Homeric" introduction (parodic, of course) into whose frame the crowd's glorification of Merdle has been inserted (concealed speech of another in another's language)'. This is followed, Bakhtin says, by 'direct authorial discourse; however, the author gives an objective tone to this "aside" by suggesting that "everybody knew" (the italicized portion). It is as if even the author himself did not doubt the fact.'[7] For Bakhtin, then, there is clearly a difference between the author's view of a matter and the subjective belief-systems of a character or the crowd.[8] The technique of pseudo-objective motivation allows the author to be distanced from a particular opinion (or conviction) while at the same time preserving the tension of a 'hybrid construction'. Thus, two stories emerge: the story told by the narrator and the characters, and the second story of the author who speaks ('albeit in a refracted way') by means of the whole: 'We puzzle out the author's emphases that overlie the subject of the story, while we puzzle out the story itself and the figure of the narrator as he is revealed in the process of telling his tale. If one fails to sense this second level, the intentions and accents of the author himself, then one has failed to understand the work'.[9] Bakhtin concludes:

---

6. Bakhtin, *The Dialogic Imagination*, p. 305. Bakhtin further comments: '*Pseudo-objective motivation* is generally characteristic of novel style, since it is one of the forms for concealing another's speech in hybrid constructions. Subordinate conjunctions and link words ("thus", "because", "for the reason that", "in spite of", and so forth), as well as words used to maintain a logical sequence ("therefore", "consequently", etc.) lose their direct authorial intention, take on the flavor of someone else's language, become refracted or even completely reified' (p. 305). While responsibility for discerning *pseudo-objective motivation* falls on the reader, Bakhtin clearly is interested in establishing certain controls, and the thus the technique is not arbitrarily invoked.
7. Bakhtin, *The Dialogic Imagination*, p. 306
8. Bakhtin, *The Dialogic Imagination*, pp. 312-13.
9. Bakhtin, *The Dialogic Imagination*, p. 314.

As we have said above, the narrator's story or the story of the posited author is structured against the background of normal literary language, the expected literary horizon. Every moment of the story has a conscious relationship with this normal language and its belief system, is in fact set against them, and set against them *dialogically*: one point of view opposed to another, one evaluation opposed to another, one accent opposed to another (i.e., they are not contrasted as two abstractly linguistic phenomena). This interaction, this dialogic tension between two languages and two belief systems, permits authorial intentions to be realized in such a way that we can acutely sense their presence at every point in the work.[10]

Bearing the above discussion of *pseudo-objective motivation* in mind, I would like to expand on Polzin's earlier work and suggest that Bakhtin's theory of hybrid constructions and *pseudo-objective motivation* may illuminate certain aspects of 2 Samuel 3, an episode that features the assassination of Abner (commander-in-chief of Israel's 'northern alliance') and King David's apparent innocence. My contention is that not only does consideration of *pseudo-objective motivation* serve to illustrate the versatility of Bakhtin's theory, but also has useful application in the analysis of this highly intriguing portion of biblical narrative.[11] To anticipate my conclusion, I am suggesting that *pseudo-objective motivation* is a helpful critical category for assessing 3.36-37, the capstone of a chapter that is fraught with ambiguous political motives and public opinions:

> All the people noticed this, and it was good in their eyes; indeed, everything the king did was good in the eyes of the people. Hence all the people knew, even all Israel, on that day, that it was not from the king to cause the death of Abner son of Ner.

Commentators have generally recognized—though often for different reasons—the importance of this narrational discourse. On the one hand, this series of utterances is often interpreted as an unequivocal defense of David's innocence in the matter of Abner's assassination. As such, the lines would represent the 'author's opinion', and thus function as an apology for the king. On the other hand, some commentators are inclined to believe that the king's conduct is not as pure as the driven snow in the murky episode of

10. Bakhtin, *The Dialogic Imagination*, p. 314.
11. Another instance of *pseudo-objective motivation* in the Deuteronomistic History may be seen in 2 Sam. 16.22-23. The context is Ahithophel's advice to Absalom: 'So they pitched the tent for Absalom on the roof, and Absalom entered the concubines of his father in the eyes of all Israel. Now the advice that Ahithophel gave—in those days—was just as though one was inquiring of God. Thus was all the advice of Ahithophel: also with David, and also with Absalom.' There seems to be some distance between the narrator and the commonly held opinion as far as the counsel of Ahithophel is concerned. Rather than an 'authorial endorsement' of this matter, the seemingly divine nature of Ahithophel's counsel is rather stated as an issue of public opinion.

Abner's demise, despite the successful public relations event of Abner's funeral where the king assumes the central role of chief mourner and eulogist. My interest in 2 Sam. 3.36-37 is as follows: Whose perception is captured through this series of lines? In other words, does this series of lines represent 'truth' from the author, or is the narrator in fact refracting a piece of 'public opinion', the perception of '*even all Israel*' on that day? Reading this episode alongside Bakhtin's category of *pseudo-objective motivation*, I argue the latter: the Deuteronomist provides the reader with the angle of the crowd in 3.36-37, and such a move is consistent with the larger strategies of characterization that can be seen in the larger episode. In order to frame my argument, I need to explore some of the dynamics of 2 Samuel 2 and 3, and draw attention to the manner in which the Deuteronomist portrays the major characters in this narrative stretch.

2. *The Unleashing of Abner in the House of Saul*

As 2 Samuel 2 unfolds, there is a power vacuum after the death of Saul and political factions have emerged. David has been crowned as king of Judah in Hebron, but Saul's son Ishbosheth has been installed as king of the northern tribes primarily through the efforts of Abner, the commander of Saul's army. McCarter notes that the 'precipitating factor' that leads to open warfare in this chapter is 'probably David's attempt to treat with the lords of Jabesh-gilead, a gesture that Ishbaal must have regarded as a direct challenge to his authority'.[12] There is certainly a measure of simultaneity here: at the same time that David makes his overtures to the northern community of Jabesh-gilead, Abner is taking Ishbosheth on a coronation tour with a host of northern stops.[13] Such parallel actions suggest that Abner and David are foregrounded as rivals. As this narrative stretch continues, this is not the only occasion where Abner and David mirror one another through their actions. Furthermore, it is symbolically appropriate that Abner takes Ishbosheth to Mahanaim (מחנים, 'two camps'), since it evokes memories of the Jacob/Esau struggle in Genesis. As Fretheim comments, 'The name Jacob gives to the place, Mahanaim (its location is uncertain; it must have had some link with Jacob), "two camps [or companies]", refers to God's company and his own or to the two divisions of his own people'.[14] This allusion to Genesis 32

---

12. P.K. McCarter, *II Samuel: A New Translation with Introduction, Notes, and Commentary* (AB, 9; Garden City, NY: Doubleday, 1984), p. 97.

13. On this technique, see S. Talmon, 'The Presentation of Synchroneity and Simultaneity in Biblical Narrative', in J. Heinemann and S. Werses (eds.), *Studies in Hebrew Narrative Art throughout the Ages* (Scripta hierosolymitana, 27; Jerusalem: Magnes Press, 1978), pp. 9-26.

14. T.E. Fretheim, 'The Book of Genesis', in *NIB*, I, pp. 319-674 (562).

in 2 Sam. 3.8, if it be such, would underscore the 'elect' vs. 'non-elect' dynamic at work in this narrative, with Jacob representing the election of David and Esau the rejection of Saul.[15]

At least two elements in the aftermath of the battle that begins at the pool of Gibeon (2 Sam. 12.12-32) are important for Abner's characterization.[16] First, during his retreat from the battle of Gibeon, Abner conducts a lengthy running dialogue with the light-of-foot Asahel. Taking exception to this single-minded pursuit, Abner breathlessly commands Asahel to 'turn aside'. Asahel, though, is unwilling to heed Abner's imperatives. Abner's final command to Asahel in 2.22 is telling: 'Again Abner was saying to Asahel, "Turn away from following me! Why should I strike you to the ground? How could I lift up my face to Joab your brother (ואיך אשא פני אל יואב אחיך)?"'[17] While it is not exactly clear what Abner means with the idiom 'lift up my face', one certainly can infer that there is a measure of fear or respect for Joab, and perhaps even an anticipation of retribution should he kill Asahel. Hence, it is significant that a number of terms in this running dialogue occur later in the story of Joab's purported 'revenge'. Most striking of these terms is the anatomical place of execution, the 'fifth [rib]' (חמש). Just as Abner stabs Asahel in the חמש (2.23), so Joab will later stab Abner in the same region, חמש (3.27).

After Abner's killing of Asahel, a second important element for Abner's characterization emerges in 2 Sam. 2.26-27: the ensuing 'hilltop' dialogue with Joab. With the Benjaminites having rallied around him and taking their stand at the top of a hill, Abner has a distinct strategic advantage as he addresses Joab: 'Does the sword continually have to devour? Don't you know that bitterness lies at the end of this? For how long will you not order

---

15. See R.C. Heard, *Dynamics of Diselection: Ambiguity in Genesis 12–36 and Ethnic Boundaries in Post-Exilic Judah* (Atlanta: Society of Biblical Literature, 2000). Serge Frolov ('Succession Narrative: A "Document" or a Phantom?', *JBL* 121 [2002], pp. 81-104 [100]) notes that Mahanaim and Bahurim—ostensibly Saulide towns—will later support David during another monarchic crisis: 'Mahanaim, the capital of Ishbosheth and Abner, becomes the base of David's operations, and one of those who provides David's army with foodstuffs is Machir ben Ammiel from Lo-Debar, the former host of Mephibosheth (2 Sam. 17.27-29; cf. 2 Sam. 9.4)'.

16. Polzin, *David and the Deuteronomist*, p. 28: 'numbers appear to perform symbolic functions within the story. In the tournament, "twelve versus twelve" probably has tribal significance mirroring the conflict between north and south that constituted "the long war between the house of Saul and the house of David"'. It must not be accidental that Ishbosheth's assassins hail from Gibeon. Cf. Arnold, *1 & 2 Samuel*, p. 436.

17. Note the slight expansion in the LXX: καὶ ποῦ ἐστιν ταῦτα ἐπίστρεφε πρὸς Ιωαβ τὸν ἀδελφόν σου ('And what are these things? Return to Joab your brother!'). In the LXX account, Abner asks yet another question, issues yet another imperative to Asahel, and underscores the fraternal relationship 'brother'.

the troops to turn back from after their brothers?' Robert Alter labels the bitter (מרה) remarks of Abner as a 'grim prognostication' that 'hovers over not only the continuing civil war but over the entire David story'.[18] This aligns with Polzin's observation about the larger narrative theme here: the Deuteronomistic History's 'central social message about the institution of kingship as a major cause of frequent fratricide on a tribal or national level'.[19] If Polzin is correct that 'the pursuit of brothers' is a major theme of this narrative stretch, then Abner's hesitation in killing Joab's brother *and* in offering something of a truce at the top of the hill cohere with this larger storyline. Consequently, Joab's reply is suggestive, since this is the final time in the narrative that Joab and Abner are actually recorded in dialogue: 'As God lives, if you had not spoken up, the troops would not have gone up from after their brothers until morning!' Graeme Auld notes that

> it was Abner's plea, 'Shall the sword devour forever…?' that brought an end to the internecine strife. His poignant words had their desired effect, yet Joab's reply (2.27) is far from clear. Does he mean: Had you not spoken now, we should have pursued you through the night till morning? Or: Had you not spoken the way you did this morning, none of this would have happened?[20]

By any measure, the dialogue between Joab and Abner serves to intensify their rivalry: not only are they military leaders of opposite camps, but also Abner has killed Joab's brother. These background details are crucial for understanding Abner's characterization in 2 Samuel 3, to which this analysis will now turn.

3. *House Work*

> The battle between the house of Saul and the house of David was long. David was growing stronger and stronger, but the house of Saul, they were growing weaker and weaker. There were sons born to David in Hebron. His first born, Amnon, was from Ahinoam of Jezreel. His second was Chileab, from Abigail wife of Nabal of Carmel. The third was Absalom, son of Maacah daughter of Talmai king of Geshur. The fourth was Adonijah son of Haggith, and the fifth was Shephatiah son of Abital. The sixth was Ithream, from Eglah, wife of David. These were born to David at Hebron. (2 Sam. 3.1-5)

The opening paragraph of 2 Samuel 3 establishes at least two elements that are important in the unfolding of this chapter: *division* and *strength*. First, in the context of the long struggle between the two houses, David is proving superior to the house of Saul not least because of the *division* in the latter. The very fact that the writer pointedly avoids, so it would seem, the name

---

18. Alter, *The David Story*, p. 207.
19. Polzin, *David and the Deuteronomist*, p. 49.
20. Auld, '1 and 2 Samuel', p. 231.

'Ishbosheth' suggests a degree of internal fissure within the larger 'house of Saul'. This is augmented, as Graeme Auld points out, by the use of plural participles that I have attempted to render through the translation 'but the house of Saul, they were growing weaker and weaker' (ובית שאול הלכים ודלים). Auld comments, 'There is a significant little grammatical detail at the end of v. 1 which does not show up in English translation: while David on the stronger side is obviously singular, the Hebrew treats the weakening "house of Saul" as a plural, perhaps hinting at its disunity'.[21] If the division in the house of Saul stems in part from a leadership crisis, then the *strength* of David's position is correspondingly increased.

In pointed contrast to the dwindling of Saul's house, David's 'house' is exponentially on the rise, and some commentators believe that David's multiple wives imply a series of political alliances. Along such lines, Jon Levenson and Baruch Halpern argue at length that 'marital politics' is a significant component in David's rise.[22] Furthermore, Bruce Birch remarks that the list of David's sons in 2 Sam. 3.1-5 heralds the 'the issue of succession' that will loom large in the forthcoming narrative. To be sure, names such as Amnon, Absalom, and Adonijah serve to foreshadow varying degrees of internecine strife and civil war to come. All three sons will be involved in sexual misconduct (i.e. appropriating a royal consort or daughter) of the same nature that Abner is accused of in 3.7. Consequently, 3.1-5 is not an innocent genealogical listing—it thematically foregrounds the contours of struggle in this very chapter. The listing of David's sons at this particular narrative juncture is not accidental. Not only does it anticipate the plot to come, but it also reminds the reader of the past rivalry between Saul and David.

In my view, the key issue of the rivalry that emerges in the opening paragraph is *dynasty*. In the midst of his tirade against the king in 1 Sam. 13.14, the prophet Samuel emphatically declares that Saul will not sire a lasting house: 'But now, your dynasty will not continue' (ועתה ממלכתך לא תקום). By extension, the list of David's offspring declares the opposite. If there is dynastic sterility in Saul's house, David's house has prolific virility. Therefore, just as David is becoming strong and partially gaining mastery over the house of Saul by means of wives and sons, the Deuteronomist is very deliberate in showing (in the next paragraph, 2 Sam. 3.6) that Abner is *simultaneously* adopting the same strategy. To detect that Abner is attempting to do the same thing as David is essential for understanding how the Deuteronomist is presenting Abner in 2 Samuel 3.

21. Auld, '1 and 2 Samuel', p. 231; cf. McCarter, *II Samuel*, p. 100.
22. B. Halpern and J.D. Levenson, 'The Political Import of David's Marriages', *JBL* 99 (1980), pp. 507-18. See also J.D. Levenson, '1 Samuel 25 as Literature and History', *CBQ* 40 (1978), pp. 11-28; J. Kessler, 'Sexuality and Politics: The Motif of the Displaced Husband in the Books of Samuel', *CBQ* 62 (2000), pp. 409-23.

4. Who Let the Dog Out?

> Over the course of the war between the house of Saul and the house of David, Abner had been strengthening himself over the house of Saul. (Now Saul had a concubine named Rizpah, daughter of Aiah.) He said to Abner, 'Why would you enter my father's concubine?' Abner burned with great anger on account of the words of Ishbosheth, and he said, 'Am I a dog's head in Judah? Today I have performed loyalty with the house of Saul your father—toward his brothers and friend—and I have not caused you to be found by the hand of David, yet you would assign upon me the guilt of the woman today! Thus may God do to Abner and even more, if, just as the LORD swore to David, I do not act for him: to cause the kingdom to pass over from the house of Saul, and to establish the throne of David over Israel and Judah from Dan to Beersheba!' He was not able to respond to Abner with even a word, because he feared him. (2 Sam. 3.6-11)

While there are internal fractures within the house of Saul, David is 'growing strong' (הלך וחזק) through the acquisition of wives and sons. At the same time that David is growing strong, the reader is informed in 2 Sam. 3.6: 'Abner had been strengthening himself over the house of Saul' (ואבנר היה מתחזק בבית שאול).[23] It stands to reason that wives and sons might be involved in Abner's 'strengthening', and hence the accusation fits within the context of this chapter.[24] Nomenclature is important in this stretch of text: one notes that again Ishbosheth is not named, only the generic 'and he said' (ויאמר) is used. Despite a number of English translations that periphrastically render this phrase 'And Ishbosheth/Ishbaal said...', it would seem that the writer is avoiding the proper name, even though the ostensible subject is Ishbosheth.[25] Similarly, the unnamed Ishbosheth does not specifically name Rizpah herself: at different points both names are supplied only by the narrator. Rizpah is identified as the 'daughter of Aiah' immediately preceding the accusation of Abner's violation. Such identification of Rizpah, in hindsight, will assume heightened significance in light of the disclosure that she has borne two sons to Saul (2 Sam. 21.8). The issue here could then be a struggle for *the borne supremacy*: David has political marriages and sons in Hebron, while Abner (according to Ishbosheth) is appropriating a mother who has given birth to Saulide seed. Numerous commentators agree that the

---

23. For a discussion of וְאַבְנֵר הָיָה מִתְחַזֵּק בְּבֵית שָׁאוּל, translated as 'Abner had been strengthening himself over the house of Saul', see B.K. Waltke and M. O'Connor, *Introduction to Biblical Hebrew Syntax* (Winona Lake, IN: Eisenbrauns, 1990), p. 628.

24. As Hamilton (*Handbook on the Historical Books*, p. 308) notes: 'Eight women appear in 2 Samuel 3, but not one of them ever speaks'.

25. Cf. the NRSV rendering of 2 Sam. 3.7: 'Now Saul had a concubine whose name was Rizpah daughter of Aiah. And Ishbaal said to Abner, "Why have you gone in to my father's concubine?"' The NRSV here follows Chronicles, and usually inserts 'Ishbaal' for MT אִישׁ־בֹּשֶׁת (in spite of the fact that the proper name does not occur at 2 Sam. 3.7).

Deuteronomist does not confirm or deny the charge of Ishbosheth; indeed, it is surrounded with ambiguity. At the same time, in light of the larger context of sons and lovers, there is an unpleasant suspicion that Abner is not entirely innocent.

Both the *accusation* of Ishbosheth and the *response* of Abner contain some peculiar elements. In terms of wording of the indictment itself, Ishbosheth's allegation is an indirect one, and he does not mention Rizpah's name. Nonetheless, most readers are fairly confident about the nature of the charge. Brueggemann states, 'Abner is consolidating his personal power', and 'makes a preemptive gesture by taking Saul's concubine'.[26] Ishbosheth, for whatever reason, is presented as reluctant directly to confront his military commander. In this charge, Ishbosheth's semantic choices are significant, especially his opening interrogative 'Why?' (מדוע). According to Halpern, 'Biblical Hebrew has two words for "why", and Ishbaal uses the neutral one, rather than the negative one'.[27] I have attempted to capture this perceived neutrality by translating Ishbosheth's query as 'Why would you enter my father's concubine?' This does not seem to be a 'polar question'—that is, one that requires a 'yes/no' answer. Rather, it seems that the recently hatched monarch is allowing Abner to provide an explanation of his conduct. Such a lack of ambition would imply that Ishbosheth has a healthy measure of fear or deference for Abner. More acutely for the present analysis is this fact: this is the only occasion in the narrative where Ishbosheth is afforded any direct speech. After this quarrel with Abner, Ishbosheth will be seized with vocal paralysis for the remainder of his pusillanimous reign.

5. Canine Teeth

> 'You know how European literature begins?' he'd ask, after having taken the roll at the first class meeting. 'With a quarrel. All of European literature springs from a fight. And then he picked up his copy of *The Iliad* and read to the class the opening lines. "Divine Muse, sing of the ruinous wrath of Achilles… Begin where they first quarreled, Agamemnon the King of men, and great Achilles".'[28]

So inquires Dr Coleman Silk, novelist Philip Roth's politically incorrect professor of Classics at Athena College. The intense exchange between Abner and Ishbosheth in 2 Samuel 3 is obviously not equivalent to the squabble of Agamemnon and great Achilles, but nonetheless it represents an important moment for David's epic kingship. If Ishbosheth formalizes the quarrel by

---

26. Brueggemann, *First and Second Samuel*, p. 225.
27. Halpern, *David's Secret Demons*, p. 27. The other word is 'why' (למה). Halpern is in line with a number of commentators, suggesting that Abner's activity is a tacit attempt at the throne and tantamount to usurping.
28. P. Roth, *The Human Stain* (New York: Vintage, 2000), p. 4.

posing his question about Abner's conduct in spirit of 'neutrality', then Abner counters with a biting query of his own: 'Am I a dog's head in Judah?'

Scholars have presented a number of opinions on the precise nature of this expression in light of other uses of 'dog' in the books of Samuel, but it seems safe to agree with McCarter that this is a term of opprobrium.[29] If one were to adapt a recent study by Jeremy Schipper, then the term 'dog' (כלב) becomes quite problematic for Abner. When such a term enters a *character zone* in the books of Samuel—as the examples as Goliath, David himself, Mephibosheth, and Abishai (who uses the label for Shimei)—it is often deployed 'in the company of usurpers and political enemies'.[30] When Abner snarls his 'dog' question to Ishbosheth, his words may actually work to undermine his assertions of loyalty as the speech progresses, since other speeches that involve the term 'dog' often occur in suspect political circumstances. Abner does not directly answer Ishbosheth's question, but circuitously turns his response toward his avowed loyalty (חסד) to the house of Saul and 'to his brothers, to his friend' (2 Sam. 3.8). Without pausing to specify the exact identity of Saul's 'friend', Abner articulates his recent *curriculum vitae* by telling Ishbosheth all the things he has *not* done, including: 'I have not caused you to be found by the hand of David' (ולא המציתך ביד דוד). The syntax of the final clause of Abner's response in 2 Sam. 3.8 (ותפקד עלי עון האשה היום, 'yet you would assign upon me the guilt of the woman today') is challenging to decipher, as Abner expresses anger only over the charge within the context of his חסד ('loyalty'), not an acknowledgment or denial of the charge. A number of commentators have wondered if the man 'doth protest too much'.[31]

In this generous self-appraisal Abner adumbrates a host of ways that he has manifested his constancy to Saul's house, for example, by not handing Ishbosheth over to David. In other words, Abner claims to have not been a 'turncoat'. Such a claim is surprising since Abner is now proposing to be exactly that, and transfer his allegiance to the Davidic cause. Abner's intentions are sealed with a scathing self-curse ('Thus may God do to Abner and even more, if...') and the recitation of an apparent divine promise ('...just as the LORD swore to David, I do not act for him: to cause the kingdom to pass over from the house of Saul, and to establish the throne of David over Israel and Judah from Dan to Beersheba!'). Several commentators observe that there is not a precise antecedent for this promise in the narrative hitherto. As Bruce Birch notes,

29. McCarter, *II Samuel*, p. 113.
30. J. Schipper, '"Why do you still speak of your affairs?": Polyphony in Mephibosheth's Exchanges with David in 2 Samuel', *VT* 54 (2004), pp. 344-51 (344). While Schipper is concerned with 'dead dog', my interest is with 'dog' (כלב) in general, whether living or dead.
31. Gunn, 'David and the Gift of the Kingdom', p. 16.

> We do not have any record of so specific a divine promise made to David, although his anointing by Samuel and the many references to David as God's choice for king would carry the implicit promise of such an established kingdom. Certainly there is no story of a divine oath sworn to David, but this may simply indicate the widespread recognition of divine favor attached to David and his future reign.[32]

Whether such 'widespread recognition' is implicit in the narrative is outside the scope of my analysis; rather the concern lies with Abner's problematic invocation of a supposed oath. Cheryl Exum perceives the difficulty thus: 'Particularly striking in Abner's rejoinder to Ishbosheth's question is the discrepancy between Abner's professed knowledge that Yhwh has given all Israel to David, and the fact that Abner has now been opposing Yhwh by supporting Saul's house against David. Is he, for this obstinacy, destined to die a fool's death?'[33] A further question arises: If Abner is so sure of this oath, then why does he take Ishbosheth on a coronation tour in the previous chapter (2 Sam. 2.8-9)? After Ishbosheth's inquiry and Abner's evasive response, the reader is caught between two conflicting possibilities about Abner's actions. As Polzin asks: 'Does he begin negotiations with David and use his influence to further David's cause within Israel as Ishbosheth's loyal commander, who is now falsely accused, or as a disloyal culprit who, having been caught out by his king, now makes the best of a bad situation by changing sides?'[34] Of course, the interaction between Abner and Ishbosheth in several respects will parallel the interaction between David and Joab as this chapter continues. Abner's rhetorical question that begins the about-face—'Am I a dog's head in Judah?' (הראש כלב אנכי אשר ליהודה)—is thus laced with a certain irony. Before too long, both Abner and the head (ראש) of Ishbosheth will be buried in Hebron, the city of Caleb (כלב) in Judah (2 Sam. 4.12).[35]

'Am I a dog's head in Judah?' This is not the last time Abner unleashes a rhetorical question when addressing a king. In fact, Abner uses the same strategy to begin his negotiation with David: 'Who has a country?' (2 Sam. 3.12).[36] Abner's question here is not altogether straightforward. As Birch

---

32. Birch, 'The First and Second Books of Samuel', p. 1223.
33. Exum, *Tragedy and Biblical Narrative*, p. 102.
34. Polzin, *David and the Deuteronomist*, p. 39.
35. The text of 4.12 reads: 'Then David commanded the lads, and they killed them. They severed their hands and feet, and impaled them by the pool (הברכה) at Hebron. But they took the head of Ishbosheth and buried it in the grave of Abner, at Hebron'. As Halpern (*David's Secret Demons*, p. 31) notes, 'The pool [הברכה] in Hebron is where the civil war ends, just as it began at the pool [הברכה] in Gibeon'.
36. One recalls a previous conversation between David and Abner that is also full of strange questions: 1 Sam. 26.14 reads, 'And David called to the people and to Abner the son of Ner, saying, "Will you not answer, Abner (הֲלוֹא תַעֲנֶה אַבְנֵר)?" Then Abner answered and said, "Who are you who calls to the king (מִי אַתָּה קָרָאתָ אֶל־הַמֶּלֶךְ)?".'

opines, 'the rhetorical question that begins Abner's negotiations with David is not entirely clear. It may be that the question, "To whom does the land belong?" is a reference to Abner's acknowledgment of the Lord's oath to give all of the land into David's rule (vv. 9-10).'[37] Such an interpretation is entirely possible, but it is equally plausible that Abner is speaking about *himself*. Abner is asking David to cut a covenant with him, and it stands to reason that Abner is hoping to gain something substantial from the deal. Perhaps he is angling to be the commander-in-chief of David's new united kingdom, and assumes that David is the rising tide that lifts all boats. Alternatively, he may be posturing, and intends no loyalty to David whatsoever.[38] Regardless, either scenario presumably does not include Joab, whose brother's death continues to hover over this narrative: 'Over all these events lingers the unanswered death of Asahel'.[39]

In the environment of political negotiation with Abner, David's request for Michal is intriguing. The reader recalls that on a previous occasion when Michal is an object of transaction there is deception and counter-deception (1 Sam. 18). It is possible, therefore, that the Deuteronomist invests this scene with a similar ambiance of scheming. In light of Abner's alleged appropriation of Rizpah, David's demand for Michal illustrates the political power of a royal wife and his own superior claims to the throne. This may be a veiled message that Abner should be content with a subordinate status in David's kingdom.[40]

The narrative takes an unexpected turn when David demands that *Ishbosheth* send Michal. It is not clear why this northern king would so obviously weaken his position by sending a northern sister to the southern king. A number of explanations have been proffered, with varying degrees of probability. At a minimum, Ishbosheth's actions reconfirm the internal divisions of the house of Saul: a house that is willing to undermine itself and self-destruct. A

---

37. Birch, 'The First and Second Books of Samuel', p. 1224.

38. Exum, *Tragedy and Biblical Narrative*, p. 103: 'What does Abner stand to gain by helping David establish his kingship over a united Israel and Judah? Merely the satisfaction of his anger at Ishbosheth? Ishbosheth owed his throne to Abner; does Abner want David similarly indebted? An appropriate reward for Abner would be Joab's position as commander of David's army, yet the text says nothing about Abner's future role in David's service.'

39. Brueggemann, *First and Second Samuel*, p. 223.

40. Cf. the discussion of J.W. Flanagan, 'Social Transformation and Ritual in 2 Samuel 6', in C.L. Meyers and M.P. O'Connor (eds.), *The Word of the Lord Shall Go Forth: Essays in Honor of David Noel Freedman in Celebration of his Sixtieth Birthday* (Winona Lake, IN: Eisenbrauns, 1983), pp. 361-72 (366): 'Michal provided the necessary link in the broken chain of relationships. Therefore, David demanded her return as a condition for beginning the treasonous negotiations with Abner, who as a cousin of Saul may have been a candidate himself.'

serious obstacle in returning Michal to David, however, is Paltiel, to whom Saul gives Michal in 1 Sam. 25.44. Although it is Ishbosheth who 'sends and takes' Michal from Paltiel, it is Abner who barks at the weeping husband: 'Go! Return!' (2 Sam. 3.16). Notably, the place where Abner issues this imperative to Paltiel is 'Bahurim' (בחרים), a village in Benjamin. The name of the place is derived from the verbal root בחר ('to choose'). Such a spatial setting carries a deeper symbolic import, since *choices* and *chosen-ness* are integral elements in the overarching theme of this chapter.

> Now Abner's word was with the elders of Israel, saying, 'In times past you have been seeking David to be king over you. So now, make! For the LORD has said to David, saying, "By the hand of my servant David: saving my people Israel from the hand of the Philistines and from the hand of all their enemies".' Abner also spoke in the ears of Benjamin, then Abner also went to speak in the ears of David at Hebron about all that was good in the eyes of Israel and in the eyes of the entire house of Benjamin. Then Abner came to David at Hebron, along with twenty men. David made a feast for Abner and his men. Abner said to David, 'Let me arise, so that I can go and gather all Israel to my lord the king, so they can cut a covenant with you, and you can reign over everything that your heart desires'. So David let Abner go, and he went in peace. (2 Sam. 3.17-21)

For the second time in this narrative stretch Abner uses a 'divine quotation' that does not have a verifiable antecedent: 'Now Abner's word was with the elders of Israel, saying, "In times past you have been seeking David to be king over you. So now, make! For the LORD has said to David, saying, 'By the hand of my servant David: to save my people Israel from the hand of the Philistines and from the hand of all their enemies'"' (3.17-18).[41] Abner's quotation poses a problem for commentators. For example, McCarter struggles with Abner's citation of the divine voice, suggesting that it must be 'secondary' since the quotation only makes sense within the context of the larger history: 'Note also how 18b looks ahead to the subsequent Deuteronomistic passages in its allusion to an oracle about David, which has no discernable referent apart from II Samuel 7'.[42] I concur with McCarter's identification of the difficulty—that is, Abner's words have no anchor in the previous narrative—but an alternative solution is possible. Indeed, the whole speech of Abner is problematic, even his prefatory words, 'In times past you have been seeking David to be king over you'. Alter surmises that such gestures to the northerners could be 'diplomatic invention' on Abner's part.[43]

41. I am rendering the MT (בְּיַד דָּוִד עַבְדִּי הוֹשִׁיעַ אֶת־עַמִּי יִשְׂרָאֵל) quite literally here. Many translations opt for a first common singular verb, 'I will save', but I prefer Abner's awkward syntax in this (supposed) quotation of divine speech. The very awkwardness could in fact be revealing.
42. McCarter, *II Samuel*, p. 116.
43. Alter, *The David Story*, p. 211.

It stands to reason, then, that Abner's whole speech could be a diplomatic invention. There is little doubt that the theological comment about David's divine election dovetails with the later narrative, as commentators have rightly seen. In the immediate context, however, such dovetailing does not exculpate Abner. This speech has an unintentionally prophetic resonance; in the Deuteronomist's narrative here, Abner's words are inadvertent, much like Saul's massacre at Nob in 1 Samuel 22 unwittingly intersects with the earlier prophetic word spoken against the house of Eli.

Nonetheless, if Abner is guilty of divine exaggeration, there are some implications for his characterization, as Exum shrewdly notes: 'Have the elders of Israel sought David as their king? If so, Abner has not only stood in God's way, as he revealed in his angry words to Ishbosheth, he has also opposed the will of the people. Or is Abner manipulating the elders, using a conventional rhetorical ploy to identify their interests with his?—and with God's!'[44] The reader will observe some similarities between Abner's words to Ishbosheth—where he provides divine justification for his intentions—and his speech to the elders of Israel. Such a similarity further adds to the ambiguity that the Deuteronomist is intent on clouding Abner with, and is vital to the *pseudo-objective motivation* that will be the main component of my discussion below. In the meantime, there is a measure of resolution to Abner's northern overtures. Abner duly arrives at Hebron, where David gives him a feast. Abner departs 'in peace' (בשלום) without the reader knowing exactly what Abner has gained or what he has been 'promised'—the text is silent. Furthermore, the triple repetition of 'peace' may actually be an example of narrational overstatement to indicate that all is not tranquil: in terms of timing, just as Abner departs 'in peace' (from his perspective), Joab returns from a pirating sortie. Abner's 'peace' is poised to be shattered.

6. *Reservoir Dogs*

> And behold, the servants of David and Joab were coming from the raid, and they brought a great deal of plunder with them. (But Abner was no longer there with David in Hebron, for David let him go, and he went in peace.) Now Joab and all the army had come, and they reported to Joab, saying, 'Abner son of Ner came to the king, and he let him go, and he went in peace!' Then Joab came to the king, and said, 'What have you done? Look, *Abner* came to you! Why is this: you've let him go, and off he went? You *know* Abner son of Ner! Indeed, he came to entice you—to know your ins and outs, and to know all that you're doing!' Then Joab marched out from David's presence. He sent messengers after Abner, and they brought him back from the Water-hole of Sirah, but David did not know. (2 Sam. 3.22-26)

---

44. Exum, *Tragedy and Biblical Narrative*, p. 104.

4. *Bakhtin's* Pseudo-Objective Motivation

It is a remarkable coincidence that just as Abner leaves Hebron, Joab returns after a pillaging excursion. Since such practice was common during David's fugitive period (e.g. the term 'plunder' [שׁלל] occurs in 1 Sam. 30.26), one might expect this kind of operation to be a common way to pay a few royal bills incurred by the growing Hebron court. There is of course no mention in the text that David has given the order for this particular sortie by Joab, coinciding as it does with Abner's visit. But as Bruce Birch ruminates, 'In the light of subsequent events, one wonders if Joab's absence from Hebron at the time of Abner's visit was intentional on David's part'.[45] This is one more gap in a growing list during this narrative stretch. But regardless of the gap, Auld's point seems incontrovertible: 'Joab's absence from Hebron will have been convenient for the negotiations'.[46] The reader is three times told that Abner—presumably full from David's feast—departs from Hebron 'in peace' (בשׁלום). Joab arrives in Hebron full of a 'great deal of plunder', and is informed (ויגדו, 'and they reported') that Joab was sent 'in peace'. Who are the ones who 'tell' Joab? Brueggemann comments on the active verb (נגד) and its lack of an identifiable subject: 'The narrator is cunning in his use of a verb without an antecedent. What operated, according to the narrative, was court gossip. No one can be identified who informed Joab. No one can be held accountable'.[47]

Commentators agree that Joab's vitriolic attack on David is unqualified: Joab asserts Abner's intention to deceive, and rebukes David. In the larger context of the story, his words have a certain resonance; as Alter notes 'The simple idiom for arrival [בא אל] ironically echoes Ish-bosheth's use of the very same idiom in its sexual sense ("come into", "come to bed with") in his complaint to Abner. The sexual undertone is sustained in the next verse because the prominent verb "to dupe" [פתה] has the primary meaning of "seduce".'[48] Just as Abner harshly speaks to *his* king earlier in the chapter,

---

45. Birch, 'The First and Second Books of Samuel', p. 1224.
46. Auld, '1 and 2 Samuel', p. 231.
47. Brueggemann, *First and Second Samuel*, p. 228.
48. Alter, *The David Story*, p. 213. Cf. Polzin, *David and the Deuteronomist*, p. 44: 'In my suggestion that verse 25 is a wonderful encapsulation of the larger story's account of the comings and goings of David—a mise-en-abyme of the History's primary narrative world—I am also saying something about the historical background against which this communication between anonymous author(s) and hidden audience is to be understood: I am calling verse 25 a mise-en-abyme of the History's situation of discourse. What my reading of the history of royal Israel has emphasized, time and time again, is its desire to teach an audience in exile that cherished traditions about the royal throne of David have a seductive air about them.' As Polzin continues, there is continuity between the various points in the chapter, and most attractively, further layers of connection between the representations of Abner and David: 'the omniscient narrator shields the reader from crucial information concerning the inner motivations of Abner in the mise-en-abyme of

Joab now speaks to David in a not dissimilar manner. With Abner, there is a degree of equivocation in his speech to Ishbosheth. How then should Joab's words to his king be heard? H.W. Hertzberg notices a certain open-endedness in Joab's speech: 'Whether Joab really suspects in Abner, traitor to his lord, treachery towards David, too, or whether this is merely inserted to explain his subsequent action, remains open, especially as no reply from David is recorded'.[49] Exum similarly notes, 'Does Joab believe that Abner came to deceive David or does he dissimulate to mask his jealousy for his position? These questions point to another, more problematic issue, that of the narrator's reliability.'[50]

I certainly agree with the complexity of the questions that the narrative *intentionally* invites, but rather than the narrator's reliability being at issue, I would suggest that the issue is the narrator's strategy. Specifically, consider the final clause of this paragraph, which gives reason to pause, and ask: Exactly what is it that 'David does not know'? Does he not know about Abner's motives? Or is he in the dark about Joab's motives for commenting on Abner? Does David not know that Abner has killed Joab's brother, and thus, Joab's intentions for personal revenge? Or does the king not know that Joab intends to march out after Abner? Is this plausible? Would not the king be expected 'to know'? *Should* he have known? Moreover, whose *point of view* is reflected in the clause, 'but David did not know'? It is curious that Joab says to David, 'You know Abner (ידע)'; now the narrator says, 'David did not know (ידע)'. Keeping these various questions in mind, one wonders if this clause is, at the very least, designed to alert the reader to the forthcoming complexity of narrational discourse that unfolds as this episode continues. Stuart Lasine believes that the reader is obligated to carefully discern *what* the narrator is saying, because it is so complicated:

verse 25 and of David throughout much of the primary story world of 1–2 Samuel. Given the gap in the story about the truth or falsehood of Ishbosheth's accusations of Abner, and given the narrator's habitual shielding of the inner life of David from the reader, the "real" reason for Abner's actions remains hidden from characters and readers alike just as the "real" reasons for David's actions up to this point typically remain hidden from characters ("all Israel") and readers alike.' For a lucid discussion of mise-en-abyme with respect to the ark narrative of 1 Sam. 4–6 (drawing on L. Dällenbach, *The Mirror in the Text* [trans. J. Whiteley with E. Hughes; Cambridge: Polity Press, 1989]), see Green, *How Are the Mighty Fallen?*, pp. 144-45.

49. Hertzberg, *1 & 2 Samuel*, p. 261. Note also C.F. Keil and F. Delitzsch, *Biblical Commentary on the Books of Samuel* (trans. J. Martin; Grand Rapids: Eerdmans, 1956), p. 305: 'Joab hoped in this way to prejudice David against Abner, to make him suspected as a traitor, that he might then be able to gratify his own private revenge with perfect impunity'.

50. Exum, *Tragedy and Biblical Narrative*, pp. 104-105.

To take the narrator's report at face value, however, means that we must ignore many questions raised by his account. Would David be so eager to make a covenant with a man who has already betrayed one royal figure, especially when David once told that very man that he deserved death for his failure to guard Yahweh's anointed (1 Sam. 26.16)? Would David really grieve so strongly at the death of such a person? Isn't it more likely that David would 'know' that Abner might possibly be a spy, especially considering the fact that David himself once engaged in similar activity with Achish king of Gath (1 Sam. 27) and the Ammonites still think David capable of the same hidden agenda long after the death of Abner (2 Sam. 10.3)? Could David have been oblivious to the fact that the simultaneous presence of Abner and Joab would generate a crisis in David's inner circle, not just because they would be rivals for the same post, but because of the blood feud that began with Abner's slaying of Joab's brother? Wouldn't David realize that the death of Abner would strengthen his position?[51]

The kind of queries raised by Lasine and the above commentators are not easily answered. Perhaps they are not meant to be, and this is precisely the strategy of the Deuteronomist during this stretch of text. While there are gaps that abound in the *character zones* of both Abner and Joab, David is not exactly transparent either. Recall that in 1 Sam. 26.16 David labels Abner and his men with the opprobrious epithet 'sons of death' (בני מות). Here in 2 Samuel 3 he is willing to make a deal with Abner, and in just a little while David will refer to him as 'a prince and a great man'. This is a rather dramatic about-turn. Either David is genuine in his 'conversion' with respect to Abner, or his words represent some dissembling. Hertzberg wrestles with such matters:

> This and indeed the whole account is meant to show that David could not possibly be suspected of any guilt in the matter. We should nevertheless ask, as men may have asked even at that time (cf. v. 37), whether Joab did not from the beginning have a secret understanding with David or at least whether Abner did not 'die very opportunely' for David (like Mortimer for the Earl of Leicester).[52]

There may be a slight bifurcation in Hertzberg's analysis: on the one hand, he wants to take the text at apparent 'face-value' (in Lasine's words), yet on the other hand he notices a deep narrative tension. As for the possible suspicion surrounding David, Hertzberg concludes, 'The abruptness which characterizes all David's dealings with Abner could lend support to such a view,

---

51. S. Lasine, *Knowing Kings: Knowledge, Power, and Narcissism in the Hebrew Bible* (Semeia Studies, 40; Atlanta: Society of Biblical Literature, 2001), pp. 110-11. Lasine (p. 111) further interacts with Hertzberg and asks a further question: 'And, finally, wouldn't David realize that making a public display of his grief would conveniently serve to allay any popular suspicion of his complicity in Abner's death (see Hertzberg 1964 [= *1 & 2 Samuel*], 261 on v. 37)?'

52. Hertzberg, *1 & 2 Samuel*, p. 261.

as could the king's silence at Joab's remonstrances'.[53] A key point—that both Hertzberg and Lasine view from different angles—is that the narrator's comment 'but David did not know' is somewhat set apart from normal narrational discourse. Such a distinction should be kept in mind since further instances of this kind of narration will be apparent as this chapter continues.

7. A Perfect Murder?

> Abner returned to Hebron, and Joab inclined him toward the midst of the gate, in order to speak with him in quietness. He struck him there, in the fifth rib. *He died because of the blood of Asahel his brother.* After this, David heard. He said, 'Innocent am I and my kingdom before the LORD forever, from the blood of Abner son of Ner. May it whirl around on Joab's head and on his father's whole house! May there never be cut off from Joab's house someone with an issue, or leprosy, or who grabs the spindle, or who falls on the sword, or who lacks bread!' *Thus Joab and his brother Abishai killed Abner because he put their brother Asahel to death in Gibeon, during the war.* (2 Sam. 3.27-30 [emphasis added[54]])

When Joab's messengers bring Abner back, they 'cause him to return' (וישבו, hiphil) from the 'Water-hole of Sirah'. According to BDB, and following Deut. 13.6, the designation בור הסרה could be translated 'Cistern of Treason'. There is an appropriate multivalence to this designation: Does this remind the reader that Abner has acted treasonously against his king? Or does this alert the reader that Joab is about to act against the 'official' party line of Hebron? By any measure, the Water-hole of Sirah foregrounds the spatial dimension of this episode—the key component of which is the 'gate'.

In the MT of 2 Sam. 3.27, Joab swerves Abner 'into the midst of the gate'.[55] The city gate is the place for the dispensing of justice and for the conducting of legal tribunals, as texts such as Deut. 16.18, 21.19, and 25.7 make clear. Joab steers Abner into the midst of the city gate and in broad daylight—perhaps even before the elders of the city—where he *publicly* avenges the blood of his brother. By stabbing Abner in the 'fifth rib', Polzin observes that there is a narrative 'mirroring' between this death and the previous death of Asahel in 2 Sam. 2.23: 'Abner tells Asahel to turn aside [נטה], but Asahel would not turn aside [סור], so Abner smote him in the

---

53. Hertzberg, *1 & 2 Samuel*, p. 261.

54. Italics are added to draw attention to what I perceive to be an unusual kind of narrational utterance, following Bakhtin.

55. Compare the LXX's reading: 'And he brought back Abner to Hebron, and Joab caused him to turn aside from the gate to speak with him, laying wait for him' (καὶ ἐπέστρεψεν Αβεννηρ εἰς Χεβρων καὶ ἐξέκλινεν αὐτὸν Ιωαβ ἐκ πλαγίων τῆς πύλης λαλῆσαι πρὸς αὐτὸν ἐνεδρεύων). As I discuss elsewhere in this book, in the LXX the emphasis is on the private assassination of Abner; in the MT, it is a public execution.

belly [חמש]. Similarly in ch. 3, "When Abner returned to Hebron, Joab took him aside [נטה] and there smote him in the belly [חמש]".⁵⁶ The narrator twice provides the ostensible motivation for Joab's stabbing—to avenge his brother—but could Joab's motive more complicated than this? Bruce Birch's reflection merits some attention:

> Joab must be seen as a figure with two interests that work against the acceptability of an alliance with Abner. The first is his hatred and distrust of Abner, stemming from Abner's killing of Joab's brother Asahel in the battle described in 2.12-32. Joab sees himself as the legitimate bearer of a claim for vengeance against Abner, although ordinarily bloodguilt would not be recognized for a death suffered in war—i.e., it was not considered murder. The second of Joab's interests in this matter has to do with influence on David. Joab eventually becomes commander of David's armies (8.16), but it is reasonable to think that Abner might have assumed this role if he had lived. In any case, Abner would have been a powerful and influential military adviser and leader within David's kingdom, and this would make him Joab's natural rival for David's favor.⁵⁷

Birch raises the possibility that the motives of Joab could be twofold: to avenge the death of Asahel *and* to eliminate Abner as his military and political rival. Indeed, given that Joab maneuvers Abner into the midst of the city gate, it would suggest that he wants the assassination to be publicly perceived as blood vengeance. On the one hand, the twofold mention of Joab's motive by the narrator would seem to confirm such a motive. On the other hand, such narrational comments are not overly frequent in this stretch, and hence represent a different category of utterance. The narrator's words about Joab's motives appear to resemble the above comment, '*but David did not know*', as though it were a form of understatement. Furthermore, the narrator's twin comments of vv. 27 and 30 are not identical: v. 30 adds Gibeon as the place where Asahel is put to death, and Abishai as an accomplice in Abner's killing. Despite Hertzberg's claim that the inclusion of Abishai at this point is 'an obvious mistake', I would prefer to argue that the narrational strategy is rather more complex. Abishai himself has a history of enmity against the house of Saul, and Asahel was *his* brother as well.⁵⁸ Birch points out that the two death words are different: Joab and Abishai 'kill' (הרג) Abner, whereas Abner 'puts to death' (המית) their brother Asahel.⁵⁹ In light of such data, Exum's summary is most appropriate: 'Is v. 30 simply an elaboration of v. 27? Are we to assume that Joab and Abishai together take

---

56. Polzin, *David and the Deuteronomist*, p. 37.
57. Birch, 'The First and Second Books of Samuel', p. 1225.
58. Exum (*Tragedy and Biblical Narrative*, p. 173 n. 89) mentions the desire of Abishai to kill Saul in 1 Sam. 26, only he is restrained by David: 'Not to be left out of the picture, he is associated with Joab in the murder of Abner'.
59. Birch, 'The First and Second Books of Samuel', p. 1225.

Abner aside to speak with him, yet Abner suspects nothing? In view of the high degree of textual ambiguity and the many questions surrounding Abner, it is not surprising that the account of his assassination should be so equivocal.'[60] There is a complex web of motives in this episode, and the point of the double mention of Joab's motive may direct the reader to the layers of political intrigue that surface here. Such intrigue is obviously intensified when David's reaction to the news of Abner's death is considered.

8. *The Usual Suspects*

Upon hearing the news—disclosed by an unspecified intermediary—David's first reaction is categorically to distance himself from the killing: 'Exempt am I (נקי אנכי) and my kingdom before the LORD forever, from the blood of Abner son of Ner'. While David's avowal of innocence almost certainly has a forensic nuance, what is less clear is *who* he is addressing. Since an interlocutor is not mentioned, one might assume that there is a 'public' dimension to this speech that cannot be discounted. To be sure, Abner's death is a political problem for David—and hence it is likely that he addressing a broader (presumably northern) constituency with his speech.[61] There is a certain irony in cursing Joab: just as Abner acts in his own interests over and against his king, now Joab is cursed for doing the same thing. While Abner is welcomed by David, Joab receives a vociferous oath: 'The curse here is a terrible one, similar to that on the house of Eli in I Sam. 2.31-4: the family is always to have weak members, diseased or effeminate, lacking warrior aptitude, or those doomed to violent death or poverty'.[62] The curse on Joab is not the end of David's reaction; on the contrary, the curse is only the overture to a highly public and poetic demonstration of grief.

> Then David said to Joab and all the people with him, 'Tear your clothes, be clothed in sackcloth, and lament in front of Abner!' *But King David was walking behind the casket.* They buried Abner in Hebron, and the king lifted up his voice and wept at the grave of Abner, and all the people wept. The king chanted for Abner, and said,

---

60. Exum, *Tragedy and Biblical Narrative*, p. 105.

61. J.C. VanderKam ('Davidic Complicity in the Deaths of Abner and Eshbaal', *JBL* 94 [1980], pp. 521-39 [534]) notes that Ishbosheth/Eshbaal's murder in the next chapter will provide a similar embarrassment.

62. P.R. Ackroyd, *The Second Book of Samuel* (New York: Cambridge University Press, 1977), p. 45. On the term פלך, see S.W. Holloway, 'Distaff, Crutch, or Chain Gang: The Curse on the House of Joab in 2 Samuel iii 29', *VT* 37 (1987), pp. 370-75. After arguing that David's curse can include forced-labor as a consequence, in light of later events in the narrative, Holloway concludes: 'It is an excellent irony...that David should pray that House of Joab may never be without a corvée-worker'.

4. *Bakhtin's* Pseudo-Objective Motivation

> Like the death of a fool[63] should Abner die?
>   Your hands were not bound,
>   Your feet were not hauled out in bronze.
> Like one falls before sons of injustice,
>   You have fallen.
>
> And all the people added to weep over him.
>
> (2 Sam. 3.31-34 [emphasis added])

After issuing an imperative to Joab and the troops, there is an important statement from the narrator that provides the title 'King David'. The context for this epithet is fraught with background: David instructs his guilty colleague Joab to walk in front, while he himself walks behind. It has been observed that this occasion is the first time in the narrative that the title 'King David' is deployed: 'While David had previously been identified as "king"…this is the first formal use linking personal name and royal office. It is when the threat of the north has been decisively eliminated in the death of Abner that the throne is secure enough to warrant this powerful phrase.'[64] Glancing ahead in the narrative, the title 'King David' will be used at least fifty more times in the story. Glancing backward in the narrative, the title 'King Saul' has been used only once (1 Sam. 18.6). In my view, the Deuteronomist strategically uploads this title precisely at this moment (2 Sam. 2.31) to stress the 'Davidic advantage' resulting from the fall of Abner, who presently occupies the coffin behind Joab and in front of David. The scenic description of the funeral march is emphasized here to provide the framework for hearing the funeral lament of King David: in other words, the lyrics of grief need to be heard in the context of the funeral march that ends at the grave of Abner. Thus, these are not private words of grief but a public eulogy with all the ceremony of a state occasion.

A brief survey of recent secondary literature on this passage evinces a range of reactions to David's requiem for Abner. Some commentators hear in these words soaring lyrics of lament and pathos.[65] Other commentators

---

63. The term 'fool' (נָבָל) forms a word-play with the name 'Nabal' (נָבָל). Note Polzin's (*David and the Deuteronomist*, p. 218 n. 9) suggestive comment: 'Since Abner's power over Israel still poses a threat to David in spite of their covenant, Abner's association with Nabal in this chapter remains a narrative possibility. Abner's angry response to Ishbosheth, "Am I the head of Caleb which belongs to Judah?"—if indeed this is the correct translation of [הֲרֹאשׁ כֶּלֶב אָנֹכִי אֲשֶׁר לִיהוּדָה] in verse 8—recalls the theme of David's increasing control over Caleb, which culminated in his marriage to the widow of Nabal the Carmelite. At the same time, the Deuteronomist may be using David's lamentation over Abner to liken the deceased to Nabal: "Does Abner die as Nabal died?" (v. 33).'

64. Brueggemann, *First and Second Samuel*, p. 230.

65. Bergen, *1, 2 Samuel*, p. 314: 'David had been traumatized by the shocking turn of events that day'. Cf. Mullen, *Narrative History and Ethnic Boundaries*, pp. 240-41.

hear someone who may not be completely blameless putting on a public relations show that is worthy of a Western-style politician. As Brueggemann notes, 'We need not doubt David's genuine respect for Abner, but the funeral is also a media event. It is like a US president with the returned body of a soldier from an unauthorized war. The president must lead national mourning, which is genuine, but at the same time must stage a media event designed to legitimate policy.'[66]

There is of course a certain poignancy to Brueggemann's words in light of recent events in a more contemporary era. But with respect to David's situation in 2 Samuel 3, Brueggemann is proposing that the ceremony is somewhat contrived, and that the lengthy procession becomes a prolegomena for the funeral speech itself. In terms of the dynamics and dimensions of David's eulogy for Abner, Hertzberg notes: 'The verse, skillfully constructed and subtly expressed, laments that this noble man was done to death like a fettered law-breaker, attacked by robbers: "but the malefactor was not he—it was rather those who stabbed him in the back" (Gressmann)'.[67] If we consider the position of Hertzberg and Gressmann, then the implication is that David is publicly characterizing Joab (and Abishai) as 'robbers' and criminals. For the postmodern reader it is a matter of proper jurisprudence that the chief suspect in any murder trial should be presumed innocent. The court of public perception, though, has not always been so generous, and the Davidic court appears to be no exception. It is of course possible for someone to be innocent, but if no one believes you, then there is a problem: 'David is the chief of the mourners for Abner, and although his sentiments may be genuine, it is clear that his mourning bears political significance'.[68] It is significant that David begins his tribute to the deceased with a rhetorical question. While one guesses that the audience for this question is the northern league, David immediately changes gears and addresses the dead man himself. By virtue of this words, there is a dramatic sense of personal involvement here with a double efficacy: David simultaneously distances himself from Joab while appearing to draw near to the beloved memory of the departed.

66. Brueggemann, *First and Second Samuel*, p. 230.
67. Hertzberg, *1 & 2 Samuel*, pp. 263-64; cf. H. Gressmann, 'The Oldest History Writing in Israel', in D.M. Gunn (ed.), *Narrative and Novella in Samuel: Studies by Hugo Gressman and Other Scholars 1906–1923* (trans. D.E. Orton; JSOTSup, 116; Sheffield: Almond Press, 1991), pp. 9-58. For a study of David as a 'soldier-poet' in the narrative, see A.R. Ceresko, 'A Rhetorical Analysis of David's "Boast" (1 Samuel 17.34-37): Some Reflections on Method', *CBQ* 47 (1985), pp. 58-74.
68. Birch, 'The First and Second Books of Samuel', p. 1226. See also Exum, *Tragedy and Biblical Narrative*, p. 106.

4. *Bakhtin's* Pseudo-Objective Motivation

9. *The Latest Opinion Polls*

> Then all the people came to implore David to eat on that day. David swore an oath, 'Thus may God do to me, and even more, if—before the sun goes down—I taste bread or anything'. *But all the people noticed, and it was good in their eyes; indeed, everything the king did was good in the eyes of the people. Hence all the people knew, even all Israel on that day, that it was not from the king to cause the death of Abner son of Ner.* The king said to his servants, 'Don't you know that a prince and a great man has fallen in Israel today? So I am today a tender and an anointed king. But these men—the sons of Zeruiah—are too severe for me. May the LORD repay the one doing evil according to his evil deeds!' (2 Sam. 3.35-39 [emphasis added])

As this long and complex episode begins to move toward a conclusion, a key feature that several commentators discuss is the various levels of 'knowledge' that are reported. Specifically, the reader may wonder what David *does* know, what David *does not* know, and *when* does he know or not know. Further, in terms of knowledge, the crucial lines for this chapter are 2 Sam. 3.36-37: 'But all the people noticed, and it was good in their eyes; indeed, everything the king did was good in the eyes of the people. Hence all the people knew, *even all Israel*, on that day that it was not from the king to cause the death of Abner son of Ner.' Surely this is not a simple case of the narrator merely disclosing information, nor does this line represent the 'author's opinion'; this line rather seems to capture the public opinion 'on that day'. Perhaps even more than just generic public opinion, this line also refracts the beliefs of a more specific constituency—'all Israel'—which in this politically charged episode sounds more like the Saulide northern tribes in particular. It is my contention that 3.36-37 bears a striking resemblance to *pseudo-objective motivation* that Bakhtin theorizes, and thus the viewpoint of these lines does not represent the opinion of the author, but rather presents the general consensus of public opinion 'on that day' when Abner is lamented by David. Polzin poses a trenchant question, as he asks, 'What is the basis for the people's acceptance of David's acts of mourning as authentic signs of his innocence in the death of Abner? The narrator makes the claim that this is merely an instance of what the people *habitually* think and feel about David.' Polzin continues:

> However, the narrator's words are much more than a statement of the people's thoughts and feelings about David. What sounds loud and clear through the piling up of universals ('all the people', 'everything that the king did', 'so all the people and all Israel') is the narrator's distance from the people's wholesale acceptance of David, even in this instance when such confidence in him, as the reader well knows, turns out incidentally to be justified'.[69]

---

69. Polzin, *David and the Deuteronomist*, p. 40.

Even though one may quibble with Polzin's notion of 'justified' in this context, the use of *pseudo-objective motivation* here equips the reader with a unique perspective from which to view the events of this chapter. To adapt the words of Walter Brueggemann: 'in response to the death of Abner, David issues an extravagant disclaimer, taking great care to assign the death to Joab (2 Sam. 3.28-29)'. But 'the narrative [also] adds: So all the people and all Israel understood that day that the king had no part in the killing of Abner son of Ner. (2 Sam. 3.37) The rhetoric at least invites suspicion. Apparently some thought David was implicated in the death.'[70] Brueggemann argues that there is a 'careful and seemingly exaggerated rhetoric of 2 Samuel 3', and consequently one may indeed deduce that the subtext of the line is that *there is an air of doubt* that envelops David in this matter. If so, then David's executive sensibilities are graphically displayed here: the extravagant mourning ritual for Abner is politically endearing, and David is successful insofar as public relations are concerned. Yet as the episode concludes, there are more questions than answers about David's knowledge. As Polzin notes, the king's 'funerary deportment' is convincing enough, but further questions linger:

> the narrator's voice in vv. 36-37 clearly distances itself from its reference both to the people's wholesale pleasure in David and to their knowledge of David's innocence in the death of Abner. How can the narrator be so intent on making sure that readers know of David's innocence in the crime, only then to sound a note of caution about how easily the people of Israel were won over to David's side by his funerary deportment? How are David's seductive power over all Israel and Israel's knowledge of David's innocence bound up with the Deuteronomist's presentation of David in the History?[71]

10. Conclusion

In my opinion, the idea of *pseudo-objective motivation* seems amenable for helping a reader to navigate the multifaceted issue of David's apparent innocence in 2 Samuel 3. The questions raised by Polzin in the quotation above are not easily answered, but the note of 'caution' sounded by the narrator is surely a matter that needs to be addressed. If David's funerary deportment is choreographed as a public relations stratagem to persuade Israel of his own non-involvement in Abner's assassination, then he is clearly successful: in terms of the *perception* of the crowd, the king is without guilt. For the Deuteronomist, the literary strategy of creating some distance from the realm of public opinion is important for David's characterization. After all,

---

70. W. Brueggemann, *1 & 2 Kings* (Macon: Smyth & Helwys, 2000), p. 35.
71. Polzin, *David and the Deuteronomist*, p. 36.

4. *Bakhtin's* Pseudo-Objective Motivation 63

David is one of the most complex figures in ancient literature.[72] While David is God's anointed choice and the kingdom of Israel is a 'gift', there remain a host of human dynamics in this narrative.[73] One can immediately see that *pseudo-objective motivation* has great versatility at this key point in the larger story: there is a subtle undermining of the crowd and popular opinion while simultaneously the reader is exposed to a critique of power and self-aggrandizement. Such a critique of Israel's monarchy, it would stand to reason, must be close to the Deuteronomist's heart in light of both God's promise to David and the collapse at the end of 2 Kings 25. Hugh Pyper considers the utterance of 2 Sam. 3.36-37 to be a significant moment. According to him, 'David's mourning is public and theatrical with a seemingly staged ritual where the people urge him to eat and he publicly refuses. The point is explicitly made that this pleased the people, and that they then understood David was completely blameless in this matter'. Pyper continues:

> Is this the noble-hearted king acknowledging the death of a worthy adversary and a potential ally? A more suspicious reading might wonder how far all this is convenient to the king, or to the image of the king. One might also see a veiled criticism in the very explicitness of the account as it appears here in 2 Samuel. The wide-eyed acceptance of the king's innocence goes beyond what might be expected, raising the doubts that superfluous assurances always raise. By the conclusion of the episode, David ends up with a rival eliminated and the blame placed on Joab's personal vendetta. The leader of the still-disaffected tribes is removed in a way that leaves David as a viable candidate to step into his place'.[74]

Building on Pyper's analysis, I would argue that *pseudo-objective motivation* is a helpful critical category for considering this episode because so many key elements in the forthcoming narrative are exposed here: personal 'conflict' with Joab illustrates the internal tensions David himself will experience, while political tensions with the northern tribes foreground the dark undercurrent of conflict that is barely disguised on the surface. The 'superfluous assurances' of 2 Sam. 3.36-37 indicate that knowledge and tacit approval of the crowd could be temporary; in other words, public opinion seems to support the idea that Joab is the architect of Abner's demise. However, just as hostility with the northern tribes festers below the surface for much of the story, so there is a seed of conflict between David and Joab sown in this episode that will germinate later in the narrative.

72. G. Josipovici, *The Book of God: A Response to the Bible* (New Haven: Yale University Press, 1988), pp. 191-209.

73. Gunn, 'David and the Gift of the Kingdom', pp. 14-45.

74. H.S. Pyper, 'Reading David's Mind: Inference, Emotion and the Limits of Language', in A.G. Hunter and P.R. Davies (eds.), *Sense and Sensitivity: Essays on Reading the Bible in Memory of Robert Carroll* (JSOTSup, 348; Sheffield: Sheffield Academic Press, 2002), pp. 73-86 (78).

In terms of this personal conflict with Joab, it would seem that in 2 Samuel 3 Joab absorbs the brunt of bad publicity in order for David's innocence to be recognized. Notably, Joab's conduct will be not dissimilar in ch. 11 —sacrificing a contingent of soldiers to facilitate the cover-up—yet in so doing Joab arguably gains something of an upper hand on the king that will continue for a considerable narrative stretch. Of course, there is a pointed contrast in ch. 19. While here in ch. 3 David's astute political imagination is evidenced—with Joab on the receiving end of a scathing curse—later in the story the roles are diametrically reversed after the rebellion of Absalom: in 19.7 Joab is the one who practices some political choreography ('So now arise, go out and speak kindly to your servants, for I swear by the LORD, if you do not go out, surely not a man will pass the night with you, and this will be worse for you than all the evil that has come upon you from your youth until now'). The reversal is apparent: David issues the imperatives to Joab and swears an oath in ch. 3, whereas Joab issues the imperatives to David and swears an oath in ch. 19. Consequently, the events of ch. 3 have far-reaching implications.

In terms of the public ledger, Hertzberg observes that David's inner circle will not be the same: 'Here, for the first time, internal difficulties at the court are brought to light, difficulties over which the king does not have complete mastery'.[75] For David personally, the events of 2 Samuel 3 mark the beginning of a new level of struggle. As Birch notes, 'David will have to deal with the Abners and the Joabs, the civil wars and the Philistine wars, his own faithfulness and the seductions of his own power'.[76] Having said this, it may be somewhat artificial to bifurcate the 'public' and the 'private' careers of David, especially since this is not the last one hears about the demise of Abner: the aged king reviews the matter of Abner's death in his final words to his son Solomon (1 Kgs 2).[77] Whether David has long been planning the demise of Joab cannot be determined. However, the conflict between Joab

---

75. Hertzberg, *1 & 2 Samuel*, p. 262.
76. Birch, 'The First and Second Books of Samuel', p. 1217.
77. See further Frolov, 'Succession Narrative', pp. 81-104, and especially his interaction with the work of J.S. Ackerman (p. 99): 'Ackerman argues that 2 Sam. 20 traces the political split between Israel and Judah that also began under the איש לאהלו slogan (1 Kgs 12.16) to the psychological split between public and private within David's personality (Ackerman, "Knowing Good and Evil", p. 48). There is no doubt that it is possible to read 2 Sam. 20 together with 1 Kgs 12; but why not do this the other way around? Viewed against the backdrop of Sheba's semicomic rebellion, Jeroboam's revolt looks doomed from the outset; 2 Sam. 20 foreshadows therefore the ultimate failure of the northern kingdom.' I would add that such failure is hinted at even earlier than 2 Sam. 20, and that the ultimate failure of the north is introduced as early as 2 Sam. 3. Moreover, the motif of powerful generals undermining their sovereigns will be a hallmark of the northern political experience.

4. *Bakhtin's* Pseudo-Objective Motivation

and Abner certainly serves to presage the fragile north–south relations that will plague David (e.g. Sheba son of Bicri) and Solomon (e.g. Jeroboam son of Nebat) in the days ahead.

I will conclude by arguing that the technique of *pseudo-objective motivation* is useful to consider when reading 2 Samuel 3 because of the insights in this chapter regarding the theme of Davidic election. Unlike the northern kingdom in the Deuteronomistic History, the promise to David in 2 Samuel 7 results in far more stability. The utterance of 3.36-37 needs to be considered as something akin to *pseudo-objective motivation* because it captures an important theological angle of the narrative. In the episode of Abner's demise, David has a good return at the polls. In terms of public opinion, notwithstanding the negative 'media hype' surrounding Abner's death, David remains popular. Yet the same crowd—'even all Israel'—will soon be responding to the rebellious lyrics 'What share have we in Jesse?' The utterance of 3.36-37 thus serves to focus attention on God's promise as the central reason for stability of the Davidic kingdom, and not simply effective political decision-making. This chapter is replete with machinations, including highly suspicious invocations of (alleged) divine discourse. This chapter is also bursting with political maneuverings, including questionable loyalties and self-serving motives. Yet through such utterances as 3.36-37, the Deuteronomist reminds his exilic audience that no amount of scheming and maneuvering can jeopardize the divine guarantee to the Davidic throne.[78] Whether David is popular and 'innocent' in the eyes of the public is essentially immaterial: no Abner can break a Davidic king, and no popular uprising can stand in the way of the promise.[79] On the contrary, so much of the

---

78. See J.P. Fokkelman, *Narrative Art and Poetry in the Books of Samuel. III. Throne and City (2 Sam. 2–8 and 21–24)* (Assen: Van Gorcum, 1990), p. 76, for the discourse of Abner that he puts in 'inverted commas', as it were: 'Up to now all this is in the inverted commas which a cynical reception wants to put round the speech of someone who, in reality, is engaged in the perpetration of power politics and is almost sadistically harassing his puppet with pious words. But the curious thing about this is that the thesis "Abner as willing instrument of God" seen on the level of a higher plane is still seriously legitimized in the scheme of the writer. In the long run Abner is a character who is allowed to come forward several times as an actor in a design which stretches far back, and of which David's career is merely a part. On a spiritual level the weakness of Ishbosheth and the strength of Abner provide the leverage used by God to realize David's ascendancy.'

79. David is often described as אִישׁ כִּלְבָבוֹ ('a man according to his [God's] heart'), based on the words of Samuel in 1 Sam. 13.14. Regarding this phrase, McCarter (*I Samuel*, p. 229) comments as follows: 'This has nothing to do with any great fondness of Yahweh's for David or any special quality of David, to whom it patently refers. Rather it emphasizes the free divine selection of the heir to the throne (*nāgîd*, "prince"), as the alternative to the endurance of Saul's "kingship [dynasty!] over Israel forever"... As its use in 14.7 shows, the expression [כלבב], "according to (one's) heart", has to do with an individual's will or purpose. Compare Ps 20.5 [יִתֶּן־לְךָ כִלְבָבֶךָ]...' Note the further

northern kingdom's political life seems foreshadowed here—the power of military figures, the executions, the internal strife—yet inexorably the divine will prevails.[80]

reflection of J. Goldingay, *Old Testament Theology*. I. *Israel's Gospel* (Downers Grove, IL: InterVarsity Press, 2003), p. 557: 'David is a king "according to Yhwh's heart" (e.g. 1 Sam. 13.14). Other occurrences of such phrases imply this need not suggest he is a king who shares Yhwh's priorities or way of thinking. It simply identifies David as the king whom Yahweh personally chose and made a commitment to. For theological as well as practical reasons the people will thus have a hard time removing this king whom they anointed. He is more like a lifetime president than one who needs periodic reelection. Yhwh is committed to David independently of commitment to the people as a whole.'

80. Cf. McCarter, *II Samuel*, p. 83. Note also Brueggemann, *First and Second Samuel*, p. 232: 'in the midst of bargains, killings, and funerals, in the midst of seizing concubines (Abner) and guarding preeminence (Joab), there is another power and purpose at work. The promise of Yahweh functions, hidden, in the midst of human action.' Brueggemann then summarizes: 'The narrator lets us see the operation of Yahweh's determined promise through these unwitting characters, their devious words, and their self-serving actions. Through the sordid narrative, the kingdom has advanced a step toward Jerusalem.' Cf. B.S. Childs, *Introduction to the Old Testament as Scripture* (Philadelphia: Fortress Press, 1979), pp. 276-77.

5

NATHAN: PROPHET, POLITICIAN, AND PLAYWRIGHT

In the book of Samuel–Kings, the prophet Nathan has evoked a variety of responses from commentators over the years. G.H. Jones has undertaken the most complete study of the prophet, and compiled a variety of opinions on his role and personality.[1] Nathan is variously described as an enigmatic 'counselor', a 'public functionary at the royal court', an 'indigenous Jebusite court official' co-opted into the new regime, a 'minister with special responsibilities in the immediate entourage of the king', a 'person involved in a political intrigue for whom the label "prophet" is a misguided addition', and not least, 'a typical political schemer who depended entirely on human means to achieve his purpose'.[2] Moreover, numerous scholars have concluded that a montage of sources is used in the sections of text where Nathan appears.[3] Hence, the composite nature of Samuel–Kings results in incoherence with respect to his overall presentation in the narrative, due to a perceived tension between an original core tradition and later additions.[4] The present chapter is a study in characterization; it will examine the three episodes where Nathan the prophet appears in Samuel–Kings, and evaluate these episodes from a literary approach to see if this provides a new perspective on the matter of Nathan's character and role in the narrative. The three episodes which feature Nathan are: 2 Samuel 7 (where he is involved in the divine word concerning the temple and house of David), 2 Samuel 12 (where he makes two appearances: first to deliver a message to David about his sin, and then a momentary appearance to deliver a message to David about his son), and 1 Kings 1 (where he is a key player in the process of Solomon's accession to the throne).

---

1. G.H. Jones, *The Nathan Narratives* (JSOTSup, 80; Sheffield: JSOT Press, 1990).
2. Jones, *The Nathan Narratives*, pp. 20-21, 145.
3. McCarter, *II Samuel*, pp. 210-31; cf. A.A. Anderson, *2 Samuel* (WBC, 11; Dallas: Word Books, 1989), pp. 109-16.
4. Jones, *The Nathan Narratives*, pp. 143-47.

1. *Episode 1: 2 Samuel 7.1-17*

> Now when the king dwelt in his house, and the LORD had given him rest from all his enemies round about, the king said to Nathan the prophet, 'See now, I dwell in a house of cedar, but the ark of God dwells in a tent'. And Nathan said to the king, 'Go, do all that is in your heart; for the LORD is with you'. (2 Sam. 7.1-3)[5]

Many commentators have been puzzled by the lack of genealogical data for Nathan. He is simply referred to as 'the prophet' and first appears here in dialogue with the king. Without attempting to resolve this issue, two things can be mentioned in passing. First, it is notable that during David's periods of *inactivity*, Nathan the prophet is particularly active. Second, the almost casual manner in which David initiates conversation with the prophet suggests a kind of intimacy. But in this conversation, what is David *looking for* when he consults the prophet about the incongruity between his house of cedar and the ark in the midst of curtains? Is he seeking a divine oracle, or some general *human* encouragement? Nathan's exegesis of David's query indicates that human encouragement is sufficient, which he promptly provides. But it is evident that both are being somewhat indirect in their speech. The assumption here is that Nathan must discern that David is referring to the construction of a temple, a project which receives the prophet's unqualified endorsement. This affirmation is complicated, though, in this episode's next scene:

> But that same night the word of the LORD came to Nathan, 'Go and tell my servant David, "Thus says the LORD: Would you build me a house to dwell in? I have not dwelt in a house since the day I brought up the people of Israel from Egypt to this day, but I have been moving about in a tent for my dwelling. In all places where I have moved with all the people of Israel, did I speak a word with any of the judges of Israel, whom I commanded to shepherd my people Israel, saying, 'Why have you not built me a house of cedar?'" Now therefore thus you shall say to my servant David, "Thus says the LORD... Moreover the LORD declares to you that the LORD will make you a house. When your days are fulfilled and you lie down with your fathers, I will raise up your offspring after you, who shall come forth from your body, and I will establish his kingdom. He shall build a house for my name, and I will establish the throne of his kingdom for ever. I will be his father, and he shall be my son. When he commits iniquity, I will chasten him with the rod of men, with the stripes of the sons of men; but I will not take my steadfast love from him, as I took it from Saul, whom I put away from before you. And your house and your kingdom shall be made sure for ever before me; your throne shall be established for ever."' In accordance with all these words, and in accordance with all this vision, Nathan spoke to David. (2 Sam. 7.4-8a, 11b-17)

---

5. Throughout this chapter longer quotations from the biblical text follow the RSV translation.

5. Nathan: Prophet, Politician, and Playwright

2 Samuel 7 has elicited an immense amount of commentary over the ages, as is evidenced by the massive bibliography pertaining to this material. Source-critical archeologists have excavated layers of compositional strata in this chapter, while other scholars have debated that from a form-critical viewpoint it could be seen as the work of one author.[6] There is general agreement, though, of the importance of this chapter within the narrative of David. Walter Brueggemann refers to this chapter as 'the dramatic and theological center of the entire Samuel corpus'.[7] Accordingly, there has been some analysis of 2 Samuel 7 from a literary perspective. Lyle Eslinger's helpful study has illuminated the mingled shades of 'rhetoric and persuasion' in the chapter.[8] Further, Robert Polzin has drawn attention to the 'complex voice structure through which the oracle conveys meaning'.[9] Consider his following remarks:

> The narrator reports God's words in direct discourse in such a way that there are four levels of reported speech within them. God's exact command to Nathan is the first level: 'Go and tell my servant David' (v. 5a). God's words then descend to a second level by reporting exactly what Nathan is to say to David: 'Thus says the LORD' (v. 5b). God's words reach a third level when Nathan directly reports the words of God he introduced through 5b: 'Would you build me a house...?' (vv. 5c-7). Finally, God's words in verses 5-7 conclude with a fourth level of reported speech in which God reports himself as never having said, 'Why have you not built me a house of cedar?' (v. 7b). We see the complexity in verses 4-7 when we simply describe its voice structure: the narrator (v. 4) quotes God (v. 5a) quoting Nathan (v. 5b) quoting God (vv. 5c-7a) quoting himself (v. 7b).[10]

It should be emphasized that David does not hear this word directly—it is mediated by means of Nathan, after he receives the nocturnal vision. At the conclusion of this lengthy divine speech, the narrator reports: 'In accordance with all these words, and in accordance with all this vision, Nathan spoke to David'. I would like to argue that the complex rhetorical structure of these divine words indicates that this address is *not solely intended for the king*. Of course David and his house are the subjects, and it is their future which is the central issue. But it should be stressed that by virtue of the *style* of this discourse, Nathan is also part of the intended audience. He is certainly commanded to 'Go and tell David'; the sense, however, is that he is to listen carefully to these words before relaying them. The complexity of this speech

---

6. Summarized in Anderson, *2 Samuel*, p. 114. An extensive overview of the scholarship on the editorial history of the passage is provided in McCarter, *II Samuel*, pp. 220-24.
7. Brueggemann, *First and Second Samuel*, p. 253.
8. L. Eslinger, *House of God or House of David: The Rhetoric of 2 Samuel 7* (JSOTSup, 164; Sheffield: JSOT Press, 1994).
9. Polzin, *David and the Deuteronomist*, p. 71.
10. Polzin, *David and the Deuteronomist*, pp. 71-72.

in 7.3-16 is designed, among other things, to communicate four points to Nathan. First, the prophet is rebuked for blithely encouraging David: 'Go, do all that is in your heart; for the LORD is with you'. The rather acerbic edge to the divine words illustrates that the LORD is not pleased with either Nathan or David's presumption,[11] and unlike the two of them, speaks of 'building a house' without any indirection whatsoever. Second, the prophet receives something of a theological education. Eslinger successfully draws attention to the rhetorical subtleties of this passage. However, one could take it a step further and suggest that part of the rhetorical thrust is aimed at educating the prophet. Third, Nathan receives instructions that are *minutely specific*—even to the point whereby *indirect discourse* is employed. This is designed to show the prophet how important this message is, and that it is imperative that he deliver it flawlessly. In other words he is being instructed not to tell the king simply to 'Go, do all that is in your heart', but rather to speak in consonance with the divine instruction. Fourth, Nathan the prophet is given insight into the future promises to David's house. Specifically, because this divine message is mediated through him, Nathan *knows about the promise to David regarding 'the one who will issue from his loins'*—seemingly a son yet to be born—who will sit on the throne of Israel in an eternally established kingdom. In sum, these four factors illustrate that the divine discourse certainly functions as a rebuke to Nathan, but also serves to acquaint the prophet with the divine plans for David's future offspring and provide him with the necessary motivation for his own later actions in the narrative. If a reader is seeking a motivation for the prophet's conduct in subsequent episodes, it may be that this speech provides Nathan with a sense of a divine mission.

2. *Episode 2: 2 Samuel 12.1-15, 24-25*

And the LORD sent Nathan to David. He came to him, and said to him, 'There were two men in a certain city, the one rich and the other poor. The rich man had very many flocks and herds; but the poor man had nothing but one little ewe lamb, which he had bought. And he brought it up, and it grew up with him and with his children; it used to eat of his morsel, and drink from his cup, and lie in his bosom, and it was like a daughter to him. Now there came a traveler to the rich man, and he was unwilling to take one of his own flock or herd to prepare for the wayfarer who had come to him, but he took the poor man's lamb, and prepared it for the man who had come to him.' Then David's anger was greatly kindled against the man; and he said to Nathan, 'As the LORD lives, the man who has done this deserves to die; and he shall restore the lamb fourfold, because he did this thing, and because he had no pity'. Nathan said to David, 'You are the man. Thus says

---

11. Eslinger, *House of God or House of David*, p. 26.

5. *Nathan: Prophet, Politician, and Playwright*

the LORD, the God of Israel, "I anointed you king over Israel, and I delivered you out of the hand of Saul..."' David said to Nathan, 'I have sinned against the LORD'. And Nathan said to David, 'The LORD also has put away your sin; you shall not die. Nevertheless, because by this deed you have utterly scorned the LORD, the child that is born to you shall die.' Then Nathan went to his house. (2 Sam. 12.1-7, 13-15)

An interpretive issue which immediately arises is whether Nathan is reciting this story about the 'two men in one city' on his own authority, or if this is part of a divine plan to trip David in self-judgment. This is an important question for Nathan's characterization and will be discussed in a moment. I would begin, though, by arguing that Nathan invents this 'affair of the ewe-lamb'. Stylistically its 'emphatically rhythmic character, with a fondness for parallel terms' and words that are rare in biblical prose seems 'to make clear its own status as a traditional tale and poetic construction'.[12] Indeed, there is another example of the exact same kind of story in ch. 14, which unambiguously is invented for similar reasons.[13] It seems plausible, therefore, to understand an element of connection in the two stories. Of course, if this is so obviously an example of literary invention, why would David not have recognized it as such (as he does in ch. 14)? Alter suggests that 'Nathan may be counting on the possibility that the obverse side of guilty conscience in a man like David is the anxious desire to do the right thing', thus his 'compensatory zeal to be a champion of justice overrides any awareness he might have of the evident artifice of the story'.[14] Now, this is important in the characterization of Nathan for two reasons. First, this episode demonstrates that the prophet knows how to extort a specific response from the king. Nathan's story in vv. 1-4 depicts him as able to set a narrative before David which is designed to create a certain kind of response in the mind of his hearer. This will be crucial for the next episode. Second, this episode reveals Nathan to be a *creative purveyor of fiction*. There is a network of correspondences between Nathan's short story and the preceding narrative of David's adultery, such as 'eat, drink, lie down with, and daughter'.[15] So, despite the fact that it is a literary artifice, this story is not without its parabolic contours—the hallmark of any good novel or play, one might add. Again, as in the beginning of Episode 1 in ch. 7 of 2 Samuel, Nathan commences his words to the king by speaking on his own authority. However, the difference here in Episode 2 is that his purposes are congruent with the LORD's, and his

---

12. Alter, *The David Story*, p. 257.
13. Rather than referring to these narratives as 'juridical parables', Pyper describes them as 'oath-provoking stories' since their primary function is to induce the king to swear an oath. See Pyper, *David as Reader*, p. 109.
14. Alter, *The David Story*, p. 257.
15. Cf. Polzin, *David and the Deuteronomist*, pp. 120-26.

creative embellishment of the parable (while slightly risky in light of his previous divine rebuke) indicates that he has learned from his first mistake.

Episode 2 has another brief appearance by the prophet at 12.24-25:

> And David consoled Bathsheba, his wife, and went in to her, and lay down with her, and she bore a son, and she called his name Solomon. The LORD loved him, and sent by the hand of Nathan the prophet, and he called his name Jedidiah, on account of the LORD.

A host of commentators have noted that this second appellation could be a throne name, although it is perplexing why it would not recur at a later point if this was the case.[16] G.H. Jones observes 'the naming of Solomon as Jedidiah, which was an obvious variant on the name David, does not necessarily mean that Solomon had from an early date been designated as crown-prince'.[17] Conversely, it could mean exactly that, at least in the mind of the prophet who has been divinely sent with this name. Fokkelman notes that this scene 'becomes a foreshadowing of the succession in I Kings 1'.[18] Alter builds on this by suggesting that 'perhaps the second name, indicating special access to divine favor, reflects a political calculation on the part of Nathan: he is already aligning himself with Solomon (and Bathsheba), figuring that in the long run it will be best to have a successor to David under some obligation to him'.[19] Finally, one might infer that through this 'naming' Nathan makes a connection between Jedidiah and the divine words of ch. 7—that is, the son mentioned in 7.12 ('who shall come forth from your body, and I will establish his kingdom') is understood by the prophet to be Solomon/Jedidiah. This short scene should not be dismissed when considering Nathan's characterization, as it is integral to understanding his sense of divine mission (or at least the motives for his actions) in 1 Kings 1.

3. *Episode 3: 1 Kings 1.1-31*

The context of Episode 3, one recalls, is the aged infirmity of King David, and the self-exaltation of Adonijah. Adonijah has gathered around him a number of confederates, but notably absent is Nathan the prophet—who is twice mentioned by the narrator in vv. 8 and 10 of ch. 1: 'Adonijah sacrificed sheep, oxen, and fatlings by the Serpent's Stone, which is beside En-rogel, and he invited all his brothers, the king's sons, and all the royal officials of

---

16. See, e.g., N. Wyatt, '"Jedidiah" and Cognate Forms as a Title of Royal Legitimation', *Bib* 66 (1985), pp. 112-25.

17. Jones, *The Nathan Narratives*, p. 49.

18. J.P. Fokkelman, *Narrative Art and Poetry in the Books of Samuel*. I. *King David* (Assen: Van Gorcum, 1981), p. 92.

19. Alter, *The David Story*, p. 263.

Judah, but he did not invite Nathan the prophet or Benaiah or the mighty men or Solomon his brother'. At this point in the narrative, Nathan enters the stage:

> Then Nathan said to Bathsheba the mother of Solomon, 'Have you not heard that Adonijah the son of Haggith has become king and David our lord does not know it? Now therefore come, let me give you counsel, that you may save your own life and the life of your son Solomon. Go in at once to King David, and say to him, "Did you not, my lord the king, swear to your maid-servant, saying, 'Solomon your son shall reign after me, and he shall sit upon my throne'? Why then is Adonijah king?" Then while you are still speaking with the king, I also will come in after you and confirm your words.' (1 Kgs 1.11-14)

Nathan initiates dialogue with Bathsheba 'the mother of Solomon' and commences with a question—one which draws attention to the perilous current events of Adonijah's exploits, reinforced by referring to him as 'the son of Haggith' (which emphasizes the maternal rivalry he intends to exploit). It is noteworthy that Adonijah has not become king at this point in the narrative, but this fictional elaboration by the prophet heightens the efficacy of his speech to Bathsheba.[20] He also alludes to the impotence of the king and his lack of knowledge of such current events. Casting himself in the role of an adviser deflects attention from anything which he stands to gain if this plan works. The plan revolves around 'an oath' regarding the succession to the throne. As every commentator agrees, there is an ambiguity surrounding this oath, because the narrative does not record such an oath made by David. Even in the place where it might be expected, 2 Sam. 12.25, it is conspicuously absent. Moreover, by framing the oath in the form of a question, the prophet cannot be legally guilty of perjury. Is Nathan fabricating this scenario? There are grounds for suspecting that he is, not the least being that he has done something similar before. In Episode 2 he probably employs a literary artifice to procure a certain response from David, one which is consonant with the divine plan. It appears that this is a similar case. He instructs Bathsheba to speak such words to the king, and assures her that he will appear to 'fill up her words':[21]

---

20. Nelson, *First and Second Kings*, p. 16, comments as follows: 'Adonijah's sacrifice meal was not necessarily the occasion for an unauthorized coronation, although the wily Nathan makes it out to be just that. It may have been only a way of building good will among his potential supporters. Although the narrator leaves our suspicions unconfirmed either way, most commentators have for some reason bought Nathan's story at face value.'

21. The Hebrew verb מלא should be translated more literally as 'fill up' rather than 'confirm' (as RSV); 'confirm' has the sense of validating or authenticating what has been said hitherto, whereas Nathan's speech is designed to accomplish the intended effect of Bathsheba's discourse to David. Nathan's machination is not to corroborate her witness or verify her story, but rather to finish rhetorically what she begins.

> So Bathsheba went to the king into his chamber (now the king was very old, and Abishag the Shunammite was ministering to the king). Bathsheba bowed and did obeisance to the king, and the king said, 'What do you desire?' She said to him, 'My lord, you swore to your maidservant by the LORD your God, saying, "Solomon your son shall reign after me, and he shall sit upon my throne". And now, behold, Adonijah is king, although you, my lord the king, do not know it. He has sacrificed oxen, fatlings, and sheep in abundance, and has invited all the sons of the king, Abiathar the priest, and Joab the commander of the army; but Solomon your servant he has not invited. And now, my lord the king, the eyes of all Israel are upon you, to tell them who shall sit on the throne of my lord the king after him. Otherwise it will come to pass, when my lord the king sleeps with his fathers, that I and my son Solomon will be counted offenders.' (1 Kgs 1.15-21)

As several scholars have pointed out, Bathsheba makes a number of key alterations to Nathan's instructed speech. For example, she transforms the 'third-person question' which Nathan presented into an emphatic vow made by David, crucially adding the weighty phrase 'by the LORD your God'.[22] Furthermore, she adds a list of conspirators to her speech, throwing in the name of 'Joab commander of the army'. Given David's hostility to 'the sons of Zeruiah' in general and Joab in particular (who was responsible for the death of Absalom), this could be a prudent move. In studying the character of Nathan, though, the question is: Was he anticipating Bathsheba to be such a master rhetorician and skilled improviser, or was this simply a convenient serendipity? While there is no textual anchor on this point, the balance of evidence would have to incline toward Nathan calculating that she was the right candidate for such a speech. Does the prophet give the queen the 'essential information' and count on her to embellish the rest as she sees fit?[23] Bathsheba's name means 'daughter of an oath'—it may be a shrewd move by the prophet to employ the 'daughter of an oath' to persuade the king that he did swear an oath. Meanwhile, as if on cue, Nathan arrives in the inner chamber to 'fill up her words':

> While she was still speaking with the king, Nathan the prophet came in. And they told the king, 'Here is Nathan the prophet.' And when he came in before the king, he bowed before the king, with his face to the ground. And Nathan said, 'My lord the king, you must have said, "Adonijah shall reign after me, and he shall sit upon my throne". For he has gone down this day, and has sacrificed oxen, fatlings, and sheep in abundance, and has invited all the king's

---

22. R. Alter, *The Art of Biblical Narrative* (New York: Basic Books, 1981), pp. 98-99, additionally observes that this phrase affixes 'a higher order of binding solemnity to the vow. Perhaps Nathan as a man of God was nervous about taking His name in vain (especially, of course, if the whole idea of the pledge was hoax) and so omitted that phrase from his instructions.'

23. Fokkelman, *King David*, p. 356.

5. Nathan: Prophet, Politician, and Playwright

sons, Joab the commander of the army, and Abiathar the priest; and behold, they are eating and drinking before him, and saying, "Long live King Adonijah!" But me, your servant, and Zadok the priest, and Benaiah the son of Jehoiada, and your servant Solomon, he has not invited. Has this thing been brought about by my lord the king and you have not told your servants [*qere* = servant] who should sit on the throne of my lord the king after him?' (1 Kgs 1.22-27)

I would contend that this final speech of Nathan provides a number of key moments in his characterization. To begin, Nathan's entrance to the king's chamber is formally announced with the appellation 'the prophet'.[24] Since on previous occasions he has delivered the divine word to David, there is a corresponding authority to Nathan's persona, perhaps heightened by this manner of announcement.[25] Noticeably, in his opening words to the king there is no mention of the 'oath', which readers may have been anticipating. While this may be surprising for a moment, his first words indicate the direction of his rhetorical strategy. Although some translators render Nathan's commencement in v. 24 as a question, the syntax makes better sense as a flat statement, and dovetails with Bathsheba's emphatic declaration 'you yourself swore' with the addition of the pronoun before the second person singular verb: 'You yourself (evidently) said, "Adonijah shall be king after me"... For he has gone down today and has sacrificed...'[26] So Nathan implies that David has indeed sworn an oath, but one which is antithetical to that which he and Bathsheba discuss. Not only does the prophet avoid mentioning the oath of Bathsheba concerning Solomon, he appears to invent a completely different one for another son of David. This must reveal something of his character, as he has the nerve to play dangerously with a supposed oath to Adonijah, which is extremely risky though in the end highly effective.[27] Further, his strategy for kindling the wrath of David is to draw

---

24. B.O. Long, *1 Kings, with an Introduction to Historical Literature* (FOTL, 9; Grand Rapids: Eerdmans, 1984), p. 38, notes 'Nathan's posture is remarkable. In contrast to the more confrontational Bathsheba, who retains nonetheless a certain deportment, Nathan is the observant, almost dispassionate servant who speaks carefully and politely (note the author's extra descriptive touch, "he bowed...*face to the ground*", v. 23; cf. v. 16). But he makes no accusations save the mild one that *perhaps* (it is really left only as a possibility) the king has neglected to inform him of a succession to the throne.'

25. Contrast v. 13, where Bathsheba receives no formal announcement. Cf. J.T. Walsh, *1 Kings* (Berit Olam; Collegeville, MN: Liturgical Press, 1996), p. 16.

26. Cf. the translation and comments of S.J. DeVries, *1 Kings* (WBC, 12; Waco, TX: Word Books, 1985), pp. 15-16. DeVries notes that this statement is an 'ironic exaggeration', and the fact that 'Nathan feels the need to inform the king in detail shows that he does not actually believe that David ordered Adonijah's coronation, an attitude which his question of v 27 underscores'.

27. Cf. Fokkelman, *King David*, p. 354.

him into the narrative account of this *injustice*, forcing the king to make a judgment. The same tactics are used in Episode 2 with the story of the 'two men in one city'. Finally, he concludes with a note of reproof: 'Has this decision proceeded from my lord the king, and you have not caused your servant to know who will sit on the throne of my lord the king after him?'[28] As Fokkelman puts it, 'one must be extremely sure of one's calculations in order to express such outright provocation so dispassionately'.[29] The net effect, though, is that Nathan's calculations are correct, and the king acts exactly as he and Bathsheba would have wished—within an hour, Solomon is anointed king with Nathan and Zadok presiding over the ceremony.

4. *Conclusions*

By way of conclusion, consider two remarks on the characterization of Nathan. First, in contrast to those who would view the Nathan narratives as a stretch of discourse that does not yield a homogeneous product in the end, I would submit that from a literary perspective, there is a consistency of characterization and inherent character development in the presentation of Nathan the prophet. I would argue that each of the three episodes build one on the other, and draw a network of references back and forth. The portrait of Nathan is presented through a series of increments, commencing with the theophany concerning David's house and culminating in the coronation of King Solomon. It appears that these episodes are linked, and reveal a prophet with a growing sense of divine purpose (even resorting to rather dubious means) in securing the throne for the specified son of the king. Second, there is a richness and a complexity in the portrait of Nathan that has hitherto not been discussed at any great length. Some useful work has been done by G.H. Jones, but virtually none of his book includes (or builds on) analysis which utilizes a literary methodology. Narrative-orientated studies in the future may uncover a good deal more about the figure who stage-manages the installation of Solomon with a prophet's authority, with the savvy of a smooth politician, and with the flair of a good playwright or literary artist. The term 'literary artist' may in fact be an appropriate one, since Nathan goes on to forge a successful literary career once Solomon is established. After all, the Chronicler reminds us in 1 Chron. 29.29 and 2 Chron. 9.29 that we can read all about the events of the reigns of David and Solomon in the book of Nathan the prophet.

---

28. On the syntax of Nathan's final utterance to David, see GKC §150f.
29. Fokkelman, *King David*, p. 361.

6

LAYERS OF AMBIGUITY IN 2 SAMUEL 11.1

The events of 2 Samuel 11 are often referred to as a profound turning point in the narrative of David. To this juncture in the story, the career of David has been predominantly a success in military, political, and perhaps personal terms as well. Moreover, the episodes recorded in 2 Samuel 7, where David is divinely promised a lasting dynasty, provide evidence of a king who also is a religious success. While there are undercurrents of David's life in the narrative that are certainly less than favorable, the surface presentation (since his emergence in 1 Sam. 16 as Saul's court musician and the triumph over Goliath in 1 Sam. 17) is mainly positive.[1] This sense of achievement is poised decisively to change in the episode of 'David and Bathsheba'. Considering the narrative material from 2 Samuel 9 and following, it is difficult to argue against (at least in this section) a portrait of David as a kingly victor. He has reduced the rival house of Saul to the lowly Mephibosheth, a crippled subaltern who becomes dependent on the royal house for his daily bread. He has effectively (if only temporarily) obviated the threat posed by the neighboring Ammonites, and 2 Samuel 10 portrays this conflict as one where David's nation is in a position of strength, and the hired Arameans are subdued. Thus David's dominion is becoming increasingly secure, and according to Everett Fox: 'As ruler of a small empire, as a military and political success, David seems to be the king with everything, including multiple wives and sons to succeed him'.[2] Yet Fox continues by noting that in the midst of these moments of triumph, the 'turning point of II Samuel'

---

1. Cf. Polzin, *David and the Deuteronomist*, p. 119: 'The success and adulation that have constantly accompanied David up to now were only questioned by the Deuteronomist's subtle hints, which, here or there, helped us to wonder whether there was more— or less—to David than met the eye. In previous chapters and a previous book [*Samuel and the Deuteronomist* (Bloomington: Indiana University Press, 1993)], I have suggested some of these indirect challenges to the narrator's surface adulation of David.'
2. E. Fox, *Give Us a King! Samuel, Saul, and David* (New York: Schocken Books, 1999), p. 187.

occurs with the events of 2 Samuel 11.[3] In his frequently cited literary analysis of ch. 11, Meir Sternberg has drawn attention to the layers of ambiguity and indeterminacy in this narrative.[4] His interpretation focuses on the details of ch. 11, but in an important footnote Sternberg argues that it 'gains support from the structure and progress of the text as a whole'. He then proceeds to discuss the location of ch. 11 within the larger narrative of David:

> On the one hand, it [2 Sam. 11] is preceded by a consistently favorable presentation of David as a God-fearing, successful, and victorious king. On the other hand, it is followed by a long chain of mishaps and disasters: the aftermath of the Bathsheba affair, Tamar's rape and Amnon's murder, Absalom's usurpation of the throne, the Sheba ben Bichri rebellion, the three-year famine, and the census followed by the plague. Within the composition of the book, therefore, [2 Sam. 11] is a central chapter in that it pinpoints the where and why of David's change of fortune.[5]

1. *2 Samuel 11.1: The Overture to a Narrative 'Fraught with Ambiguity'*

Assuming, then, 2 Samuel 11 represents a definitive turning point of the David narrative, it is notable that this episode exemplifies the literary art of intentional ambiguity. In a helpful overview of the range of ambiguities in this episode, Gale A. Yee provides the following definition: 'Literary ambiguity is the narrative's quality of indeterminateness, its equivocation. The story is open to several interpretations at once, each supported by the text itself. Being thus polyvalent, the text summons the reader to "fill in the gaps" which the narrative in its ambiguity leaves open.'[6] For instance, at crucial points in the narrative the reader may ask the question: Does Uriah know (or suspect) what David has done and why he has been summoned to return to Jerusalem from the battlefield?[7] Moreover, does David suspect that Uriah

---

3. Fox, *Give Us a King!*, p. 187. Cf. Alter, *The David Story*, p. 249.
4. Sternberg, *The Poetics of Biblical Narrative*, pp. 186-229. Sternberg's original article (with M. Perry) was published in 1968 in Hebrew, but revised for his influential 1985 book version. A helpful theoretical exploration of indeterminacy from a biblical standpoint is provided by M. Fox in his 'The Uses of Indeterminacy', *Semeia* 71 (1995), pp. 173-92. Cf. S. Lasine, 'Indeterminacy and the Bible', *HS* 27 (1986), pp. 48-80.
5. Sternberg, *The Poetics of Biblical Narrative*, pp. 528-29.
6. G.A. Yee, 'Fraught with Background: Literary Ambiguity in 2 Samuel 11', *Int* 42 (1988), pp. 240-53 (240-41).
7. Sternberg, *The Poetics of Biblical Narrative*, pp. 186-222. See also M. Bal, *Lethal Love: Feminist Literary Readings of Biblical Love Stories* (Bloomington: Indiana University Press, 1987), pp. 10-36.

may know, or is his mounting frustration as the episode continues due to Uriah's apparent naïveté? Clearly these ambiguities are irresolvable, but there is a compelling argument that they are an intentional strategy of the author.[8]

In this chapter I would like to suggest that the tone of the larger ambiguities of 2 Samuel 11 is sounded through the subtleties of the opening verse. There has been much discussion in the secondary literature surrounding a number of difficult aspects of this verse.[9] However, the argument here is that in a chapter fraught with polyvalence, 2 Sam. 11.1 plays an integral role in establishing its own set of ambiguities, and hence functions as an overture to the chapter as a whole. Two issues in this verse will be focused on. First, there is a *textual ambiguity* in 2 Sam. 11.1. Do 'messengers' go forth at the return of the year (following the MT), or 'kings' (as many ancient versions and some Hebrew manuscripts)? The semantic uncertainty surrounding 'kings' and 'messengers' is an intriguing ambiguity in light of the ensuing developments in the story. Second, in 2 Sam. 11.1 David 'sends' Joab and the army to besiege the capital city of the Ammonites while David himself remains in Jerusalem. This emphasis on the sending of Joab while David 'sits' in Jerusalem is an instance of *motivational ambiguity*, and is crucial for the unfolding narrative. My contention is that these undecidable elements can be understood as functioning as an overture to the story as a whole, and serve to engage and prepare the reader for a host of ambiguities that will follow in this episode. Consider, therefore, the opening verse of 2 Samuel 11:

> In the spring of the year, the time when kings go out to battle, David sent Joab with his officers and all Israel with him; they ravaged the Ammonites, and besieged Rabbah. But David remained at Jerusalem. (NRSV)

---

8. Cf. W. Brueggemann, *Theology of the Old Testament* (Minneapolis: Fortress Press, 1997), p. 111: 'In regard to David's affront against Uriah by the hand of Joab in 2 Samuel 11, Meir Sternberg has nicely explored the teasing quality of the narrative. The narrator presents David so that neither the king nor the reader knows how much Uriah knows about David's conduct. If David knew that Uriah knew about his violation of Uriah's wife, David could proceed on one basis with Uriah. If David knew that Uriah did not know about his affront, David could proceed in another way. But David does not know what Uriah knows, and neither does the reader. David's not knowing is not a lack of historical information, but a rhetorical strategy in which the reader must inevitably participate.'

9. In addition to the studies cited below, a number of text-critical issues in 2 Sam. 11.1-4 are addressed in I. Teshima, 'Textual Criticism and Early Biblical Interpretation', in J. Krašovec (ed.), *The Interpretation of the Bible* (JSOTSup, 289; Sheffield: Sheffield Academic Press, 1998), pp. 165-79.

2. Do Kings or Messengers 'Go Forth' in 2 Samuel 11.1a?

The David–Bathsheba–Uriah affair is framed by the international conflict with the Ammonites.[10] 2 Samuel 10 records the gradual escalation of the war, and concludes with Israel having an advantage. 2 Samuel 11.1 seems to demarcate a resumption of this conflict, and hence the verse opens a new chapter in the confrontation. The temporal setting for this episode in the increasingly complex narrative of David's life has been translated numerous ways, and scholars have a variety of opinions regarding the meaning of the chronological reference of 2 Sam. 11.1a (ויהי לתשובת השנה). Some contemporary English versions (such as NJB, NEB, NJPS) reflect a more literal rendering of the Hebrew, opting for 'At the turn of the year'. But, as is evident in the NRSV translation above, 'springtime' is also an option (followed by NIV and NKJV), assuming that the 'return of the year' is commensurate with the 'spring season'. This is the idiomatic rendering suggested in standard reference works: BDB glosses ויהי לתשובת השנה as '*at the return of the year*, i.e. of spring', similar to KB, 'at the return of the year, *the next spring*'.[11] The meaning in this case would be that military campaigning is most effective in the drier season associated with the spring weather; 'At the turn of the year' in 2 Sam. 11.1 would then be located within this common pattern of military action. Hence, A.A. Anderson regards this phrase as 'a general reference indicating the period between the heavy winter rains and the harvest... This would be an appropriate time for military exploits.'[12] Uriel Simon further suggests that in this verse 'that serves as the link between the history of the war and the episode of David and Bathsheba (11.1), the narrator makes clear that in the second year of the war the initiative passed to David. The temporal setting...informs us that this time David is not reacting to an enemy thrust but is guided by the calendar.'[13] At the conclusion of the

---

10. Cf. D.F. Payne, '1 & 2 Samuel', in D.A. Carson *et al.* (eds.), *New Bible Commentary, 21st Century Edition* (Downers Grove, IL: InterVarsity Press, 1994), pp. 296-333 (327): 'Ch. 10, taken by itself, is all about a successful Israelite campaign against the Ammonites, and resumes the record of David's victories begun in ch. 8. It is in fact a link chapter, because this particular military campaign had its effects in Jerusalem. One of the Israelite soldiers who fought in Transjordan was Uriah, whose wife Bathsheba was seduced by David in her husband's absence. Subsequently David made use of the warfare to bring about Uriah's death. Thus chs. 10–12 link the theme of warfare with affairs at the royal court.'

11. See BDB, p. 1000 (with cross-references for לִתְשׁוּבַת הַשָּׁנָה listed as 1 Kgs 20.22, 26; 2 Chron. 36.10; and the parallel text to 2 Sam. 11.1; 1 Chron. 20.1); KB, p. 1043.

12. Anderson, *2 Samuel*, p. 153. Anderson translates the phrase, 'In the following spring of the year, when the kings march out to battle...' (p. 151).

13. U. Simon, *Reading Prophetic Narratives* (Bloomington: Indiana University Press, 1997), p. 96. An alternative view is advanced by McCarter (*II Samuel*, p. 285): 'the reference here is not to the marching out of kings in general but of some specific kings...

rainy season, Simon argues, David sends his troops for a second time to Ammon, and the events of 2 Samuel 10 are about to have a sequel. However, the issue in 2 Sam. 11.1a is not so simple. In light of a textual ambiguity in the opening half of the verse, our question becomes: At the return of the year, is it 'kings' or 'messengers' that go forth?

Commentators have long wrestled with manuscript variations in 2 Sam. 11.1a. As the NRSV translation above indicates, a rendering such as 'In the spring of the year, the time when *kings* go forth to battle' has widespread support.[14] The textual issue, however, is not so clear as these translations may indicate. The standard MT reads המלאכים ('the messengers', *hml'kym*), whereas other manuscript traditions and ancient versions read המלכים ('the kings', *hmlkym*).[15] Alter summarizes the apparent confusion as follows:

This can only refer to the coalition of Aramean kings summoned by the Ammonites in 10.6'. McCarter continues: 'A literal translation of the opening clause is "And it was at the return of the year..."' (p. 285), and concludes that the temporal phrase 'the return of the year' therefore 'does not refer to the spring season but rather to the coming around again of the time of year at which the Aramean kings marched to the aid of the Ammonites. That is, the siege of Ammon began at a time one year after the beginning of the clash described in 10.8ff.' Cf. Smith, *A Critical and Exegetical Commentary on the Books of Samuel*, p. 317: 'The time seems to be fixed at a year after the embassy to Hanun. The return of the season was a fitting time to refresh the king's memory of the insult.' M. Garsiel ('The Story of David and Bathsheba: A Different Approach', *CBQ* 55 [1993], pp. 244-62 [251-52]) outlines a number of reasons against the notion that 'the return of the year' indicates the spring season (when in fact it may be harder for invading armies to find water, cross rivers, etc.), and concludes: 'The most reasonable interpretation of the temporal indications in 2 Sam. 11:1 is, therefore, that a year after the Syrian alliance in aid of the Ammonites against Israel had failed, David, recognizing that the Syrians would not come to Ammon's help again because some of them made peace with Israel after the failure of that alliance, sent Joab and the army to complete the conquest of Ammon' (cf. Mauchline, *First and Second Samuel*, p. 247).

14. Cf. KJV: 'And it came to pass, after the year was expired, at the time when kings go forth *to battle*'; NASB: 'Then it happened in the spring, at the time when kings go out *to battle*'; NIV: 'In the spring, at the time when kings go off to war'. Note that each of these translations have an aspect of paraphrase, adding the term 'war' or 'battle', and each translation also opts for 'kings' as opposed to 'messengers'. R.D. Bergen comments on the NIV translation in particular: 'The NIV's rendering rejects the MT at this point, choosing to follow the variant textual traditions of the LXX, Vg, Josephus, and 1 Chron. 20.1. However, the MT reading is both comprehensible and thematically useful here: it should not be rejected' (Bergen, *1, 2 Samuel*, p. 367).

15. McCarter (*II Samuel*, p. 279) defends his 'kings' decision by citing 'MT[MSS], LXX, OL, Targ., Vulg., and I Chron 20.1' as opposed to the MT: 'We follow the versions in assuming that the reference is to the marching out [צאת] of "the kings" (*hmlkym*; cf. I Chron 19.2) in 10.2'. Moving toward the interpretive side, Smith (*A Critical and Exegetical Commentary on the Books of Samuel*, pp. 317-18) comments: 'The interpretation seems especially unfortunate, in that the example of David shows that kings did not regularly go out to war, but sometimes sent their armies. We might suppose indeed that

'There is a cunning ambiguity here in the Hebrew text. The received consonantal text reads *mal'akhim*, "messengers", though many manuscripts show *melakhim*, "kings".'[16] Alter's use of the term 'ambiguity' is helpful for the present purposes, as it suggests that there may be something more complex in this sentence, rather than simply a scribal error (which is the standard line of reasoning).[17] Of course, as Polzin points out, there are a number of reasons why 'kings' is a natural reading. First, throughout the Deuteronomistic History kings are more likely to 'march out' (צאת) than messengers. Second, there are other instances where David does not go forth into battle, and this could be some sort of foreshadowing (see 2 Sam. 18.2-4; 21.17). Thus, David's remaining in the capital city while his troops are away in battle could be construed as a prolepsis or a precedent. Third, in terms of 'the immediate story, the reference to kings going forth (to battle) sets up an ironic contrast between the beginning and the end of the verse, that is, between what normally takes place at this time of the year on one hand, and this particular instance on the other, when "David was remaining at Jerusalem" (v. 1)'.[18]

There is a possibility, though, that 'kings' may be what text critics refer to as a *lectio facilior*, whereby the scribes and translators of the ancient versions provided an easier and smoother reading.[19] If one assumes that

---

there is a covert condemnation of David for not doing as kings (on this theory) usually do. But this seems far fetched. The supposition of Kimchi therefore claims attention which is that the time designated is *the season of the year when the kings* [of Syria] *made their invasion*. If however we go so far, it is better to accept [המלאכים] and understand *at the season of the year when the messengers of David first went forth.*'

16. Alter, *The David Story*, p. 249. Cf. BDB, p. 521.

17. Since Alter quotes Polzin in his next sentence, and subsequently builds on the latter's insight, it may be helpful to cite Polzin's (*David and the Deuteronomist*, p. 109) comments in more detail: 'It may be that there is no more deliciously ambiguous verse in all the [Deuteronomic] History than 2 Samuel 11.1: do "kings"…or "messengers"…go forth in the spring of the year? The question is an ancient one, for early textual witnesses already testify both to the widespread presence of "messengers", indicated by an aleph [א] in the disputed word, and also to "kings", indicated by the absence of the aleph. It is commonly assumed that one must make a choice here, whether on textual, literary-historical, or other grounds, and it is not difficult to mount a defense of either alternative.'

18. Polzin, *David and the Deuteronomist*, p. 109. Cf. Steussy, *David: Biblical Portraits of Power*, p. 18.

19. See B. Albrektson, 'Difficilior lectio probabilior: A Rule of Textual Criticism and its Use in Old Testament Studies', in A.S. van der Woude (ed.), *Remembering All the Way* (OTS, 21; Leiden: E.J. Brill, 1981), pp. 5-18. Cf. Simon, *Reading Prophetic Narratives*, p. 291: 'even without the unequivocal testimony of the parallel text in 1 Chron. 20.1, of the ancient versions, of the Aleppo Codex, and of a number of medieval manuscripts, the *qere* seems more plausible since it relates the temporal setting to the season of

'messengers' is the *lectio difficilior*—that is, the harder reading, based on the text-critical principle that the more difficult reading is to be preferred in the first instance—then Polzin's suggestions for taking 'messengers' seriously are compelling.[20] He notes that reading המלאכים sets up a situation whereby David is acting at a distance, and David as a dispatcher of messengers is a theme throughout the episode: 'the chapter's subsequent emphasis on messengers as the means by which things get done is a plausible argument for the going forth of messengers in its opening verse'.[21]

If David is portrayed in this opening verse as one who sends, then this episode is indeed one where 'messengers' go forth—even if the reader is expecting to encounter 'kings' as the subject of 'going forth'. המלאכים is clearly the more difficult reading, but in Polzin's judgment, 'the *lectio difficilior* ought to be retained, even as its dual reference is to be emphasized'.[22] If, as is most compelling, this is a conscious word-play, then 'we cannot rule out...that the wordplay itself was well-known, even traditional, at the time of its usage in this narrative'.[23] In light of this 'textual and compositional ambivalence', Polzin concludes that the issue of 'kings' or 'messengers' is

the year appropriate for warfare rather than to the previous dispatch of messengers which, timewise, is quite irrelevant to the present context.'

20. Cf. Fox (*Give Us a King!*, p. 197), where 2 Sam. 11.1 is translated as 'Now it was at the turning of the year, at the time of kings' going-forth'. With respect to the 'messengers' of the MT, Fox notes: 'Either meaning is attractive given the story; I lean toward "kings" as an indictment of David's being at the palace and not with the troops'.

21. Polzin, *David and the Deuteronomist*, p. 111. Cf. GKC §23g.

22. Polzin, *David and the Deuteronomist*, p. 112. J. Rosenberg (*King and Kin*, p. 126) reflects on the 'kings/agents' dilemma: 'While it seems unwise to accord conflicting versions of a biblical word *equal* weight (the two words, after all, are spelled differently, and only one of the two can occupy the textual space accorded it), the fact that the ambiguity exists at all suggests that conflicting interpretative pressures (what Barthes in another context called *pressions de lisibilité*) may themselves have helped shape the history of the text. This is, after all, the first place in the Bible that a leader of Israel stays off the battlefield in time of war, and the question of the role of agents in the conduct of kingly business returns again and again throughout the story (and, indeed, throughout the court history). Since a king, as defined in I Sam. 8, is *himself* an agent of the people, and his exit to battle a constitutive moment of his authority, we find ourselves with an oddly convoluted inversion of kingly function in the king's preference of agents to represent him.' For the reference to Roland Barthes, see 'La lutte avec l'ange: Analyse textuelle de Génèse 32.22-33', in R. Barthes *et al.*, *Analyse structurale et exégèse biblique* (Neuchâtel: Delachaux et Niestlé, 1971), pp. 26-39 (31); ET R. Barthes, *Image, Music, Text* (trans. S. Heath; New York: Hill & Wang, 1977), pp. 125-41.

23. Polzin, *David and the Deuteronomist*, p. 112. Fokkelman (*King David*, p. 51) prefers 'messengers', as it 'provides the advantage of integration by establishing a temporal relationship between the action in 11.1 and 10.1-5. Simultaneously, the motif of the campaign, 11.1b-d, is kept alive for us. In this way, an individual adjunct of time follows a general one: "And it happened with the coming (literally: return) of the new year, at the

too intricately ambiguous to be the result simply of textual or editorial misadventure, and, consequently, one does not have to choose between kings and messengers, because both meanings hover over the verse from the start—whatever one may decide about original orthography. The verse clearly doubles back on itself in a marvelous display of narrative virtuosity: at a time when kings go forth, David did not, making a time, therefore, when messengers must go forth; at a time when messengers go forth, David, remaining in Jerusalem, sent Joab, his servants and all Israel to ravage Ammon. I suppose this circular progression of meanings may have happened by chance, but almost everything we know about this chapter and the History conspires against a merely happy accident.[24]

There is a creative argument, therefore, for retaining the ambiguity of 'kings *and* messengers' in 2 Sam. 11.1, an ambiguity which, I would argue, heightens the irony which follows in the remainder of this verse, and stretches until the end of this long chapter 'fraught with ambiguity'. First, this tension between king and messenger prepares the reader for the situation of David 'sitting' at home (described at the end of v. 1): even as it is the customary time of year for kings/messengers to be active on the battlefield, David is a sedentary monarch.[25] Second, there is an additional tension between king and messenger in 2 Sam. 11.3, one that is intensified because of the ambiguity here.[26]

3. *Why Does David Remain in Jerusalem?*

As the narrative of 1 Samuel makes clear, David is undoubtedly a popular leader. The people of Israel are enamored with David because he 'led them in all their campaigns' (1 Sam. 18.16)—and clearly this is vital in his rise to

(same) time as the envoys (i.e. diplomats, consolers) had marched out, that David sent out Joab, etc."—which creates the implication of the revenge for the envoys' humiliation having been aptly timed'.

24. Polzin, *David and the Deuteronomist*, p. 111.

25. Rosenberg does not view this 'sedentary' position as negative: 'The pointed reference to David's remaining in Jerusalem, in any case, makes clear to us that war is being conducted in a very different way from that of the archaic tribal muster, whose dynamics (and defects) we are familiar with from the song of Deborah (Judg. 5). The rational and bureaucratic mode of statecraft that is David's specific innovation has better uses for the king than the charismatic and warlord functions that elevate a man to kingship in the first place. The advantages of a sedentary monarch are both practical and symbolic: as strategist, the king can move troops and materiel with greater freedom than his location in the heat of battle would permit... David's genius as a monarch is here shown resting in his overcoming a certain literalism of kingly function that had plagued both the reign and mental tranquility of Saul' (*King and Kin*, pp. 126-27).

26. As discussed in the next chapter, though, in 2 Sam. 11.3b there is an ambiguity as to whether the speaker is King David or an unnamed messenger.

6. *Layers of Ambiguity in 2 Samuel 11.1*

power. There is something enigmatic, then, in that the central action of David in this opening scene of 2 Samuel 11 is his dispatching of Joab and the troops to engage in battle *without* the presence of the king himself. Scholars are divided on the issue of whether David's abstaining from battle is a positive, negative, or ambivalent characterization. Sternberg argues at length that the expositional data in v. 1 is arranged in a 'conspicuously asymmetrical' manner, such that the comparatively short second part of the verse ודוד יושב בירושלם ('and David stayed in Jerusalem') arrests the reader's attention.[27] Noting that the verb 'stayed' (ישב) can literally be translated 'sat' ('and David *sat* in Jerusalem'), Sternberg argues that the various features of this verse 'direct the reader to view the king (who tarries at home) in ironic contrast to all the others (whom he has sent to make war)'.[28] Consequently, the question is then posited: 'What is the king doing in his city while the nation is fighting in the field?'[29] These details, in Sternberg's opinion, are organized as a contrastive analogy, and serve 'to construct metaphoric linkages—based on parallelism—by turning an ironic spotlight on what takes place in the city'.[30]

In contrast, Garsiel has a different interpretation, and poses the question: 'Was it in fact standard practice in that era for kings to participate personally in every battle?'[31] Although Garsiel hedges his argument by admitting that the question clearly cannot be answered with absolute certainty, he evaluates the 'advantages' and 'disadvantages' of a king remaining in his capital city during a military campaign, and concludes: 'David's preferring to stay in Jerusalem does not imply a failure in his royal duty'.[32] However, Garsiel's

27. Sternberg, *The Poetics of Biblical Narrative*, p. 193.
28. Sternberg, *The Poetics of Biblical Narrative*, p. 194.
29. Sternberg, *The Poetics of Biblical Narrative*, p. 194. Cf. Whedbee, 'On Divine and Human Bonds', p. 153: 'Right from the outset we are alerted that King David is fundamentally a man out of place and out of time. Kings normally go to battle in the spring of the year—but King David stays at home. Why? What does this signify? Is it necessary for the king's protection? Is it necessary for the king to be on the home front to attend to affairs of state? As the story turns out, it seems almost as if David had two choices: to make war—which was his duty as Yahweh's anointed—or to make love, which normally has the potential for new life but here will lead to death. David is portrayed as a man in the wrong place at the wrong time—hence a prime candidate for temptation and fall.'
30. Sternberg, *The Poetics of Biblical Narrative*, p. 195.
31. Garsiel, 'The Story of David and Bathsheba: A Different Approach', p. 249.
32. Garsiel, 'The Story of David and Bathsheba: A Different Approach', pp. 249-50. As he further states, 'This interpretation undermines Perry and Sternberg's contention that David is viewed with irony, when they write that "the phrase which speaks of kings going forth (to war) turns a spotlight on the king who stays at home". The two principal words here, "to war" and "the king" (David), are in fact absent from the text: they have been added by Perry and Sternberg.'

list of 'advantages' of a king remaining the capital are not entirely convincing, and it would appear that the syntax of the entire verse would militate against Garsiel's position. Why, one could then ask, does the biblical narrator not record that David is absent from the battlefield in 2 Samuel 10, when clearly he is remaining at home, (presumably) in Jerusalem? Sternberg's argument could be enhanced by suggesting that the final clause in v. 1 is in fact *disjunctive* syntax, yielding a translation ('*but* David sat in Jerusalem').[33]

A compelling case can be made that there is a narrative signal here, as Sternberg intuits, drawing attention to the public/private dichotomy that will be unveiled in the next lines of the chapter. Consequently, while the narrator stops short of outright indictment, there is yet another *purposeful* (i.e. intentional) layer of ambiguity that should be retained—just like the ambiguity that should be retained between 'kings' and 'messengers' earlier in 2 Sam. 11.1a.[34] After all, one may infer with Polzin: had David been where the military action was, he 'would never have seen Bathsheba when he did, and the history of the house of David might have been different'.[35]

The reason for David remaining in Jerusalem while his troops go forth to battle the Ammonites may be ultimately undecidable, but it obviously is key to the fate of the story. As 2 Samuel 11 continues, Uriah himself seems to exploit the 'dissonance' by emphasizing the troops on the field, while seemingly alluding to the contrast of the king at home.[36] Hence this detail of the king remaining in Jerusalem acts as a destabilizing factor in the narration here, and makes Uriah's comments later in the narrative more severe.[37] Uriel

---

33. The final clause completes the irony of this opening exposition, with the disjunctive 'but...'. In normal Hebrew syntax of a narrative such as this, sentences generally commence with 'and' followed by a verb, hence the translation here often replicates that style: 'And it was at the return of the year...and David sent (lit. "and sent David"—as the subject follows the verb in this and other Semitic languages)...and they destroyed...' As the final clause, then, one might expect 'and dwelt David in Jerusalem'. In this case, however, a noun clause is deployed by the narrator, and this has the effect of heightening the disjunctive aspect (read irony) to the entire situation, '*but* David sat in Jerusalem'.

34. Cf. Yee, 'Fraught with Background', p. 252.

35. Polzin, *David and the Deuteronomist*, p. 109.

36. Cf. Yee, 'Fraught with Background', p. 253.

37. Cf. Brueggemann, *First and Second Samuel*, p. 273: 'These four words at the end the verse ["David stayed in Jerusalem"] change the subject of the narrative. All the terror of war and the confusion of battle are bracketed out, making way for another kind of terror and confusion. There is a powerful silence back in Jerusalem with this king, who now seems so settled and sure that his mind—and body—can wander from the military action. David has ceased to be chieftain and now relies on agents to do his work. He has ceased to be the king requested by Israel who would "go out before us and fight our battles" (I Sam. 8.20)'. See also Steussy, *David: Biblical Portraits of Power*, p. 18: 'This opening verse, so often overlooked by interpreters eager to get to the scandal, foreshadows the problem of a king misusing his privilege'.

Simon further reflects that the statement 'David remained in Jerusalem' is ironic when considering the auxiliary indication of time (the season when kings or messengers *should* go forth), and hence this emphasis provides an overt criticism of David:

> The interpolation of the entire story of the sin and its punishment within the frame story of the war requires that later events precede earlier ones; hence we read of the military victory not against the background of the secret transgression (in accordance with the sequence of events) but against that of the anticipated punishment, which thereby casts its terrible shadow on the victory. In this way, the structure of the story hones its response to the riddle of David's kingdom from the day it reached its political and military zenith—the great disparity between might and peace abroad and weakness and dissension at home. The king who sinned in his palace, during and by means of the war, will not be punished by an enemy sword, aimed at the king on the battlefield, but by the sword of his sons, directed at a father in his own house.[38]

4. *Conclusion*

> Narrative ambiguity is a deliberate stylistic device which engages the reader, seizes the imaginative processes, and creates an interaction with the characters of the story that a more explicitly detailed account does not allow to happen.[39]

After this *overture of uncertainty* in the opening verse of 2 Samuel 11—where one is unsure if 'kings' or 'messengers' go forth at the turn of the year, and ponders the reasons for David remaining in the capital city of Jerusalem rather than journeying to the capital city of Rabbah—the reader is prepared to encounter a host of more elaborate ambiguities that will be unfolded in the ensuing incidents: whether Uriah knows or suspects what David has done, if Bathsheba is in any degree complicit in the matter, whether Joab is suspicious about events in Jerusalem, and so forth. In light of the uncertainties in the opening verse, readers are sufficiently prepared to encounter a narrative

---

38. Simon, *Reading Prophetic Narratives*, p. 98. He also comments (p. 100): 'The anatomy of the sin begins with the short exposition in which the military background (which, as we have seen, belongs to the frame story) is pulled toward the plot by the prominence accorded to a crucial point: "At the season when kings go out [to battle], David remained in Jerusalem". The king's remaining at home during wartime is not considered to be sin; but it is a moral flaw that casts a shadow on his devotion to his people and his solidarity with his warriors. What is more, it resembles the hole in the fence that beckons to a thief. Readers are invited to wonder: what is the stay-at-home king about to do?' Of course, the last time David is the subject of 'sit' (ישׁב) is in 2 Sam. 7.18. It may be possible to construct an argument that the divine promises about a 'lasting house' triggers a new complacency in David.

39. Yee, 'Fraught with Background', p. 240.

'fraught with background' and ambiguity, and therefore 2 Sam. 11.1 is a fitting overture to the David and Bathsheba episode. Both Polzin and Sternberg draw attention to the *constructive force of ambiguity* in this episode, and suggest that this intentional strategy of the biblical writer serves to enhance characterization and invite the audience to ponder more deeply the actions and words of the king. Indeed, Walter Brueggemann theologically reflects on the broader purpose of such literary strategies in the Hebrew Bible:

> These rhetorical strategies of metaphor, hyperbole, and ambiguity—to which could be added irony, incongruity, and contradiction—are not marginal or incidental to the text. They are the very stuff of the Old Testament. We have no Old Testament text without them, for they form the way this textual community gives voice to its reality, its life, and its life with God.[40]

Finally, it should be emphasized that 2 Sam. 11.1 is a complex verse simply by virtue of the momentous events it serves to introduce. If indeed 2 Samuel 11 and 12 represent the 'great turning-point of the David story', then it should not be surprising that the opening sentence is packed with meaning. But there is another feature here that is generally eschewed in the secondary literature: namely, the prominence afforded to Joab. As David's key commanding officer, Joab will play a complex and indispensable role in these chapters. At the very least, this opening verse firmly establishes Joab in a position of military authority, as commanding officer, with the troops under his command. This deserves attention because David will, in due course, call on this very figure of authority to dispatch an order not to destroy a foreign capital, but rather a foreign soldier within the ranks of Israel's troops. Joab has a pivotal position in the story, and the opening verse underlines this in the strongest institutional terms.

---

40. Brueggemann, *Theology of the Old Testament*, p. 111. Cf. Yee, 'Fraught with Background', pp. 252-53: 'The ambiguity of narrative has an importance theologically as well as literarily. The ambiguity of biblical narrative, the fictive world, reflects the ambiguity of the so-called "real" world. The readers encounter the same equivocal, ambivalent state of affairs in real life that they do in the realm of the story. The process of moral decision-making in real life, then, is similar to the process by which readers judge the morality of a character's actions. The latter involves a complex interaction with the characters, bringing into play the readers' personal experiences. These historically conditioned experiences inform their judgments about the morality of a particular character's deeds. When the readers "fill the gaps" of the story, they have a base to assess the reliability of the omniscient narrator's final judgment over the characters. The narrator's final statement is all the more powerful because it carries with it the commitment of the readers who have come to the same stance.'

7

THE ROYAL CONSCIENCE ACCORDING TO 4QSAM^A

1. *Introduction*

In a recent article in *Dead Sea Discoveries*, Alexander Rofé discusses a 'small variant' of Exod. 2.3 attested in 4QExod^b, a textual detail pertaining to the transport of the ark of Moses to the Nile River.[1] The NRSV renders Exod. 2.3 as follows: 'When she could hide him no longer she got a papyrus basket for him, and plastered it with bitumen and pitch; she put the child in it and placed it among the reeds on the bank of the river'. However, 4QExod^b contains an additional three words at 2.3b, where Moses' mother commands her maid: ותואמר לשפחתה לכי ('*She said to her maid, "Go!"*').[2] Rofé's reasons for adjudging this addition 'secondary' need not be repeated here, but clearly there are some literary implications of this variant. Consider a gloss of Exod. 2.3 that includes the Qumran addition in italics:

> But when she could no longer hide him, she took a papyrus ark for him, and coated it with tar and pitch. Then she put the child into it. *She said to her maid, 'Go!'* And she set it among the reeds by the bank of the Nile.

In terms of plot and character, the additional three words of the 4QExod^b fragment (ותואמר לשפחתה לכי) produce some interesting variations. In 2.3a, the mother of Moses is portrayed as patiently covering the little ark with tar and pitch, and then setting the infant inside. Yet at 2.3b the Qumran fragment concludes the verse with the mother's slight loss of nerve or perhaps hesitation about actually delivering the fragile vessel to the 'lip of the Nile'. The servant girl herself receives the imperative, and obediently does as she is instructed. A reader may assume that the maid knows the mind of Moses' mother, and that the mother plans to float the child on the river. Alternatively, it is conceivable that the mother merely says 'Go', and the enterprising

---

1. A. Rofé, 'Moses' Mother and her Slave-Girl according to 4QExod^b', *DSD* 9 (2002), pp. 38-43. Rofé is discussing the text as presented in E.C. Ulrich *et al.*, *Qumran Cave 4. VII. Genesis to Numbers* (DJD, 12; Oxford: Clarendon Press, 1994) (hereafter DJD 12), pp. 79-95.

2. Based on the reconstruction of F.M. Cross in DJD 12, p. 87. Cross also notes that no other ancient textual witness contains this phrase.

maid takes initiative and places the ark and its precious cargo among the reeds of the Nile. Either way, the servant girl herself is depicted as a courageous servant involved in defying the edict of Pharaoh to save the child, and in this regard she fits into a larger motif of women who take risks (e.g. the midwives in 1.15-21) on behalf of the Israelites in Exodus 1–2. Moreover, there is a balanced structure to the story, in that a female servant carries the ark of Moses *to* the river, and another female servant lifts the ark *out of* the river (2.5). As Rofé observes, 'In this way, there resulted a nice symmetry between both "mothers" of Moses, Jochebed and Pharaoh's daughter. One sent her maid to place the basket in the reeds; the other sent her maid to take the basket from the reeds.'[3]

2. *A Roof with a View*

Enough has been said, I trust, concerning the richness of minor characterization that the 4QExod[b] variant brings out in this passage.[4] In light of Rofé's analysis of Exod. 2.3, I would like to suggest that there is a not dissimilar variant of 2 Sam. 11.3 attested in 4QSam[a], with a number of intriguing literary possibilities. The MT reads 'And David sent and inquired about the woman, and he said, "Is this not Bathsheba, the daughter of Eliam, the wife of Uriah the Hittite?"', but 4QSam[a] includes the phrase '...Uriah the Hittite *armor-bearer of Joab*?' (ונשא[נ] כלי יואב).[5] For my purposes, the issue here is not necessarily the perceived 'originality' of this variant (or matters of textual or compositional history), but rather some literary implications that arise when the additional designation 'armor-bearer of Joab' is considered against the backdrop of the broader narrative canvas.[6] Most readers would

---

3. Rofé, 'Moses' Mother and her Slave-Girl according to 4QExod[b]', p. 43.
4. Cf. U. Simon, 'Minor Characters in Biblical Narrative', *JSOT* 46 (1990), pp. 11-19.
5. E.C. Ulrich, *The Qumran Text of Samuel and Josephus* (Missoula, MT: Scholars Press, 1978), p. 173. Josephus (*Ant.* 7.131) also includes this detail. Anderson (*2 Samuel*, p. 151) also notes the 4QSam[a] variant, opining that it is an 'explanatory gloss'. Cf. McCarter, *II Samuel*. NAB renders 2 Sam. 11.3 as 'David had inquiries made about the woman and was told, "She is Bathsheba, daughter of Eliam, and wife of (Joab's armor-bearer) Uriah the Hittite".'
6. Note that Uriah does refer to the general as 'my lord Joab' in the king's presence (11.11). Hence, the 4QSam[a] variant could quite conceivably be classed as a 'scribal performance' (cf. R.F. Person, 'The Ancient Israelite Scribe as Performer', *JBL* 117 [1998], pp. 601-609), influenced by the biting irony of Uriah's words to David. There is also the matter of 2 Sam. 23.37 (cf. 1 Chron. 11.39), 'Naharai of Beeroth, the armor-bearer of Joab son of Zeruiah' (נשא כלי יואב בן צרויה). An impressive argument for the inner logic of this variant is articulated by Polak, 'David's Kingship', pp. 134-35. Polak draws attention to the similar roles of Joab in both this narrative of 2 Sam. 11 and the rebellion of Absalom later. Polak writes (p. 134): 'The main point, however, concerns the

agree that this vocational epithet affects the narrative presentations of both Joab and Uriah in this episode. On the one hand, it locates Uriah within the larger matrix of the 'master/armor-bearer' motif, exemplified by Jonathan's armor-bearer in 1 Samuel 14, and also the David/Saul relationship as David is introduced to the royal court (see 1 Sam. 16.21, 'and he loved him greatly, and he became his armor-bearer [ויהי לו נשׂא כלים]'). On the other hand, the variant could grimly accentuate Joab's Machiavellian cunning, as he is willing to sacrifice his own armor-bearer to safeguard the king's cover-up operation, and, by extension, protect his own interests as commander of the national troops.

Consequently, the 4QSam^a variant raises several interpretive issues for the characterization of both Joab and Uriah in this narrative. Some further complications surface when considering 'David's troubled conscience' which emerges in this episode, poignantly crystallized in 2 Sam. 11.3. As I discussed in the previous chapter, 2 Samuel 11 represents a decisive moment in King David's career. Walter Brueggemann reflects, 'We are now at the pivotal turning point in the narrative plot of the books of Samuel. We are also invited into the presence of delicate, subtle art.'[7] Further, Meir Sternberg's analysis of 2 Samuel 11 has drawn attention to a host of gaps and ambiguities in this chapter, and Robert Alter argues that in 2 Samuel 11 and 12, 'it seems as though the writer has pulled out all the stops of his remarkable narrative art in order to achieve a brilliant realization of this crucially pivotal episode'.[8] Bearing in mind the host of narrative subtleties and ambiguous overtones in this pericope, consider 2 Sam. 11.1-3 with the 4QSam^a addition in italics:

---

relation between Joab and Uriah. Unlike the MT and LXX, the Samuel Scroll from Qumran has Uriah introduced as [נ]ושׂא כלי יואב (11.2), a detail also mentioned by Flavius Josephus (*Ant.* 7.7.1 §131). The content of this surplus is highly untypical of explanatory glosses, and therefore the longer reading seems original. It implies an extremely involved introduction, which presents Bathsheba in her relation to Eliam, and to Uriah, who is related to Joab.' After surveying other such 'introductions' to characters in various biblical texts, Polak (p. 135) remarks that the phrase [נ]ושׂא כלי יואב 'could easily have been omitted, since the introduction of Bathsheba is quite elaborate even without it. Of course, the mention of Joab in the introduction of the man who is to be killed by his co-operation with the king (cf. 13.1-2) exhibits the bitter irony characteristic of this narrative. More importantly, it creates a deep psychological tension, as Joab inevitably was quite close to the man he had to kill by the king's order. This tension adds another dimension to Joab's sarcastic message after Uriah was killed.' For further details on Joab's 'sarcastic message' to David in 2 Sam. 11.19-21, see the next chapter of this book.

7. Brueggemann, *First and Second Samuel*, p. 271.
8. Sternberg, *The Poetics of Biblical Narrative*, pp. 186-229; Alter, *The David Story*, p. 249.

> It was at the return of the year, the time when kings/messengers go forth, and David sent Joab and his servants with him, and all Israel, and they ravaged the Ammonites and besieged Rabbah, but David sat in Jerusalem. It was the time of the evening, and David arose from his couch, and walked upon the roof of the king's house, and saw a woman bathing from the roof, and the woman was very beautiful to look upon. And David sent, and inquired concerning the woman, and he said, 'Is this not Bathsheba, daughter of Eliam, wife of Uriah the Hittite *armor-bearer of Joab*?'

By any measure, the question posed in 2 Sam. 11.3b represents a warning to the king.[9] Most translations render the response to David's instruction in the form of a reply, presumably from a messenger-figure who is dispatched with the commission to discover the woman's identity. The NIV, for example, adds the subject 'man': 'The man said, "Is this not Bathsheba...?"' Compare also the NRSV: 'David sent someone to inquire about the woman. It was reported, "This is Bathsheba daughter of Eliam, the wife of Uriah the Hittite".' One could ask whether or not this is the expected response from a servant returning from an assignment—a rhetorical-sounding query framed in the negative with a hint of dissatisfaction, '*Is this not* Bathsheba...?'—as a servant would perhaps reply with a more efficient 'she is A, daughter of B, wife of C'. While this sense is conveyed in the NRSV, it would seem that the interrogative aspect (הלוא זאת בת־ישבע) should be retained for a number of literary reasons. The information is framed as an implicit warning designed to stir the conscience of the king regarding the identity of the woman who happens to live next door to him: '*Is this not* Bathsheba, daughter of Eliam, wife of Uriah the Hittite *armor-bearer of Joab*?'[10]

---

9. For whatever reasons, David has not gone forth to battle the Ammonites and participate in the siege of Rabbah (2 Sam. 11.1). If there is irony and ambiguity in the opening verse of this episode, it is certainly continued in the next sentence of the narrative. There is a second temporal reference in as many sentences, and the second is meant to reflex back to the first: 'It was the turn of the year' (when the kings/messengers go forth—but David remains in Jerusalem) followed by 'It was the time of the evening' (when David sallies forth from his couch where he is reclining, many miles from the siege led by Joab). Espying the beautiful woman bathing, David's action is 'to send', and for the second time in as many verses he is once more engaged in the activity of sending; on this occasion, the task is to gather intelligence on the identity of the bather. Cf. Brueggemann, *Theology of the Old Testament*, pp. 364-65: 'David is regularly critiqued in commentary for having stayed behind in time of war, sending Joab in his place... David is the sender, the instigator of the battle, but David runs no risks. Indeed, he has time for much other "sending" of a destructive kind (see the verb in vv. 3, 4, 6, 12, 14).'

10. This question also highlights the kind of dualism that reverberates throughout the rest of the episode—the conflict between the 'outer man' (the king and military leader) and the 'inner man' (the very fallible human being with struggles and temptations). Here, David displays an 'innocence' for his public audience by feigning ignorance as to the woman's identity, but privately he must know exactly who she is, and this long statement

There are, then, numerous issues for the 'royal conscience' that are contained in this question concerning Bathsheba's identity. If indeed, as the NRSV and NIV render the verse, it is an unnamed 'messenger' who delivers this question, it is a rather bold and brave underling who registers a virtual objection and warning to the king. The question needs to be posed, however, as to whether this possibly might be David's own 'stream-of-consciousness' that is refracted in 2 Sam. 11.3b. In a chapter so 'fraught with ambiguity',[11] could this 'conscience' issue be one further example of narrative drama designed to draw the reader into its literary web? R.C. Bailey has already argued that 2 Sam. 11.3b is an example of inner direct speech; according to this proposition, the query 'Is this not Bathsheba, daughter of Eliam, wife of Uriah the Hittite *armor-bearer of Joab*?' is articulated *by David himself*. Surveying 2 Sam. 11.3 as a whole, Bailey notes that a new subject for the verb 'and he said' is not introduced, and that there is sequence of verbs which precede this one ('and he said'), each having David as the subject.[12] Bailey suggests,

> It should be noted that generally this third-person verb is attributed to an anonymous speaker who 'answers' David's inquiry. The structure of 2 Sam. 11.3, however, demonstrates that there is no other subject introduced in the verse. Similarly, there is no use of *l* [ל] to indicate David has become the indirect object of the verb. Thus syntactically it appears that all three verbs have David as the subject.[13]

---

of her name and familial connections, commencing with a negative exclamation, demarcate the issues at stake in an unambiguous manner: '*Is this not* Bathsheba, *daughter* of Eliam, *wife* of Uriah the Hittite?'

11. Yee, 'Fraught with Background', pp. 240-41.

12. Bailey, *David in Love and War*, p. 85. Citing Bailey, J.C. Exum (*Fragmented Women: Feminist [Sub]versions of Biblical Narratives* [Philadelphia: Trinity Press International, 1993] notes: 'It is not clear who says these words, whether David or an attendant, but, in any event, 'Is this not Bathsheba?' suggests that someone else is looking too.'

13. Bailey, *David in Love and War*, p. 94. Bailey (p. 94) further notes: 'The story line offers further confirmation of the correctness of this interpretation of the verbs in v. 3. The verb [אמר] follows [דרש], which points to an inquiry for information. Similarly, it is followed by a "speculative identification" of the woman [הלוא זאת]. It would appear, therefore, that the statement in v. 3b is the "inquiry" [דרש] of David in search of the confirmation of the identity of the woman.' To supplement Bailey's reading on this point, I would suggest that this does not have to be limited to David's speculative inquiry, but rather might also be the king's own conscience informing him of the woman's identity, her family lineage (as the daughter of one of his warriors according to 2 Sam. 23, and consequently the granddaughter of Ahithophel), and her status as a married woman (the wife of Uriah, also a warrior listed in 2 Sam. 23; moreover, one who is currently away on the battlefield, and therefore this husband is not a factor). McCarter (*II Samuel*, p. 277) discounts this option in his translation: '[He] sent out inquiries about the woman. "Isn't she Bathsheba daughter of Eliam", someone said, "the wife of Uriah the Hittite?"'

Hence, when Bailey considers that there is not an explicit marker denoting a change in the subject of the verb, it could plausibly mean that David is the speaker (or thinker) of these words—after all אמר is a verb that can also mean 'to think' as well as 'to say' in Hebrew.[14] If the notion of inner direct speech is taken seriously, an alternative way of rendering this portion of text (assuming the king remains the subject) could be, 'And David sent, and inquired concerning the woman, *and he thought*, "Is this not Bathsheba, daughter of Eliam, wife of Uriah the Hittite, *armor-bearer of Joab*?"'[15] In my view, such a reading is highly defensible in light of other instances in Hebrew narrative where ויאמר should be translated 'and he thought'. For example, 1 Sam. 18.11, 'And Saul hurled the spear and he thought (ויאמר), "I will pin David on the wall"'.[16] Another useful example is 2 Kgs 20.19, 'Then Hezekiah said (ויאמר) to Isaiah, "The word of the LORD which you have spoken is good". For he thought (ויאמר), "Will there not be peace and security in my days?"'[17] Fortuitously, both of these examples also represent a royal stream-of-consciousness from Saul and Hezekiah respectively, and both kings are negatively characterized through these examples of inner discourse.

3. *A Sovereign Soliloquy?*

There is a defensible argument, it would seem, that David asks the question of 2 Sam. 11.3b *internally*. Exactly why he 'inquires' (דרש) as to the woman's identity in 11.3a remains obscure, and would have to be understood as something of a formality. But my point here would be: whether

---

Anderson also inserts a different subject for the verb 'and he said' (ויאמר): 'So David sent someone and made inquiries about the woman, and he reported…' (*2 Samuel*, p. 150).

14. Cf. BDB, p. 56; *HALOT*, p. 66; *DCH*, I, p. 324.

15. If 2 Sam. 11.3b included a qualifying phrase such as, 'said in his heart' (i.e. 'to himself')—for example, as in Gen. 17.17, 'Then Abraham fell on his face and laughed, and said to himself (ויאמר בלבו)…', or Gen. 27.41, 'Now Esau hated Jacob because of the blessing with which his father had blessed him, and Esau said to himself (ויאמר עשו בלבו)…'—the ambiguity would of course be resolved.

16. The MT reads ויטל שאול את־החנית ויאמר אכה בדוד ובקיר. Cf. the rendering of ויאמר by McCarter (*I Samuel*, p. 184: 'thought').

17. The MT reads ויאמר חזקיהו אל־ישעיהו טוב דבר־יהוה אשר דברת ויאמר הלוא אם־שלום ואמת יהיה בימי. T.R. Hobbs (*2 Kings* [WBC, 13; Waco, TX: Word Books, 1985], p. 285) renders this line as 'But to himself he said, "Why not …?"' Hobbs (p. 295) further notes that this inner speech is revealing: 'The clay feet of Hezekiah are now apparent'. Cf. M. Cogan and H. Tadmor, *II Kings: A New Translation with Introduction and Commentary* (AB, 11; New York: Doubleday, 1988), p. 258: 'For he thought: At least there will be peace and security in my lifetime'. Cogan and Tadmor also note that this inner thought shows Hezekiah's 'self-concern' (p. 260) and 'unseemly pride' (p. 262). See also the discussion of B.O. Long, *2 Kings* (FOTL, 10; Grand Rapids: Eerdmans, 1991), pp. 244-45.

David is the speaker (internal discourse) of these words or whether this query proceeds from an unidentified subordinate may be yet another level of ambiguity in this narrative, with consequences for the remainder of 2 Samuel 11 and beyond.[18] If this is a moment in biblical prose when the royal conscience is stirred and motives are questioned, then the interior angle of the king's mind that is briefly divulged is paramount for the delineation of character and the conflict generated in the narrative. Even if an unnamed servant poses the question to David, the audience is nonetheless provided with a 'struggle' between king and servant on the roof at this early stage in the narrative, and it serves to tangle David's motives in a more intricate net.[19] But if, as a reader may be inclined to think, this question marks the stirring of *David's own* conscience (meaning that he is aware of the woman's identity *before* sending his agent to 'take her'), then the result is a narrative that is further fraught with complexity.[20] When the 4QSam[a] variant ('...*armor-bearer of*

---

18. Cf. the footnote of J.W. Wesselius, 'Joab's Death and the Central Theme of the Succession Narrative (2 Samuel ix—1 Kings ii)', *VT* 40 (1990), pp. 336-51 (347): 'It seems likely that David's unusual words in 2 Sam. xi 3, "Is not she Bathsheba, daughter of Eliam, the wife of Uriah the Hittite?", indicate some consideration on the part of David, apparently leading to the conclusion that he could do what he wanted without fear for the consequences'.

19. The same 'roof' (גג) features tragically in Absalom's rebellion (2 Sam. 16.21-22), as the counsel of Ahithophel (the father of Eliam) is followed and a tent is erected on the 'roof' (גג) of the king's house to defile the concubines. The struggle of David's conscience on the roof in 11.3 presages the struggle of Absalom's rebellion to come.

20. This example of 2 Sam. 11.3b would correspondingly provide an instructive example of 'stream-of-consciousness', defined as a 'term coined by William James in *Principles of Psychology* (New York: Dover Publications, 1918) to denote the flow of inner experiences. Now an almost indispensable term in literary criticism, it refers to that technique which seeks to depict the multitudinous thoughts and feelings which pass through the mind. Another phrase for it is "interior monologue"' (J.A. Cuddon, *A Dictionary of Literary Terms and Literary Theory* [Oxford: Basil Blackwell, 3rd edn, 1991], p. 866). If, as is suggested above, 2 Sam. 11 is the great turning point of David's reign, then this could be construed as a brilliant literary device for showing the king's thought process at this crucial juncture—a far more sophisticated literary device (the subject of the verb is deliberately obfuscated to create a range of possibilities in the reader's mind) than is often acknowledged, and one could argue that this is a vital part of the theological vision of this narrative since it provides the reader with an inside view of David's conscience before his great fall. In their influential text, *The Nature of Narrative*, Scholes and Kellogg contend that in 2 Sam. 11, 'Bathsheba's beauty is presented impersonally, as a fact, and not from David's point of view or in terms of his reaction to seeing her. The inward life is assumed but not presented in primitive literature, whether Hebraic or Hellenic' (R. Scholes and R. Kellogg, *The Nature of Narrative* [New York: Oxford University Press, 1966], p. 166). The present argument would pose a challenge to this observation about 'primitive' literature, which may in fact be more sophisticated than such critics have discerned hitherto. See Sternberg, *The Poetics of Biblical Narrative*, p. 525.

Joab?') is thus considered as a trajectory of David's own mind, a host of narrative forces further collide around the identity of Bathsheba and the tessellated network of relationships that are involved in David's decision. Frank Polak touches on some of the wider reaches of 2 Sam. 11.3 and the 4QSam^a addition:

> The Qumran reading also sheds new light on the tale of Absalom's death. First of all, one notes the structural opposition: Uriah, Joab's armourbearer, must die by the express order of David; Absalom, David's son, is killed by Joab, against David's express interdiction. The latter scene, then, is the counterpart of the former one. Moreover, after hitting Absalom with three arrow-heads (שלחים) [18.14, LXX], Joab has him killed by ten of his armourbearers. Among the many other reminiscences one must mention the 'roof of the gate' on which the spy stood in order to inform the king of any news (18.24). This roof is an echo of the roof on which David was walking when he espied Bathsheba (11.2). Another intriguing detail is the mention of the wall (18.24: אל גג השער אל החומה), reminding us of the wall from which Uriah was hit (מעל החומה, 11.24), as was Abimelech (11.21; this sound constellation is similar to המלחמה, vv. 7, 15-20, 25). The town gate appears in the pericope of Uriah's death in the heroic attempt to use the counter-attack for forcing a way into the town (11.23). All these features enhance and deepen the intricate connection between these two tales. Absalom's death is an act of divine retribution for the murder of Uriah.[21]

4. Conclusion

To summarize and conclude, I would suggest that the 4QSam^a variant ('...*armor-bearer of Joab*?') merits interpretive attention for three reasons. First, the addition emphasizes the significance of 2 Sam. 11.3b in terms of its *literary foreshadowing* of the climactic events of this 'turning point' episode in David's life. Clearly, the question posed in 11.3b points ahead to Ahithophel's future involvement, since Ahithophel, according to 2 Sam. 23.34, is the father of Eliam and thus grandfather of Bathsheba. Ahithophel's role in the ensuing civil war is thus anticipated in this verse. But 2 Sam. 11.3b also alerts the reader to the complex role of Joab in 2 Samuel 11, especially in the liquidation of Uriah, and in the rest of the David narrative. By extension, just as Eliam's daughter Bathsheba and father Ahithophel are important players in the immediate wake of 2 Samuel 11, Joab is a pivotal figure as well, and according to the 4QSam^a variant, Joab and Uriah have a deeper relational connection than is represented in the MT.

---

21. Polak, 'David's Kingship—A Precarious Equilibrium', pp. 135-36. One would further note that in Judg. 9.54 Abimelech is run through by 'the lad who carried his armor' (הנער נשא כליו).

7. *The Royal Conscience*

Second, the 4QSam[a] variant underscores the *ambiguity of conscience* presented in this episode: is the question of Bathsheba's identity posed by a messenger, or is the king himself responsible for this utterance? One could argue that the 4QSam[a] addition certainly preserves, if not enhances, the drama of this syntactic ambiguity. The forthcoming civil war beginning in 2 Samuel 15 and its key players are thus registered in David's mind from the outset. In a narrative 'fraught with ambiguity', this ambiguity of whether David himself is the speaker of these words (including the 4QSam[a] variant) adds one more level to the narrative sophistication, and accentuates the *drama of conscience* played out in the royal mind. Is this a remarkably well-informed messenger delivering a memorandum of veiled rebuke to the sedentary monarch (who is *not* out with the troops battling the Ammonites)? Or is this a Davidic stream-of-consciousness unveiling a struggle in the royal conscience at this precipitous moment for king and nation? Such a question is only complicated by the presence of Uriah's vocational epithet (*'armor-bearer of Joab'*) in the Qumran fragment. In this chapter I have proposed a new reading of 2 Sam. 11.3—including the 4QSam[a] variant—suggesting that there is an intentional ambiguity as to whether this is a question from a servant or a royal soliloquy. On the one hand, it could possibly be a messenger of the king, who frames his 'response' in order to prick the royal conscience. On the other hand, my reading entertains the possibility that 11.3b (including [ונ]ושא כלי יואב) proceeds from the mind of King David. This ambiguity is one of many in a narrative episode that represents a watershed moment in David's career.

Finally, the presence of this 4QSam[a] variant provides evidence that 2 Samuel 11—the turning point of the David story—was vigorously read and viewed as highly important to early readers of this narrative, and illustrates the vitality of this verse and its dramatic purpose at such a decisive moment of David's reign.[22] Naturally there are arguments that the 2 Sam. 11.3b variant attested in 4QSam[a] is secondary, much like the Exod. 2.3b variant attested in 4QExod[b] as described by Alexander Rofé. However, appropriating the work of Rofé and Uriel Simon, I would conclude that this variant testifies to the often underrated role of minor characters within the artistic economy of biblical narrative, and thus for the history of interpretation of 2 Samuel 11 it is an issue that deserves further consideration.[23]

---

22. See further C.A. Evans, 'David in the Dead Sea Scrolls', in S.E. Porter and C.A. Evans (eds.), *The Scrolls and the Scriptures: Qumran Fifty Years After* (Roehampton Institute London Papers, 3; JSPSup, 26; Sheffield: Sheffield Academic Press, 1997), pp. 183-97.

23. Rofé, 'Moses' Mother and her Slave-Girl according to 4QExod[b]'; Simon, 'Minor Characters in Biblical Narrative'.

8

Joab and the Risks of Reader-Response Criticism

Within the narrative material of Samuel–Kings, David has a complex relationship with his commanding officer, Joab. From the opening of 2 Samuel until the final speech of David in 1 Kings, Joab is a pivotal figure—arguably, Joab's actions are virtually indispensable for David retaining his hold on power. There are a number of crucial interactions between David and Joab throughout the narrative which underscore the complexity of their relationship. A key event occurs in 2 Samuel 11, where David writes Joab a letter commanding the death of Uriah the Hittite. In this instance Joab apparently operates as a 'reader-response critic' who engages in a creative interpretation of the text. After reading the written correspondence, it is evident that Joab subtly changes the king's orders, yet David palpably benefits from his general's deceptive actions and interpretive decisions surrounding the royal missive. It is notable that similar patterns of hermeneutical strategy by Joab are seen earlier in the narrative, and recur at later points in the story. Following a brief discussion of reader-response criticism and outlining its applicability to Joab, this chapter will briefly explore and locate the narrative of 2 Sam. 11.14-25 within the wider narrative pattern of Joab as a 'reader' of literary texts, people, situations, and even 'scripture'. This chapter then concludes with a summary of insights that emerge from observing Joab as a reader-response critic and an interpreter of King David's words and actions.

In terms of definition, reader-response theory is concerned with the relationship between a literary text and a reader. The primary emphases of this theory are the various ways in which a reader 'participates' in the process of interpreting a literary text and the hermeneutical dynamics of this relationship. In other words, reader-response criticism is predominantly interested in a reader's contribution toward a text's meaning and interpretation.[1] As such, reader-response criticism is less interested in the 'text in-and-of-itself', and more interested in the interaction of a reader with the literary text.[2] For a

---

1. Cuddon, *A Dictionary of Literary Terms*, p. 770.
2. S. Mailloux, *Interpretive Conventions: The Reader in the Study of American Fiction* (Ithaca, NY: Cornell University Press, 1982), p. 20. Cf. E. Freund (*The Return of the Reader: Reader-Response Criticism* [London: Methuen, 1987], p. 5) who notes that

reader-response critic, the crucial point for this chapter is that reading is not necessarily restricted to the *discovery* of meaning, but that reading can also involve the *creation* of meaning.³ Following this line in a recent study of Amos 7, F.O. García-Treto has utilized the reader-response theory of Stanley Fish, and helpfully summarizes as follows:

> Fish postulates that there is no such thing as 'simply reading', a hypothetical activity that would imply 'the possibility of pure (that is, disinterested) perception'. Rather, a reader—or a reading—always proceeds from the basis of certain 'interpretive decisions' which in turn lead to the adoption of 'interpretive strategies' that produce or determine the reading. Interpretive strategies, in fact, 'are the shape of reading, and because they are the shape of reading, they give texts their shape, making them rather than, as it is usually assumed, arising from them'.⁴

The contention of the present chapter is that Joab strikingly conforms to the profile of a reader-response critic according to the parameters delineated above. While the episode of 2 Sam. 11.14-25 clearly does not label Joab as a reader, it seems reasonable to assume that he reads David's letter addressed to him. From his reading, it is evident that Joab makes a series of 'interpretive decisions' regarding David's literary correspondence. In effect, Joab *creates* and defines the meaning of the letter by means of the interpretive strategy he adopts. The suggestion here is that his action and status as a reader of the written word provides an important means of access into his personality as presented in the narrative. Moreover, this act of reading not only has ramifications for the portrait of Joab which emerges from the episode, but also for the wider narrative of Samuel–Kings. Consequently, the examination of 2 Sam. 11.14-25 that follows below is particularly concerned with Joab's posture as a reader-response critic in the narrower context of 2 Samuel 11, as well as some of his other hermeneutical moves within the broader narrative of David's reign.

1. *The Epistle of David (2 Samuel 11.14-15)*

The events of 2 Samuel 11 are framed within the context of Israel's conflict with the Ammonites, and Joab is highlighted in the opening sentence of the

---

reader-response criticism asks the question 'what happens—consciously or unconsciously, cognitively or psychologically—during the reading process?'

3. Mailloux, *Interpretive Conventions*, pp. 20-21.

4. F.O. García-Treto, 'A Reader-Response Approach to Prophetic Conflict: The Case of Amos 7.10-17', in J.C. Exum and D.J.A. Clines (eds.), *The New Literary Criticism and the Hebrew Bible* (JSOTSup, 143; Sheffield: JSOT Press, 1993), pp. 114-24 (115). See S. Fish, *Is There a Text in This Class? The Authority of Interpretive Communities* (Cambridge, MA: Harvard University Press, 1980), pp. 167-73.

chapter (v. 1). As it is customary for agents[5] to go out to war in the spring, Joab is sent with the troops to destroy Rabbah, the capital city. However, the disjunctive syntax of the final clause in the Hebrew text foregrounds the contrasting actions of David and Joab: Joab is sent to war, 'but David remained in Jerusalem'.[6] Joab is next mentioned in v. 6, where he receives a terse message from the king: 'Send to me Uriah the Hittite'. It is conceivable that Uriah knows, or at least suspects why he has been summoned away from armed combat to return to Jerusalem.[7] Greeting Uriah with the rather banal inquiries—about the welfare of Joab, the welfare of the army, and the welfare of the battle—may not be the most convincing subterfuge on the king's part. The audience naturally conjectures that David is anxious for Uriah's return to Jerusalem in order to *rendezvous* with his wife Bathsheba, and so impart the paternity of the incubating child to the legal husband. Uriah, though, does not prove compliant. David is increasingly desperate, and undoubtedly it is significant that he calls on his commanding officer to be the 'hatchet man'.[8] 2 Samuel 11.14-15 records the king embarking on a unique epistolary enterprise, as he composes a letter with specific instructions for his general:

> In the morning, David wrote a letter to Joab, which he sent by the hand of Uriah. He wrote in the letter, 'Give Uriah to the front of the face of the strongest battle. Then withdraw from him, so that he may be struck down, and die.'

Both the courier and content of David's letter to Joab in v. 14 are peculiar. The letter clearly amounts to a death warrant for Uriah. Whether it is a prudent move to send it by means of Uriah himself is questionable, but in any case David expects that the letter, presumably sealed, will not be prematurely opened by its conveyor. Of course, if Uriah is oblivious to the adultery, 'he has in any case no personal motive to look at the letter'.[9] If, on

---

5. As discussed in Chapter 6, R. Polzin discusses at length the ambiguity in the Hebrew text as to whether 'kings' or 'messengers/agents' should be read in the MT. The ambiguity is laced with irony since messengers are deployed throughout 2 Sam. 11, including, of course, the irony of Uriah as messenger and Joab's use of the messenger. See Polzin, *David and the Deuteronomist*, pp. 109-12. Cf. Rosenberg, *King and Kin*, p. 126.
6. Cf. Exum, *Tragedy and Biblical Narrative*, p. 126: 'By not going forth to war, David brings the war home'.
7. Sternberg, *The Poetics of Biblical Narrative*, pp. 186-222. Sternberg's original article (with M. Perry) was published in 1968, and he notes a host of responses debating the thesis of whether Uriah 'knows'. Cf. Bal, *Lethal Love*, pp. 10-36; Yee, '"Fraught with Background"'.
8. Brueggemann, *First and Second Samuel*, p. 276.
9. Alter, *The David Story*, p. 253. For a visual exegesis of Rembrandt's painting and a cultural analysis of the various 'roles' of a letter read by Bathsheba, see M. Bal, 'De-disciplining the Eye', *Critical Inquiry* 16 (1990), pp. 506-31.

the other hand Uriah does know, perhaps 'he is accepting his fate with grim resignation, bitterly conscious that his wife has betrayed him and that the king is too powerful for him to contend with'.[10] From a literary viewpoint, it is certainly intriguing to see David employ Uriah himself as the courier of this malignant epistle, as it causes one to speculate how Joab may have reacted.[11] The contents and directions to Joab within the missive are equally odd.[12] To this point in the narrative David has shown himself to be a competent military and political leader. The imperatives to his general concerning Uriah display evidence of neither. In military terms, it would be most unlikely for a field marshal to issue an order for the troops simply to withdraw and abandon a colleague. In political terms, if Uriah is publicly killed through such a withdrawal, then surely the reasons for this *de facto* assassination will be suspected. Therefore, in light of these factors, the reaction of Joab is telling. Joab's reading of David's epistle leads to a creative encounter and interpretation of the text: he proceeds to disregard the 'letter' of the king's orders, while at the same time being faithful to the spirit of the author's intention.

2. *Joab as a Reader-Response Critic of the Epistle of David (2 Samuel 11.16-17)*

> And, while Joab was watching the city, he stationed Uriah at the place where he knew that there were valiant men. The men of the city came forth. They fought with Joab, and some of the army, some of David's servants, fell. Also, Uriah the Hittite died. (2 Sam. 11.16-17)

The narrator affords him no direct speech in vv. 16-17, but Joab is described as 'watching the city'. While this depiction of a watchful Joab contrasts with

---

10. Alter, *The David Story*, p. 253. As Alter notes, a mediating position is argued by Garsiel, 'The Story of David and Bathsheba', pp. 256-59.

11. Cf. McCarter, *II Samuel*, p. 287: 'On the motif, widespread in world literature, of the messenger carrying his own death warrant, see Gunkel 1921.132 [*Das Märchen im Alten Testament* (Religionsgeschictliche Volksbücher, 2; Tübingen: J.C.B. Mohr, 1921)]. Perhaps the most interesting illustration is found in the *Iliad* (6.168-90), where the Argive king Proteus, suspecting Bellerophon of adultery with the queen, arranges for the young man's death by sending him to Lycia with a coded message asking the Lycian king, Proteus' father-in-law, to put him to death.'

12. A recent monograph by Pyper, *David as Reader*, draws particular attention to a pair of texts where David 'reads' (or at least 'hears') the words of others and provides an interpretive response. In a lucid review of Pyper's book, H.C. White summarizes the thesis: 'Pyper sees such an internal act of interpretation as a model of "reading": the character's utterance mimics the interpretative role of the narrator thereby providing a model by which the external reader may access the meaning of the story' (*CBQ* 60 [1998], pp. 341-42). Pyper's thesis could perhaps be extended to include 2 Sam. 11.14-15, where the narrator provides a concrete image of David, not 'as reader', but David 'as writer'.

the earlier images of a reclining David, the main inference here is that Joab, after reading the letter, is waiting for the opportune moment to implement his own version of David's plan. Instead of the logistically inane 'advance and withdraw' scheme composed by the king, Joab does something rather different from what is inscribed in the letter. A central argument of the present chapter is that how a character reads can function as an important means of indirect characterization in biblical narrative. Hugh Pyper cites the work of literary theorist Inge Crosman Wimmers, noting that in her study on the poetics of reading, 'she looks at the way in which a reader can gain information about characters, but also be led to judgments about various possible strategies of reading, from the display of characters in the act of reading'.[13] Joab as a reader of the king's epistle is performing a crucial act of interpretation, and makes strategic decisions based on signs, cultural codes, military conventions, but, most significantly, his knowledge of David.

A number of commentators point out that Joab modifies David's orders as imprinted in the letter. Kyle McCarter economically remarks, 'Joab does not follow instructions exactly, but he gets the job done'.[14] With more attention to detail, Robert Alter begins to search for possible reasons behind the change of the king's order: 'Joab, then, coldly recognizes that in order to give David's plan some credibility, it will be necessary to send a whole contingent into a dangerous place and for many others besides Uriah to die'.[15] In a highly perceptive study of 2 Samuel 11, Meir Sternberg delineates the 'subtle differences between...the order of execution and the execution of the order... It is better for many to fall, [Joab] decides, than for the conspiracy to stand revealed.'[16] The term 'conspiracy' raises an interesting question, then, surrounding the motives for changing David's order, and the larger reasons for Joab's interpretive strategy here. As with Uriah in Jerusalem, the audience may inquire: Does Joab know, or suspect, or deduce from the contents of the letter the impetus for David sending an elite soldier[17] to his death? This is an important question because it helps to explain *why* Joab acts as a reader-response critic with respect to David's letter.

---

13. Pyper, *David as Reader*, p. 35. Cf. I.C. Wimmers, *Poetics of Reading: Approaches to the Novel* (Princeton, NJ: Princeton University Press, 1988). The contention here is that a great deal can be learned from watching Joab in the act of reading. Moreover, when Joab is viewed as a reader *within the text* his actions parallel the reader *of the text*, who undertakes a similar kind of literary interpretation.

14. McCarter, *II Samuel*, p. 287. Cf. Garsiel, 'The Story of David and Bathsheba', pp. 259-60.

15. Alter, *The David Story*, p. 254.

16. Sternberg, *The Poetics of Biblical Narrative*, p. 214.

17. The list of David's primary warriors in 2 Sam. 23 features 'Uriah the Hittite' as the final name (v. 39).

On the matter of whether Joab suspects David's reasons for writing the letter in the first place, A.A. Anderson is doubtful, and concludes: 'It is unlikely that Joab, at this stage, knew the reason for Uriah's liquidation'.[18] On the contrary, there are grounds for submitting that Joab does know the real purpose for the execution of Uriah; hence, he modifies David's directive precisely because he is aware of the extenuating circumstances that have led to this strange order from the king. But, as written in the letter, the king's orders are 'impossibly clumsy (perhaps an indication that the Machiavellian David has suddenly lost his manipulative coolness): if the men around Uriah were to draw back all at once, leaving him exposed, it would be entirely transparent that there was a plot to get him killed'.[19] As it turns out, the 'watchful' Joab clearly recognizes the folly of David's plan and executes his own redaction of the king's orders. Two points arise here which will be developed below. First, Joab's reader-response criticism of the royal letter is ultimately beneficial for David. Second, Joab's method of creative interpretation has antecedents in the wider narrative, and his stance as a reader-response critic can in fact be anticipated as early as the 'Abner affair' of 2 Sam. 3.22-39.

3. *Retrospective: Joab's 'Hermeneutic of Suspicion' in the Abner Affair*[20]

A central point of the present study is that Joab creatively interprets the king's words in 2 Samuel 11 for politically astute reasons. Joab's reader-

---

18. Anderson, *2 Samuel*, p. 155. Brueggemann suggests that Joab reads 'between the lines of the dispatch' and 'knows what is expected', but this has to do with modifying the king's order as opposed to providing grounds for a motive (*First and Second Samuel*, p. 276).

19. Alter, *The David Story*, p. 254. If Uriah is oblivious to David's adultery and the contents of the letter, at this point he may have preferred Joab to be a deconstructionist rather than a reader-response critic.

20. As critical concepts, 'reader-response criticism' and 'hermeneutics of suspicion' are often used by literary theorists who are highly self-conscious of the creation of meaning in a text through the interaction of reader and text (including the cultural and ideological assumptions involved in such a process), and/or as a tool of discourse that seeks to reveal an underlying ideology behind the writing of a text in the first instance. In the present chapter, such terms are clearly used in a more general sense as a way of accessing Joab as reader of text and situation. To be sure, Joab does not offer the kind of critical awareness expressed in many postmodern studies. However, as general categories of Joab's *reading strategies* as a means of indirect characterization, these concepts are heuristically useful for illustrating Joab's own political agenda at work during his various moments and processes of interpretation. See I.W. Provan, 'Why Barzillai of Gilead (1 Kings 2:7)? Narrative Art and the Hermeneutics of Suspicion in 1 Kings 1–2', *TynBul* 46 (1995), pp. 103-16.

response criticism of David's letter, though, has roots earlier in the narrative which serve to clarify his actions in the Uriah incident. If the episode of Uriah the Hittite is compared with the earlier execution of Abner in 2 Sam. 3.22-39, several patterns of correspondence emerge that illuminate Joab's later reading of David's letter.

The Abner affair also involves an interpretive strategy on Joab's part. In 2 Sam. 3.24-25, Joab accuses David of not being sufficiently aware of Abner's devious intent. It is conspicuous that David does not affirm or deny Joab's imputation, and it is after this silence that Joab draws Abner apart 'deceptively' in 2 Sam. 3.27 and delivers the lethal blow to his favorite target, the 'fifth rib'.[21] Joab appears to exercise a hermeneutic of suspicion toward both the actions of Abner and the silence of David. David's very public avowal of innocence does not lack melodrama as he elaborately calls down curses and composes lyrics to distance himself from this heinous deed and its perpetrators, but makes no move to rid himself of Joab and his brother Abishai; in fact 'he continues to depend on their activity as strongmen'.[22]

In addition to the display of creative hermeneutics, another crucial similarity between the Abner episode (2 Sam. 3.22-39) and the Uriah affair (11.14-25) is that in both, Joab censures David for inferior political judgment. Joab's acerbic rebuke of ch. 11 is more subtle and will be discussed in a moment. In 3.24-25 the rebuke is straightforward, as Joab upbraids David: 'What have you done?... You know Abner son of Ner! Indeed, to entice you he came, to know your going out and your coming in, and to know all that you are doing.' According to Joab's interpretation, Abner is a dangerous dissembler, and the audience may well concede that he has a point. First, according to 2 Sam. 3.6 Abner's powerbase in the north is 'growing in strength'.[23] Second, since Abner has defected once, there is the continual risk that he may turn again.[24] Third, Abner shows all the signs of having royal ambitions, especially if (as Ishbosheth alleges) he appropriates Saul's

---

21. David's silence on the crucial matter of Abner's reliability is unexpected. Until this juncture in the narrative, David has taken a multitude of opportunities to unleash his political rhetoric. The reader may have anticipated that David would defend Abner's newly found loyalty to him. David's silence—especially considering Joab's personal sense of affront with respect to Abner—indicates yet another contour of their 'entangled and stratified' relationship (E. Auerbach, *Mimesis: The Representation of Reality in Western Literature* [trans. W.R. Trask; Princeton, NJ, Princeton University Press, 1953], p. 12). There is a subsequent execution involving the 'fifth rib' (החמש) at 2 Sam. 20.10, the stabbing of another rival to Joab and threat to David's stability, Amasa.

22. Alter, *The David Story*, p. 216.

23. Cf. G.G. Nicol, 'The Death of Joab and the Accession of Solomon: Some Observations on the Narrative of 1 Kings 1–2', *SJOT* 7 (1993), pp. 135-51 (141-42).

24. Cf. Wesselius, 'Joab's Death and the Central Theme of the Succession Narrative', p. 338. It may be added that Abner refers to Judah contemptuously in 2 Sam. 3.8.

concubine (3.7).[25] Of course, as the narrator reminds the audience in 3.30, the motives here are intricately tangled since Joab desires revenge on Abner for stabbing his brother Asahel in the 'fifth rib', and may also perceive that Abner is a threat to his job security.[26] But the argument that David ultimately profits from Abner's execution is hard to resist: a potentially dangerous and unreliable foe is eliminated, and the north is considerably weakened. Despite David's elaborate protest, as Niels Peter Lemche and James VanderKam maintain, the transition to the throne of the united kingdom is perhaps smoother without Abner.[27]

So, in the Abner affair of 2 Samuel 3, David benefits from Joab's hermeneutic of suspicion just as he benefits from his interpretive creativity in the Uriah affair of 2 Samuel 11. Furthermore, in both episodes Joab concludes that David is being tactically unwise. The rebuke of 3.24-25 ('What have you done...?') is scathing and delivered face-to-face. There is a somewhat different tone and overtures of sarcasm in the veiled rebuke contained in the reply to David's letter, further evidencing Joab's unique style of literary interpretation.

4. *Joab's Reply, and his Reading of the Abimelech Narrative (2 Samuel 11.18-22)*

> And Joab sent, and reported to David all the affairs of the battle. He commanded the messenger, saying, 'When you are finished speaking of all the affairs of the battle to the king, if it should be that the anger of the king flares up, and he says to you: "Why did you draw near to the city to fight? Did you not know that they would shoot from the wall? Who struck down Abimelech son of Jerubbesheth? Was it not a woman? She threw upon him an upper millstone from the wall and he died in Thebez! Why did you draw near to the wall?"—then you should say, "Also, your servant Uriah the Hittite is dead".' The messenger left, and went and reported to David all for which Joab sent him. (2 Sam. 11.18-22)

Commentators have put forward a number of suggestions as to the purpose of Joab's cryptic instruction to the messenger. Robert Bergen perceives an ambivalence: 'Whether the comparatively lengthy set of guidelines...was

---

25. For an appraisal that David earlier pronounces judgment on Abner, see F.H. Cryer, 'David's Rise to Power and the Death of Abner: An Analysis of 1 Samuel xxvi 14-16 and its Redaction-Critical Implications', *VT* 35 (1985), pp. 385-94.

26. Several views for and against this position are compiled in Nicol, 'The Death of Joab and the Accession of Solomon', pp. 141-42.

27. N.P. Lemche, 'David's Rise', *JSOT* 10 (1978), pp. 2-25 (16-18), and J.C. Vander-Kam, 'Davidic Complicity in the Deaths of Abner and Eshbaal: A Historical and Redaction Study', *JBL* 99 (1990), pp. 521-39 (529-33). Though the methodologies of Lemche and VanderKam tend to differ in some respects, the conclusions are comparable.

intended to be part of the cover-up or whether Joab genuinely feared some reprisal from the king cannot be discerned from the text'.[28] On the other hand, McCarter is more convinced that there are two levels of understanding: 'It is phrased in such a way as to conceal from the messenger, and anyone overhearing his report to David, its real purpose'.[29] Walter Brueggemann expands this notion, and explains that the Abimelech reference would be part of David's guise:

> Joab must cast his report in subtle, misleading language so that only the king can understand. Joab anticipates David's heated, fraudulent objection to his strategy. Obviously it is foolish to go near the wall, for the soldiers are so exposed that they can be killed by a woman dropping a stone from above.[30]

Consequently, it seems plausible to infer from this discourse that indeed Joab is aware of exactly what David has done, a premise which is indispensable for understanding his reply to David. Moreover, Joab's rendering of David's hypothetical response is decidedly more intricate than the above commentators suggest.[31] I would argue that the intertextual reference to Abimelech not only serves as an important aspect of Joab's characterization, but provides yet another profile of Joab as a 'reader' of David and his situation in this episode. Consider the passage recounting the death of Abimelech in Judg. 9.50-54:

> Then Abimelech went to Thebez, and encamped against Thebez, and took it. But there was a strong tower within the city, and all the people of the city fled to it, all the men and women, and shut themselves in; and they went to the roof of the tower. And Abimelech came to the tower, and fought against it, and drew near to the door of the tower to burn it with fire. And a certain woman threw an upper millstone upon Abimelech's head, and crushed his skull. Then he called hastily to the young man his armor-bearer, and said to him, 'Draw your sword and kill me, lest men say of me, "A woman killed him"'. And his young man thrust him through, and he died. (RSV)

When comparing this account of Abimelech with David's predicament in 2 Samuel 11, it appears that Joab is reading the Judges narrative allegorically. In addition to the multiple layers of *double entendre* which make this a cunningly selected intertext, the appropriation of the Abimelech 'kingship'

---

28. Bergen, *1, 2 Samuel*, p. 367.
29. McCarter, *II Samuel*, p. 288.
30. Brueggemann, *First and Second Samuel*, p. 277.
31. In her engaging study of 2 Sam. 11, Bal observes that Joab's reference to Abimelech has a larger metaphorical role in the narrative. In the opening chapter of her book, her argument is framed in terms of the 'lethal woman' in the Hebrew Bible. While much of her analysis is beyond the scope of this article, Bal is quite accurate when she notes the neglect of commentators to 'shift their attention from David to Joab' when probing 2 Sam. 11.16-24 (*Lethal Love*, p. 27).

narrative further illuminates Joab's proclivity toward creative interpretation. For one, as Sternberg suggests, to be even mentioned in the same breath as a thug like Abimelech is pejorative, and has the effect of diminishing David's image: 'The more so since Abimelech fell at a woman's hands while at the head of his army: David falls at a woman's hands precisely because he plays truant from war'.[32] Joab's mocking voice of censure can no doubt be heard, as well as an ironic jab at the geophysical distance between king and military commander: while David is lounging on the elevated palace roof, his general is on foreign soil 'camped in the open fields' (as Uriah reminds the king in 11.11).[33] Sternberg continues: 'Moreover, Abimelech tried to cover up the disgrace for fear that the rumor would spread among the people'.[34] Thus one could infer that Joab is being crafty, because unequivocally David is trying to cover up his disgrace by using a soldier. In addition, Joab rhetorically emphasizes the decapitating role of 'a woman' in the intertext of Abimelech's fall, a thrust which sounds as though it is referring to the illicit liaison with Bathsheba as 'the ultimate source of this chain of disasters'.[35] This is both a unique style of satirical rebuke, and an illustration of Joab's allegorical stream of consciousness. Joab, from the audience's perspective, is toying with the king, since above all, David wants to hear the news that Uriah is dead. This is precisely the fact that Joab adroitly delays, drawing out the king's agitation as long as possible. For Joab, it may be poetic justice, since the king was equally artistic in publicly rebuking him after Abner's assassination in 2 Sam. 3.28-39.

Furthermore, what is noteworthy for the future is that Joab is using a story with parabolic contours. He will use and enhance this kind of artifice later in 2 Samuel 14 with the wise woman of Tekoa. In light of these various layers of irony and parabolic machinations, it may seem disappointing that David does not have the opportunity to hear this satirical rebuke, as implied by the manner in which Joab's response to David's letter is delivered.

---

32. Sternberg, *The Poetics of Biblical Narrative*, pp. 221-22. Cf. Bal, *Lethal Love*, p. 25: 'The comparison between the tyrant Abimelech and David is not a flattering one. But, technically speaking, David is not the one compared: it was the innocent Uriah, among other soldiers, who was neither a tyrant nor a king, whose death resembled Abimelech's.' On the contrary, the analysis here understands Joab's allusion differently. Joab's reading is that David has ventured too close to the 'roof' of Uriah's house, and has the allegorical equivalent of an 'upper millstone' dropped on his head, as punishment for getting 'too close to the wall'.

33. If Brueggemann is correct that the story of Abimelech functioned as something like a proverbial narrative for instructing soldiers in the danger of 'approaching the wall', then there is yet another shade of irony here, since the commander-in-chief would be guilty of ignoring this dictum (*First and Second Samuel*, p. 277).

34. Sternberg, *The Poetics of Biblical Narrative*, p. 221.

35. Alter, *The David Story*, p. 254.

5. *David's Interpretation of Joab's Messenger (2 Samuel 11.23-25)*

> The messenger said to David, 'Indeed, the men were mighty against us! They came out to us in the field, but we were upon them until the entrance of the gate. And the archers shot at your servants from the wall, and some of the king's servants are dead, and also your servant Uriah the Hittite is dead.' David said to the messenger, 'Thus say to Joab, "Do not let this affair be evil in your eyes, for like this and like that the sword consumes. Make your battle strong toward the city, and destroy it!" Thereby, encourage him.' (2 Sam. 11.23-25)

Being charged with the task of delivering bad news to a king who has an extensive history of killing such heralds is a daunting commission. Given the fact that David has ordered the deaths of messengers in 2 Samuel 1 and 4, it is perhaps not surprising that Joab's messenger delivers a different report to the king, conceivably in response to the primal urge of survival. After reading 11.23-24, a compelling case can be made for surmising that the messenger panics under pressure and modifies the transmission to avoid exactly what Joab has told him will happen—the anger of the king flaring up.[36] Accordingly, he adjusts the story to minimize the potential wrath, and 'offers a circumstantial account that justifies the mistake of approaching too close to the wall: the Ammonites came out after the Israelites in hot pursuit; then the Israelites, turning the tide of battle, were drawn after the fleeing Ammonites and so were tricked into coming right up to the gates of the city'.[37] The messenger, it should be underlined, is inadvertently mirroring his overseer by this action: he innovatively exegetes and changes the orders for tactical

---

36. The LXX does include 'David's speech as Joab expected him to make it' (Smith, *A Critical and Exegetical Commentary on the Books of Samuel*, p. 321). Cf. McCarter, *II Samuel*, pp. 282-83, and Anderson, *2 Samuel*, p. 155. For the purposes of the present study, the MT reading is retained, but see Chapter 9 of this book for further discussion. Bailey documents the 'problematic' aspects of text and transmission in 2 Sam. 11.19-24, and notes: 'the details of the battle descriptions in vv. 17, 20 and 23, do not completely coincide' (*David in Love and War*, p. 94). In passing, one could respond that v. 22—'The messenger left, and went and reported to David all for which Joab sent him'—reflects the perspective of the messenger himself: from his point of view, he is faithful is reporting the spirit of Joab's order, but not the letter.

37. Alter, *The David Story*, p. 255. The sub-heading of Sternberg's discussion of this passage is entitled, 'How the Messenger Fails to Carry Out Joab's Order'. The present chapter expands some of the intimations Sternberg proffers (*The Poetics of Biblical Narrative*, pp. 214-19). M.J. Steussy conjectures that the messenger clearly understands the 'cutting allusion' made by Joab: 'Possibly the messenger omits this part of his assigned report [2 Sam. 11.23-24] because he is afraid of David's reaction to the implied rebuke' (*David: Biblical Portraits of Power*, p. 78). In Steussy's view, the messenger fears that David's anger will be raised because of *the nature of the rebuke*, not the loss of soldiers. The messenger, in this case, has considerable ingenuity as a 'reader' of Joab's allegorical interpretation of the Abimelech narrative, the situation in Jerusalem, and the king's personality.

reasons. Thus it is surely ironic that the messenger operates as a reader-response critic of Joab's reply, just as Joab was a reader-response critic of David's letter.

In order to guarantee that David would be exposed to the parable of Abimelech, it may have been more prudent for Joab to send a letter instead of another reader-response critic.[38] The MT records no anger on David's part, and there is no reference to the moral lesson of Abimelech. Instead, in Fokkelman's words, 'David poses as Joab's mild and understanding superior'.[39] But even though David does not get a chance to hear the sarcastic rebuke, the image of Abimelech lingers in the reader's mind. It carries a strong thematic resonance, all the more when David commands the messenger to return to Joab, and say, 'Do not let this affair be evil in your eyes' (v. 25). As both Robert Polzin and David Jobling emphasize, there are numerous allusions in 1 and 2 Samuel to Judges, and David's final message to Joab in 2 Sam. 11.25 echoes the last sentence of Judges: 'In those days there was no king in Israel; every man did what was right in his own eyes'.[40] If having a king on the throne was intended to obviate the persistent threat of social chaos, then the situation whereby King David himself proffers this kind of counsel forebodes a return to the Abimelech era, or worse.[41] Joab's reading of the Abimelech account and its application to David's situation in 2 Samuel 11 becomes the instrument of a significant ideological reflection on the dangers of kingship. Joab's allegorical interpretation is especially acute when one considers that broader issues of kingship surround the Abimelech narrative; in 2 Samuel 11 there is a more legitimate king, but one who in this case is doing what is right in his own eyes. Polzin summarizes as follows:

> the narrator's statement about everyone doing what was right in their own eyes when there were no kings in Israel (Judg. 21.25) may invoke a contrast not between a kingless (or even judgeless) Israel, when every person did what was right in his or her own eyes, and a royal Israel, when people would begin to do what was right according to God's eyes, but rather between Israelites doing what was right in their own eyes and Israelites having to do what was right in their king's eyes. The second situation will turn out to be as bad as the first.[42]

---

38. Cf. Sternberg, *The Poetics of Biblical Narrative*, p. 215: 'Joab, with the whole war on his hands, has no time for epistolary composition. Yet the narrator also makes artistic capital out of the double shift in the form of communication, the word of mouth relayed by a fallible go-between.'

39. Fokkelman, *King David*, p. 63.

40. Polzin, *David and the Deuteronomist*, pp. 74-75. D. Jobling refers to the opening section of 1 Samuel as 'The Extended Book of Judges' (*1 Samuel*, pp. 43-77).

41. Polzin, *David and the Deuteronomist*, p. 75. Cf. P. Trible, *Texts of Terror: Literary-Feminist Readings of Biblical Narratives* (Philadelphia: Fortress Press, 1984), p. 84.

42. Interfacing with the literary critic M.M. Bakhtin, I would posit (reiterating what was said in Chapter 2) that Joab's utterance regarding Abimelech is an example of 'hidden polemical discourse' which is profoundly 'double-voiced'. For the reader, Joab's

6. Conclusion

The David and Bathsheba episode, along with its immediate aftermath, is a complex stretch of narrative which is enhanced by Joab's action and status as a 'reader' at several critical junctures. In conclusion, there are several insights that emerge when attending specifically to Joab's profile as a reader-response critic in the narrative. First, the present study suggests that Joab is presented as a creative reader of David's epistle commanding the death of Uriah. Observing the results of Joab's act of reading, it becomes apparent that his interpretive decisions are guided by a politically astute sensibility—an interpretive posture which evidently benefits the king. In so doing, Joab is consistent with his earlier actions in the execution of Abner, when he seemingly violates David's 'official' policy by exercising a hermeneutic of suspicion with regard to Abner's motives. Therefore, one can further the suggestion that Joab is presented as a character 'willing to act on his own judgment when a weak and injudicious king threatens the longevity of the kingdom'.[43] The Uriah affair is not dissimilar: David's impotence, politically speaking, contrasts with Joab's virility. Joab's interpretation of the king's letter betokens a calm and calculating demeanor, in contrast to David's lack of clear thinking and insipid orders. The reader-response criticism of the letter is more imaginative and effective than the text of the epistle itself.

The discourse of 2 Sam. 11.18-21 also provides a measure of insight into Joab's allegorical imagination. At the expense of the king, Joab provides the Abimelech 'play-within-a-play', and this stream of consciousness provides both a glimpse of his personality, and an ideological reflection on David's conduct. When Joab quotes 'scripture', not surprisingly it is from the rather grim epoch of the Judges, which in the end serves both to characterize Joab

utterance is understood as polemical (with respect to King David), and carries with it a larger authorial signal. 'Overt polemic is quite simply directed at another's discourse, which it refutes, as if at its own referential object. In the hidden polemic, however, discourse is directed toward an ordinary referential object, naming it, portraying, expressing, and only indirectly striking a blow at the other's discourse, clashing with it, as it were, within the object itself. As a result, the other person's discourse begins to influence authorial discourse from within. For this reason, hidden polemical discourse is double-voiced' (M.M. Bakhtin, *Problems of Dostoevsky's Poetics* [ed. and trans. C. Emerson; Minneapolis: University of Minnesota Press, 1984], p. 196). Cf. D.A. Bergen, 'Bakhtin Revisits Deuteronomy: Narrative Theory and the Dialogical Event of Deut. 31.2 and 34.7', *Journal of Hebrew Scriptures* 2, Article 4 (1999) <http://purl.org/jhs>. Utilizing the same critical methodology, a reading of portions of the Saul narrative is found in Green, *Mikhail Bakhtin and Biblical Scholarship*, pp. 67-134.

43. D.G. Schley, 'Joab', in *ABD*, III, pp. 852-54 (853). Cf. Schley's longer article, 'Joab and David: Ties of Blood and Power', in M.P. Graham, W.P. Brown, and J.K. Kuan (eds.), *History and Interpretation: Essays in Honour of John H. Hayes* (JSOTSup, 173; Sheffield: JSOT Press, 1993), pp. 90-105.

and operate as a thematic intertext. Hence Joab's allegorical reading of the Abimelech narrative is used by the author to provide indirect commentary on some larger problems of kingship raised in the long narrative of David's reign. Furthermore, in 2 Samuel 11 Joab is presented as a figure with the audacity to rebuke the king by means of a parabolic illustration. He may be the first, but not the only prominent leader in the narrative to do so: Nathan the prophet unleashes a parallel tactic in the next chapter, and Joab himself attempts it again in 2 Samuel 14. Moreover, Joab's direct modes of rebuke continue, as when he commands David to come to Rabbah (12.28, 'Lest I take the city, and it will be named after me'), and when David is inert after the execution of Absalom (19.5-7, 'You love those who hate you, and hate those who love you'). Joab is established as a significant voice of criticism toward the king, one who 'reads' his employer at vital points in the narrative and offsets potential crises.

Finally, an additional heuristic value of seeing Joab as a reader-response critic is that it becomes a lens for viewing the events of 2 Samuel 11, where Joab is shown to be a military commander with uncanny insight into the king's character. In the case of David's letter, it is Joab's reading *rather than David's writing* that produces the necessary cover-up of Uriah's death. When surveying the wider narrative as a whole (especially the deaths of Abner and Amasa, which arguably are indispensable for David retaining his control of the throne), Joab's actions are in some measure encapsulated in the events of 2 Samuel 11. After reading the epistle of David, he responds with a creative interpretation that undeniably differs from what is imprinted on the page. Even though David benefits from this exegetical maneuver, ironically it is this recurring pattern of interpretive creativity that ultimately leads to Joab's demise. In 1 Kgs 2.6, it is Joab's interpretive license surrounding the executions of Abner and Amasa that provide David with the necessary pretext for instructing Solomon to exercise his own hermeneutic of suspicion toward the aging general: 'Deal with him according to your wisdom, and do not let his gray head go down to Sheol in peace'. Joab's pattern of interpretive creativity thus proves to be a risky experiment. While the reader-response criticism and other strategic decisions undoubtedly work to David's advantage, in the end they ironically are used to hasten Joab's demise.

9

TWICE-TOLD TALES: ANGER MANAGEMENT AND THE MESSENGER(S) IN 2 SAMUEL 11.22-25

1. *Introduction*

Numerous commentators have drawn attention to the divergence between the MT and LXX of 2 Sam. 11.22-25, the passage where Joab's messenger delivers the news of Uriah's death to King David in Jerusalem. While the LXX presents 'David's speech as Joab expected him to make it', the MT contains a virtually opposite delivery of the message and unfolding of events in David's presence.[1] In fact, the two texts unfold such alternative readings that it is fair to say that a qualitatively different dramatic sequencing is at work in the MT and the LXX. In this chapter I will focus on some of the key differences between the MT and LXX in 2 Sam. 11.22-25, and highlight some of the literary implications that emerge when these textual trajectories are compared. My central purpose is to explore the differences in the characterizations of the messenger in the MT and LXX, since this figure is presented in quite a different light in these two accounts of the story. In the LXX, the messenger essentially follows Joab's instructions. After the wrath of David is ignited, he gives an explanation of events on the battlefield, and then shares the news about Uriah's death. In the MT, however, the messenger forestalls the king's wrath by providing an anecdotal report about the battle, one that includes the news about Uriah.

As a consequence of these dissimilar reports, the reactions of David are different in the Greek and Hebrew texts. In the MT, David hears about Uriah

---

1. Smith, *A Critical and Exegetical Commentary on the Books of Samuel*, p. 321. Cf. S. Pisano, *Additions or Omissions in the Books of Samuel: The Significant Pluses and Minuses in the Massoretic, LXX, and Qumran Texts* (OBO, 57; Freiburg: Universitätsverlag; Göttingen: Vandenhoeck & Ruprecht, 1984), p. 49: 'A large plus at 2 Sam. 11.22, which describes Joab's report to David that Uriah had been eliminated during a battle with the Ammonites, has led most commentators to correct the text in varying degrees according to the Greek text. Joab's prediction to the messenger in vv. 20f., that David will get angry at the news of the loss of some of his soldiers and will evoke the case of Abimelech's death at the wall, is fulfilled by the plus in LXX v. 22 although completely absent from MT.'

in the first instance, and his reaction is calm and collected. In the LXX, the messenger delays the news about Uriah (as per Joab's orders), and David launches into an angry reprimand that includes the Abimelech reference, as Joab predicts. To be sure, the parabolic rebuke of Abimelech cited by Joab (and reiterated by David in the LXX) serves to underscore the significance of this passage within the context of the larger Deuteronomistic History, and is the catalyst for an important reflection on kingship in this narrative as I discussed in the previous chapter. But my main focus is on the characterizations of the messenger in the Greek and Hebrew readings: I am arguing that there are distinctive literary strategies in operation in the MT and LXX, and that each captures a different psychological profile of David's reaction to the news of Uriah's death.

My general approach in this chapter is not dissimilar to that expressed by Eldon J. Epp in a recent SBL Presidential address, when he discussed some of the 'new approaches' of 'narrative textual criticism'. By narrative textual criticism, Epp explains, 'I understand to mean, simply and at a minimum, that textual variants have a story to tell—and that they allow new voices to be heard beyond the traditional call for "the original" text'.[2] 'This, for me', Epp said, 'has energized textual criticism. Establishing the earliest text-forms provides one dimension', but 'grasping the real-life contexts of variant readings adds' another dimension of 'richness by showing how Christians made meaning out of the *living* text as they nurtured and shaped it in worship and in life'.[3] Clearly Epp is referring to New Testament text criticism, but I think there is a measure of overlap with the Hebrew Bible. So, rather than pointing to mechanical processes or optical lapses that give rise to a deviation from a putative original, my purpose here is to focus instead on the comparative differences between a given text and its alternative. To that end, and to buttress my case for 2 Sam. 11.22-25, let me begin with two preliminary examples in the books of Samuel where alternative literary strategies within the Hebrew and Greek texts appear evident.

---

2. E.J. Epp, 'The Oxyrhynchus New Testament Papyri: "Not without Honor except in their Hometown"?', *JBL* 123 (2004), pp. 5-55 (9).

3. Epp, 'The Oxyrhynchus New Testament Papyri', p. 9. Cf. J.A. Sanders, 'The Task of Text Criticism', in H.T.C. Sun and K.L. Eades (eds.), with J.M. Robinson and G.I. Moller, *Problems in Biblical Theology: Essays in Honor of Rolf Knierim* (Grand Rapids: Eerdmans, 1997), pp. 315-27 (316): 'Text criticism, since the formulation of its task by Johann David Michaelis in the mid-eighteenth century, had been understood to be a part of exegesis of the text in the sense that one can better judge which reading to choose if one knows first what the fuller context is about. There can be no doubt that the observation is true. But the practice developed to the point, by the time of Julius Wellhausen's work on Samuel in the mid-nineteenth century, that text-criticism was not limited to choice among available "variants" but was obligated to include conjecture in the conviction that it was possible to reconstruct *Urtexte* of much of the biblical text.'

2. *Example A: Elkanah's Caution*

My first example comes from 1 Samuel 1, in the context of the type-scene of the barren wife who conceives a child of destiny. In his meticulous study of this chapter in a *JBL* article, Stanley Walters ruminates that the most puzzling sentence in the story of Samuel's birth is 1 Sam. 1.23, where Hannah and Elkanah are discussing when she will take the young Samuel to Shiloh, in keeping with her vow.[4] Elkanah's caution to Hannah is quite different in the MT and the Septuagint:

> MT: Her husband Elkanah said to her, 'Do what is good in your eyes, stay until you have weaned him, only may the LORD establish his word'.

> LXX: Her husband Elkana said to her, 'Do what is good in your eyes, stay until you have weaned him, but may the LORD establish that which comes out of your mouth'.

In the MT, there is a certain elusiveness to this line, as Elkanah does not specify what word of the LORD's 'he has in mind, and there is no divine promise in the story'.[5] The LXX aligns Elkanah's caution with Hannah's previous vow, and thus provides a 'referent for the "word" [that] must be fulfilled'.[6] Yet this hardly explains *how* the difference between these two texts came about, and possible reasons for the divergence has evoked considerable scholarly curiosity.[7] Walters surveys several reconstruction projects

---

4. S.D. Walters, 'Hannah and Anna: The Greek and Hebrew Texts of 1 Samuel 1', *JBL* 107 (1988), pp. 385-412 (385). See further J.E. Cook, *Hannah's Desire, God's Design: Early Interpretations of the Story of Hannah* (JSOTSup, 282; Sheffield: Sheffield Academic Press, 1999), p. 38.

5. Walters, 'Hannah and Anna', p. 385. Note the classic summary by S.R. Driver, *Notes on the Hebrew Text and the Topography of the Books of Samuel* (Oxford: Clarendon Press, 2nd edn, 1913), p. 20: 'LXX, Pesh. express the second person אֶת־דְּבָרֵךְ—in all probability, rightly. There has been no mention in the preceding verses of any word or promise on the part of God: and even in so far as it may be supposed to be involved in the *wish* expressed by Eli in *v.* 17, that has been fulfilled already in the birth of the child. "Establish thy word", i.e., give it effect, permit it to be carried out. הקים דבר is used especially of a person *carrying out* a command or injunction laid upon him, as 15, 13. Jer. 35, 16; or of Yahweh *giving effect to* His own, or His prophet's word, as I Ki. 12, 15. Is. 44, 26. Jer. 33, 14. LXX, rendering τὸ ἐξελθὸν ἐκ τοῦ στόματός σου, uses the more formal expression: see Nu. 30, 13 כל מוצא שפתיה. 32, 24 תעשו. והיוצא מפיכם. Dt. 23, 24; also Dt. 8, 3. Jer. 17, 16.'

6. Note the discussion of Campbell, *1 Samuel*, pp. 37-38. See also Eslinger, *Kingship of God in Crisis*, pp. 84-85; Alter, *The David Story*, p. 7; Hertzberg, *1 & 2 Samuel*, p. 28.

7. Walters, 'Hannah and Anna', p. 385. Note the translation of McCarter (*I Samuel*, p. 56): 'May Yahweh confirm what you have said', based on the following rationale: 'Reading *'k yqm yhwh hyws' mpyk*, lit. "May Yahweh indeed establish that which goes forth from your mouth!" with LXX (*alla stésai kyrios to exelthon ek tou stomatos sou*) and 4QSam^a, which preserves [*'k yqm yhw*]*h hywṣy' mpyk*. MT has *'k yqm yhwh 't dbrw*,

of nineteenth-century text criticism, but concludes that 'the distance between [the LXX] and the MT is so great that no theory of successive textual corruption could confidently be put forward...the Greek and Hebrew readings [are] too far apart to be linked by a single conjectural reconstruction'.[8] In keeping with the thesis of his article, Walters then reflects on the *substance* of the differences in 1 Sam. 1.23:

> The given Greek and Hebrew texts use discrete idioms, each belonging to a different universe of discourse. The MT's expression belongs to the world of the divine promise, while the Greek's belongs to the world of the human vow. This difference raises the possibility that these are separate stories, each informed and shaped by its own distinctive interests.[9]

From a literary perspective, I would sum up the differences as follows: in the LXX, Elkanah's words have a referent that is anchored within the immediate story world, whereas in the MT, Elkanah's words point to something outside or beyond the local context of articulation.

3. *Example B: The Gate of Hebron*

My second example comes from 2 Samuel 3, the context of Abner's assassination at the hands of Joab. During the prolonged conflict between David and the house of Saul, Abner has been strengthening his position, and has appropriated Saul's concubine, Rizpah. After defecting from the camp of Ishbosheth, Abner goes to Hebron to cut a deal with David. It is a remarkable coincidence that just as Abner leaves Hebron, Joab returns after a pillaging excursion. Joab is furious that David 'dismisses Abner', and he severely upbraids the newly crowned king of Judah. 'Then Joab marched out from David's presence. He sent messengers after Abner, and they brought him back from the Cistern of Sirah.' Consider now 2 Sam. 3.27:

> MT: So when Abner returned to Hebron, Joab took him aside into the middle of the gate to speak with him privately, and there he struck him in the belly [or, fifth rib] so that he died on account of the blood of Asahel his brother.

> LXX: And he brought back Abner to Hebron, and Joab caused him to turn aside from the gate to speak to him, laying wait [or setting an ambush] for him, and he struck him there in the loins, and he died for the blood of Asael the brother of Joab.

"May Yahweh establish his word!" but as yet there has been no word from Yahweh'. Cf. Ulrich, *The Qumran Text of Samuel and Josephus*, pp. 48-49, 78.

8. Walters, 'Hannah and Anna', p. 386. Cf. the complementary study of J.E. Cook, 'Hannah and/or Elkanah on their Way Home (1 Samuel 2.11)? A Witness to the Complexity of the Tradition History of the Samuel Texts', *OTE* 3 (1990), pp. 247-62.

9. Walters, 'Hannah and Anna', p. 387. For the importance of terms and phrases such as 'establish' and 'YHWH's word' in 1 Samuel, see Miscall, *1 Samuel: A Literary Reading*, p. 14; and Polzin, *Samuel and the Deuteronomist*, pp. 28-29.

The key issue within this little text-critical drama is the *spatial setting* for the *place* of execution. In the LXX, it would appear that Joab turns Abner aside *from* the city gate of Hebron where he has set an ambush for the *private* liquidation of his foe. In the MT, so it would seem, Joab escorts Abner into the very midst of the city gate for a *public* execution. In both cases, Joab's motive is explicit: to avenge the blood of his brother, whom Abner stabs in the 'fifth rib' during the aftermath of the battle of Gibeon. The city gate, as I mention in Chapter 4, is the customary venue for the dispensing of justice and for the conducting of legal tribunals, as Deut. 16.18, 21.19, and 25.7 illustrate. So, while it is possible to explain the discrepancy between the Greek and Hebrew readings in terms of scribal corruption, at least a case can be made for an alternative literary strategy at work: in the LXX, Abner is privately executed by Joab—and the killing is clouded with dubious legality.[10] In the MT, by contrast, Joab steers Abner into the midst of the city gate and in broad daylight—perhaps even before the elders of the city who have a role to play in the dispensing of justice—he avenges the blood of his brother.

In both of these examples, I would contend that a unique literary imagination could plausibly account for the divergent readings. This aligns nicely with James Sanders's reflections on the variants in 1 Samuel 1–2, as he concludes: 'Both tradents had quite different conceptions, probably culturally conditioned, of the story'.[11] With Elkanah it is the divine promise vs. the human vow, and in the 'Abner-gate' affair of 2 Samuel 3, it is the public execution vs. the private ambush by Joab—both of which testify to an alternative vision for telling the story, a vision shaped by a different set of literary sensibilities. In light of this discussion, I would like now to approach the two accounts of 2 Sam. 11.22-25.

4. *A Hebrew and a Hellenist: Tales of Two Messengers*

By way of background, in 2 Sam. 11.15 David sends Uriah to Joab as the courier of a malignant epistle.[12] 'Uriah carries the sealed but written, and

10. See Driver, *Notes on the Hebrew Text*, p. 250: 'The *middle* of the gate would scarcely be the place in which Joab could converse with Abner quietly. LXX ἐκ πλαγίων τῆς πύλης = אל יֶרֶךְ השער (see Lev. 1, 11. Nu. 3, 29. 35 Hebrew and LXX) "to the *side* of the gate", which is favoured also by the verb ויטהו "led *aside*".'

11. J.A. Sanders, 'Stability and Fluidity in Text and Canon', in G.J. Norton and S. Pisano (eds.), *Tradition of the Text: Studies Offered to Dominique Barthélemy in Celebration of his 70th Birthday* (OBO, 109; Freiburg: Universitätsverlag; Göttingen: Vandenhoeck & Ruprecht, 1991), pp. 203-17 (215). It also squares with the general tenor of Stoebe: 'each recension must be taken first of all for itself, and, insofar as possible, be understood through itself' (cited by Pisano, *Additions or Omissions*, p. 7, quoting H.J. Stoebe, *Das erste Buch Samuelis* [KAT, 8.1; Gütersloh: Gerd Mohn, 1973], p. 31).

12. Cf. Gunn, *The Story of King David*, p. 46 (citing H. Gunkel, *Das Märchen im Alten Testament*, and S. Thompson, *Motif-Index of Folk Literature* [6 vols.; Copenhagen:

hence potentially public, secret of David's crime.'[13] Effectively, Uriah is carrying his own death warrant, since David has written in his letter to Joab: 'Place Uriah in the front line of the fiercest battle and withdraw from him, so that he may be struck down and die'. To be sure, implementing such an order would be a difficult task, causing one to question the king's military intelligence at this point. In the event, Joab changes David's order: 'It came to pass, while Joab was watching the city, that he assigned Uriah to the place where he knew that valiant men were there. The men of the city came forth. They battled with Joab, and some of the army, some of David's servants, fell. Moreover, Uriah the Hittite died' (2 Sam. 11.16-17). At this point, Joab sends a memorandum to David in 2 Sam. 11.18-21:

> Then Joab sent and reported to David all the affairs of the battle. He commanded the messenger, saying, 'When you are finished speaking of all the affairs of the battle to the king, if it should be that the king's anger flares up, and he says to you: "Why did you draw near to the city to fight? Didn't you know that they would shoot from the wall? Who struck down Abimelech son of Jerubbesheth? Wasn't it a woman? She threw upon him an upper millstone from the wall and he died in Thebez! Why did you draw near to the wall?"—then you should say, "Also, your servant Uriah the Hittite is dead".'

In these instructions, it is conceivable that Joab is referring to common knowledge among Israelite soldiers that it is unwise to venture within striking distance of a city wall. As such, the Abimelech reference of Judges 9 is an apt intertext. But as Peter Ackroyd has already observed, there are several layers to this allusion:

> The story as related is grimly humorous, suggesting that in spite of Abimelech's attempt to cover up what had happened, it had become almost proverbial to refer to him with the sneering remark: 'A woman killed him'... It is also possible that the reference to Abimelech here is designed to point to a disastrous example of kingship and to imply how far David went astray from the ideal. This is another skilful cross-linkage in the whole narrative sequence.[14]

Along similar lines, a number of scholars have suggested that Joab provides in these instructions his own commentary on the events of the chapter —assuming he infers that David has had a *dangerous liaison* with Uriah's

---

Rosenkilde & Bagger, 1955–58]): 'The motif of a man carrying a written order for his own execution is widely attested in story the world over (Gunkel 1921: 132; Thompson 1955–58: K978). Its inherent qualities of irony and suspense make it the very stuff of story-telling.' Cf. C. Conroy, *1–2 Samuel, 1–2 Kings, with an Excursus on Davidic Dynasty and Holy City Zion* (Wilmington, DE: Michael Glazier, 1983), p. 116.

13. Bal, *Lethal Love*, p. 31.
14. P.R. Ackroyd, *The Second Book of Samuel* (New York: Cambridge University Press, 1977), p. 105.

wife, and so orders that the inconvenient husband be terminated. The fact that such a commentary is embedded within the instructions to the messenger appears straightforward enough: one expects the messenger to go and deliver the news to David exactly as Joab delineates. This is precisely what happens in the LXX. However, in the MT, the story is rather different, as can be seen when the two versions are compared:

> The messenger went, and came and reported to David all for which Joab sent him. The messenger said to David, 'Because the men were mighty against us! They marched out to us in the field, but we were upon them until the entrance of the gate. And the archers shot at your servants from the wall, and some of the king's servants are dead, and also your servant Uriah the Hittite is dead.' David said to the messenger, 'Thus say to Joab, "Don't let this thing be evil in your eyes, for the sword eats *like this and like that*. Make your battle strong toward the city, and destroy it!" Thereby, encourage him'.

The messenger is portrayed quite differently in the Greek reading:

> And the messenger of Joab went to the king to Jerusalem, and he came and reported to David all that Joab told him, all the affairs of the war. And David was very angry with Joab, and said to the messenger, 'Why did you draw near to the wall to fight? Did you not know that you would be wounded from off the wall? Who struck Abimelech the son of Jerobaal? Did not a woman cast upon him a piece of millstone from the wall, and he died in Thamasi? Why did you draw near to the wall?' And the messenger said to David, 'The men prevailed against us, and they came out against us into the field, and we came upon them even to the door of the gate. And the archers shot at your servants from off the wall, and some of the king's servants died, and your servant Uriah the Hittite is dead also'. And David said to the messenger, 'Thus shall you say to Joab, "Let not the matter be grievous in your eyes, for the sword devours one way at one time and another way at another: strengthen your array against the city, and destroy it, and strengthen him"'.

The messenger's report in the MT represents a startling diversion from what one would expect, given Joab's orders: it is immediately apparent that the messenger changes the story. In the broader context of 2 Samuel, this is perhaps understandable—after all, it is not easy being a 'tenure-track' messenger, surely one of the more perilous vocations in this stretch of the Deuteronomistic History. On the one hand, it is possible to argue that the messenger—fearing the wrath of the king—puts a positive spin on the tactical blunder of being too close to the wall. On the other hand, it has been argued that the messenger is cognizant of Joab's wry humor in alluding to the Abimelech episode, and connects Judges 9 with David's conduct in Jerusalem. The majority of commentators who are interested in the matter incline toward the scenario whereby Joab's envoy changes the memorandum in the interest of self-preservation: unaware that Uriah's death is actually good news for David, he blurts it out—replete with awkward syntax—without recognizing its true colors.

The manner in which the messenger commences his speech has been troubling for some scholars: ...כִּי־גָבְרוּ עָלֵינוּ הָאֲנָשִׁים ('Because the men were mighty against us...'). As Pisano remarks, 'Thenius noted that the כִּי in v. 23 with which the messenger begins his report indicates that something is missing from the text'.[15] If indeed the כִּי that begins the speech is unusual, it would be worth considering a recent proposal by Gary Rendsburg: 2 Sam. 11.23a could be another example of *deliberately confused language* designed to capture the sense of panic in the messenger.[16] In other words, there are plausible literary reasons for resisting emendation here. The messenger's speech as reported in the MT captures the dimension of nervousness in his voice when faced with the (presumably) daunting task of standing before the king and providing an account of the casualties of war. With respect to the MT as it stands, Uriel Simon stresses that there is a literary finesse and vitality of characterization in this passage, and the interaction between Joab and his messenger serves to highlight the ironic distance between Joab (on the front line) and the messenger face to face with the king in the lascivious luxury of the royal court.[17] In the MT, then, the messenger's haste to cover-up the error of going too close to the wall unwittingly underscores the fact that Joab himself has covered-up the error of the king.

When one further compares the MT with the Greek reading a number of points of contrast emerge. In the first instance, Uriah's death is disclosed at different moments. In the MT, the messenger does *not* follow Joab's orders. Instead of revealing Uriah's death *after* the outburst of anger—in accordance with Joab's instructions—the MT messenger pre-empts the course of action by mentioning Uriah's death as an appendix to his positive spin on the battle with the troops at Rabbah. In other words, Uriah's death is frontloaded in the Hebrew messenger's report, and David does not respond with any fury

---

15. Pisano, *Additions or Omissions*, p. 49.

16. G.A. Rendsburg, 'Confused Language as a Deliberate Literary Device in Biblical Hebrew Narrative', *Journal of Hebrew Scriptures* 2, Article 6 (1999), <http://purl.org/jhs>. Rendsburg cites a number of examples 'where confused language is invoked to portray confusion, excitement, or bewilderment' (1 Sam. 9.12-13; Ruth 2.7; Gen. 37.28, 30; Judg. 18.14-20; 1 Sam. 14.21; 17.38). A further possibility may be found in Gen. 25.22, the speech of Rebekah—אִם־כֵּן לָמָּה זֶּה אָנֹכִי ('If thus, why this I?')—which could be an attempt to capture her emotional and physical state in light of the sons 'crushing each other' in her womb (וַיִּתְרֹצֲצוּ הַבָּנִים בְּקִרְבָּהּ).

17. Simon, *Reading Prophetic Narratives*, pp. 110-11: 'The messenger's failure to report separately on Uriah's death retrospectively illuminates Joab's intention in doing so. Whereas the envoy, standing in person before the king, fears the monarch's ire and does everything to prevent its eruption. Joab's position vis-à-vis David is more complex, both because he can allow himself much more latitude than the envoy can, and also because of the resentment he has accumulated against his king, who on more than one occasion had expressed his revulsion at the ruthless acts of the devoted general.'

whatsoever. In the LXX, the messenger *does* follow Joab's orders. Just as Joab predicts—albeit with some slight variation—David's temper is ignited. It is only at the conclusion of David's tirade about 'getting too close to the wall' that the Greek messenger shares the detail about Uriah's death—and here it seems to be as part of the general excuse that he offers. As with the MT, in the LXX the messenger does present what I would argue is a fabricated and apologetic explanation (replete with first-person references)—but in the Greek reading the elucidation of the battle is part of the overall justification of the advance toward the city that comes after the king's angry riposte. In the LXX, the stress is on the messenger's fidelity to his orders, whereas the MT is more interested in the envoy's ingenuity and plan for avoiding the royal wrath.

Leo Perdue's analysis of 2 Samuel 11 captures the more amusing dimension of the MT: 'Fearing David's reaction, Joab carefully coaches his messenger in a bit of rhetorical psychology designed to avert the king's anticipated wrath. But, in comic fashion, the messenger, perhaps frightened, bungles his mission, awkwardly blurting out the entirety of his message.'[18] Perdue goes on to call this a 'poor performance'—an evaluation with which other readers might take issue, if they prefer to see a rather resourceful messenger desperately interested in avoiding a trip to Sheol. But I thoroughly agree that the messenger's activity deviates from Joab's directive, and is therefore 'humorous' in the Shakespearean sense. The Greek text, by contrast, does not seem overly interested in humor at this particular dispensation. The LXX messenger is a straight-laced employee who discharges his duty and is willing to endure the royal aggravation.

On balance, the Hebrew messenger is an intriguing minor figure. This is the case regardless of whether one interprets him as 'bungling' his assignment (pace Perdue), or whether one adjudges him to be 'clever enough' to avert the anger, as Dominique Barthélemy argues at length.[19] Either way, by frontloading his own spin on the battle and including the detail of Uriah's death he mitigates the prospect of a Davidic detonation. In the LXX, the messenger is more transparent—more of a predictable character that is perhaps in keeping with his commission. He also offers the expansive report, but in

---

18. L.G. Perdue, '"Is there Anyone Left of the House of Saul...?" Ambiguity and the Characterization of David in the Succession Narrative', *JSOT* 30 (1984), pp. 67-84 (76).

19. D. Barthélemy (ed.), *Critique textuelle de l'Ancien Testament*. I. *Josué, Juges, Ruth, Samuel, Rois, Chroniques, Esdras, Néhémie, Esther* (OBO, 50/1; Freiburg: Universitätsverlag; Göttingen: Vandenhoeck & Ruprecht, 1982): 'Le narrateur, tel que le *M nous fait connaître son œuvre, met en scène un messager intelligent qui, averti par Joab, présénte son récit de manière à éviter que le roi se mette en colère' ('The narrator, such as *M makes known to us his work, puts in the scene an intelligent messenger who, warned by Joab, presents his report so as to prevent the king putting himself in anger').

a defensive posture presumably adopted because of the king's unfurled fury.[20]

It should be noted that the two ways in which the messenger is portrayed serves to elicit a particular kind of response from King David. In other words, the implication of my analysis is that the manner in which the messenger is portrayed reflects the different literary interests at work: both the Greek and Hebrew texts seem to be concerned with capturing a certain profile of David's reception of the news about Uriah. There are distinct configurations of King David apparent in the MT and LXX readings—David has two quite different reactions, and each is predicated on what the messenger says.

In the LXX, David is the highly involved 'commander-in-chief' full of anger *against Joab*—ready to dispense the logistical cliché of Abimelech. Indeed, there is a certain 'realism' in the LXX: first the wrath, then the exhortation after hearing about the fatalities. Hence, the lesson of Judges 9 and the peril of getting too close to the wall is aptly invoked with respect to the siege at Rabbah. At the same time, the question remains: In the LXX, why specifically is David angry at Joab? Is he angry because of the needless 'loss of life' brought about by the tactical blunder? Or is it because Uriah—for all he knows—is still alive? Has his covert operation—set in motion by the deadly letter—failed? Is he, David, going to be found out? It is hard to deny that there is a particular drama in the LXX account of the story: a build-up of tension that is only dispelled when the faithful (and un-equivocating) Greek messenger eventually uploads the datum about the lately deceased Uriah the Hittite. It seems to me that this tension is what the Greek text is interested in producing: the wrath of David *because Uriah may not be dead*, and the diffusion of his rage when the messenger, on Joab's cue (albeit circuitously), imparts the information about Uriah's death.

H.W. Hertzberg, who prefers a hybrid text along the lines of the LXX, has an attractive proposal: 'David, perhaps disappointed at hearing nothing of Uriah, reacts with an angry outburst which would do honor to the king's consciousness of his responsibility if it did not occur in this particular context... The immediate change in David's attitude is masterfully expressed.'[21] To me, this seems close to the kind of literary logic that propels the plot of the Greek reading at this point in the Deuteronomistic History—the biting irony that David's reaction of anger at the gratuitous loss of soldiers 'would

---

20. From the messenger's perspective, surely Joab's instructions are somewhat counter-intuitive: Joab commands the messenger to give his report to the king, who in all probability will go ballistic and invoke the Abimelech analogy. *If* the king's anger flares up, Joab continues, *then* you are also to say: 'moreover, even Uriah (one of your top thirty soldiers according to 2 Sam. 23.39) is dead'. How is this detail about Uriah's death supposed to assuage the king's rage? Would the king not be *more* upset? Other things being equal, it is not at all surprising that the (MT) messenger changes the story.

21. Hertzberg, *1 & 2 Samuel*, pp. 311-12.

do honor to the king's consciousness of his [regal] responsibility' *were it not for the extenuating circumstances that surround these sordid affairs.*[22]

The Davidic reaction to the messenger in the MT, for all intents and purposes, is antithetical: because the messenger frontloads the news bulletin of Uriah's death, in the Hebrew text the reader is presented with a rather different royal colloquist. Notwithstanding the Hebrew messenger's report about the setback at the gates of Rabbah, the ill-advised venture into the range of the archer's projectiles, and the incidental fate of Uriah the Hittite—David is studiously cool, and outwardly appears very concerned about Joab. As one hears his response in the MT, the king's rejoinder to the messenger sounds radically different in the absence of any antecedent wrath: David simply gives the envoy an oral (as opposed to epistolary) memorandum to cite verbatim, 'Thus say to Joab, "Don't let this thing be evil in your eyes, for the sword eats *like this and like that*"'. These words strike Joel Rosenberg as 'the grossest kind of cynicism, in which appeal is made to the order of things, to a transcendent causality, to the natural way of indiscriminate destruction in wartime, as a cloak for [a] death [that] we know all too well was premeditated, and which wrought, in consequence of its complicated logistics, the death of numerous Israelite soldiers with no relation to the private intrigue at all'.[23] In the MT, the messenger's report and the king's outwardly imperturbable reaction draws attention to 'the incongruity between David's righteous sounding words and his secret intentions'.[24]

---

22. To appropriate the earlier studies of 'messenger stories' in the Succession Narrative by Gunn (*The Story of King David*) and G.P. Ridout ('Prose Compositional Techniques in the Succession Narrative [2 Sam. 7, 9-10; 1 Kings 1–2]' [PhD dissertation, Graduate Theological Union; Ann Arbor: University Microfilms, 1971]), one might say that the LXX generates 'a tale of suspense which at the same time, by creating a "build-up" to David's reaction of the news of the battle, serves to heighten the emotional impact of his response as well as the irony in the ambivalence of his attitude to the victory. The suspense lies not just in our being given "ample time to ponder how David is likely to receive the report" (Ridout 1971.97) but also how this is likely to affect the messenger—will he receive reward or might he, like the messengers of 2 Sam. 1 and 4 be the object of violent displeasure[?]... As it turns out the [Greek messenger] is more than equal to the task and manages to convey the news of victory [after the king's angry tirade], while the narrator then dissipates the messenger-orientated tension [through the immediate deflation] of David's emotional outburst, which then redirects the focus of the narrative' (Gunn, *The Story of King David*, p. 45).

23. Rosenberg, *King and Kin*, p. 173. As Sternberg (*The Poetics of Biblical Narrative*, pp. 220-21) comments: 'The story of Abimelech, formally invoked as a parallel to the story of the war at Rabbah, also turns out an ironic parallel to the story of the king in his city. Both kings, David and Abimelech, fall because of a woman. (So, in still another sense, does Uriah.) What is more, the notorious incident of Abimelech's death bears—for both Joab and the reader—connotations of a disgrace brought on royalty at a woman's hand.'

24. Sternberg, *The Poetics of Biblical Narrative*, p. 217.

Finally, because the Hebrew and Greek messengers are portrayed differently, they capture unique profiles of the royal psychology: the LXX highlights the startling reversal of emotion—the flare of temper and its immediate subsiding once he finally hears the news about Uriah. The MT presents another kind of Davidic response as it foregrounds 'the extent to which the king's character has deteriorated under the stress of his private emergency'.[25] Since it is my contention that there are alternative literary strategies at work in the Hebrew and Greek readings, it might be wise to return to the words of Eldon Epp, and submit that 'narrative textual criticism' can make a useful contribution to the wider debate about the rich variants in these *living* texts of 2 Samuel 11.[26]

---

25. Sternberg, *The Poetics of Biblical Narrative*, p. 217. In terms of the efficacy of the Abimelech allusion in the MT and LXX, I would argue that there is a useful comparison between 1 Sam. 1 and 2 Sam. 11. As discussed above, in the LXX of 1 Sam. 1.23, Elkanah's words have a referent that is anchored within the immediate story world, whereas in the MT, Elkanah's words point to something outside or beyond the local context of the utterance. So it is that the Abimelech reference accomplishes different things in the Greek and Hebrew texts. For the Greek text, there is an interest in having David cite the Abimelech analogy because, like the words of Elkanah in the LXX, it is anchored in the immediate context. For the MT, like the words of Elkanah in the Hebrew text, the allusion to Abimelech points to something that lies outside the immediate frame of reference. In the Greek reading, Abimelech's death is a tactical principle that becomes a moral lesson—one that is hard to miss by virtue of its twin citation by both Joab and David. In the Hebrew reading, however, the analogy is more elusive, and it is incumbent upon the reader to make the connection between Judg. 9 and the present situation. Consequently, the analogy of Abimelech works differently: in the LXX, David alludes to Abimelech as well as Joab, but in the MT, only Joab draws the connection with Abimelech and thus it has different parabolic contours. For a longer discussion of the analogy, and *who* is referred to in the 'allegory', see Bal, *Lethal Love*, pp. 10-35.

26. See further Sanders, 'The Task of Text Criticism', pp. 326-27: 'Text criticism has as its principal task locating and identifying for the translator and the student of the Bible those true variants, large or small, that survive the rigorous tests of current text-critical practice. This would eliminate eclectic texts that claim to press back toward some undefined original, but which are nothing but the product of imagination of a particular generation of scholarship. A pluriform Bible would honor the integrity of those ancient believing communities which had a different book of Samuel, or Joshua or Judges, or Exodus 35–40, or Proverbs, or Ezekiel, or whatever text, small or large, which text criticism is finally constrained to designate as a "true variant".'

10

MOTIVES FOR DEFECTION:
AHITHOPHEL'S AGENDA IN 2 SAMUEL 15–17

1. *Introduction*

The impetus for this chapter on Ahithophel's characterization in 2 Samuel 15–17 originates with an unassuming footnote in Gerhard von Rad's magisterial essay, 'Historical Writing in Ancient Israel'. While discussing the enigmatic defection of Ahithophel, David's advisor, and how this represents a serious setback for David during the rebellion of Absalom, von Rad inserts this footnote: 'Ahithophel was, of course, Bathsheba's grandfather', linking the reference in 2 Sam. 11.3 with 23.34.[1] It could be that this connection between Bathsheba's genealogical notice and the mention of Eliam as both a member of David's elite guard *and* Ahithophel's son is subtly intended to provide something of a clue for discovering Ahithophel's otherwise inexplicable motives to support the rebellion of Absalom. Ahithophel, according to 2 Sam. 15.12 and 16.23, is a key counselor of King David. Why does he seemingly abandon David and side with Absalom and his presumptuous claims to the throne of Israel?

Although this chapter is a synchronic study of the narrative in its final form, it is quite possible that historians or source critics may take issue with the notion of Ahithophel as Bathsheba's grandfather, since such a relationship is not clearly spelled out in the text. Nevertheless, from a literary perspective such an ambiguity is characteristic of the entire David story. As James Ackerman points out, 'As opposed to Homer, who tells us everything, the art of biblical narrative challenges us with what we are not told but must attempt to discern'.[2] Such ambiguities, therefore, can be understood as an intentional literary strategy. Ackerman further asks, 'Why doesn't the narrator give us more help? Suddenly we discover that we as readers are seeing the world through David's eyes as we attempt to discern good and evil,

---

1. G. von Rad, *The Problem of the Hexateuch and Other Essays* (trans. E.W. Trueman Dicken; Edinburgh: Oliver & Boyd, 1966), p. 184.
2. Ackerman, 'Knowing Good and Evil', p. 41, drawing on Auerbach, *Mimesis*.

loyalty and treachery, among his subordinates.'[3] Von Rad's observation, consequently, provides an intriguing starting point for exploring the possible reasons behind Ahithophel's defection.[4]

2. *Conspiracy Theory*

In my analysis of Ahithophel and his motives for supporting Absalom, the relevance of von Rad's footnote will emerge in due course, but first let us proceed to 2 Sam. 15.12, where Ahithophel's formal introduction occurs. After 'stealing the hearts' of the men of Israel, Absalom dispatches secret agents throughout the land to announce that he is 'king in Hebron' when they hear the sound of the trumpets. Then:

> While Absalom was offering the sacrifices, he sent for Ahithophel the Gilonite, David's counselor, from his city Giloh. The conspiracy grew in strength, and the people with Absalom kept increasing. (2 Sam. 15.12 NRSV)

The narrator here provides the formal introduction to the character of Ahithophel, and supplies some critical background information. That Ahithophel is given the epithet 'counselor of David' has a definite proleptic utility, but a slight irony as well, since his role in the narrative will be the senior advisor for Absalom's rebellion. The mention of 'David' also indicates that this insurrection is not only limited to his son, but now includes a major policy-maker in his administration. As well, in this introduction of

---

3. Ackerman, 'Knowing Good and Evil', p. 43.
4. Other exegetes have also reflected on this connection. Anderson, *2 Samuel*, p. 153, notes the reference in *Sanhedrin* 69b, 101a, and more recent scholars such as Hertzberg and Mauchline are also among those who allow for the connection. H. Gressmann, 'The Oldest History Writing in Israel', in D.M. Gunn (ed.), *Narrative and Novella in Samuel* (trans. D.E. Orton; JSOTSup, 116; Sheffield: Almond Press, 1991), pp. 9-58 (39), earlier remarks: 'As Bathsheba's grandfather he [Ahithophel] was an enemy of David'. From a literary angle, a narrative connection such as this can profitably be explored, but it is useful to note that 'older' critical methods also consider the links between David, Bathsheba, and Ahithophel. Cf. D. Daube, 'Absalom and the Ideal King', *VT* 48 (1998), pp. 315-25 (320): 'Ahithophel is the only member of David's inner circle to defect. A blow all the more terrible as his judgment ranks highest by far: "as if a man had inquired at the oracle of God, so was the counsel of Ahithophel both with David and with Absalom" (2 Sam. xvi 23). When he now advocates the atrocious handling of the concubines, there must be special, weighty motivation. It can be traced: he is paternal grandfather of Bathsheba (2 Sam. xi 3, xxiii 34), once treated by the king with the same ruthlessness'. Daube also implies Bathsheba's complicity in David's plot against Uriah: 'From the moment Bathsheba sends David the warning about her pregnancy to after her husband's end not a syllable is devoted to her. Yet, manifestly, the scheme by which Uriah would look the father could not be embarked on without her being fully informed and, indeed, fully co-operating—on whatever grounds' (p. 321). Cf. Bailey, *David in Love and War*, p. 88, who suggests a 'co-partnership' between David and Bathsheba with political ends.

Ahithophel the narrator twice provides a reference to his ancestry: that he is a 'Gilonite' (הגילני), and his hometown of 'Giloh' (גלה). This emphasis is not superfluous, for these references play a role in his overall characterization. The narrator makes it clear that the presence of Ahithophel is a major component of Absalom's stratagem. Immediately after the summoning of Ahithophel, the reader is informed that the conspiracy 'grew in strength'. Ahithophel's introduction, then, presents him as a main player in this drama.

When assessing Ahithophel's characterization, the immediate question is why this royal counselor abandons David in a moment of desperate crisis and sides with Absalom. It is at this point that von Rad's footnote is useful, and through these cross-references (2 Sam. 11.3 and 23.34) one can suggest that the narrator provides an invitation to speculate about Ahithophel's motives for defection. In 2 Samuel 11, David remains in Jerusalem while his troops are battling the Ammonites, and from the roof of his palace espies a woman bathing. Inquiring as to her identity yields an interesting response: 'Is this not Bathsheba, daughter of Eliam (אליעם), wife of Uriah the Hittite?' The value of this reference to 'Eliam' is realized in 23.34, the list of David's men of valor. In v. 34b, the list includes 'Eliam (אליעם), son of Ahithophel the Gilonite'. From a literary standpoint, this connection is worth exploring, as it forms a plausible nexus among these characters. For this chapter, the assumption is that these verses combine to provide the audience with a signal to form a link between these events and the characters in the narrative. If such a correlation is made, the motive for Ahithophel's defection becomes more clear: David's affair with his granddaughter and subsequent treatment of Uriah gives him a reason to harbor enmity.

After his formal introduction in 15.12, Ahithophel is mentioned again in 15.31, as David is told that Ahithophel is numbered among the conspirators. At this, David prays 'Turn into foolishness the counsel of Ahithophel, O LORD'. The prayer is seemingly answered when David then encounters Hushai the Archite, whom he implores to return to Jerusalem with the express purpose of 'making ineffectual' the advice of Ahithophel, and generating a subterfuge of their own (v. 34). Kyle McCarter states, 'Hushai is quite literally the answer to a prayer, for it is he who will defeat the counsel of Ahithophel'.[5] Baruch Halpern builds on this observation:

> As David retreats across the Qidron Valley and up the Mount of Olives, bareheaded and barefooted, he calls on Yahweh to confound the counsel of Absalom's advisor, Ahithophel of Giloh. Just as he reaches the crest of the Mount of Olives, 'where one prostrates oneself to God(s)', Hushai crosses his path. David now recognizes the providential hand behind the human appearances, especially as the signal comes at a shrine'.[6]

5. McCarter, *II Samuel*, p. 377.
6. Halpern, *David's Secret Demons*, p. 44.

David is aware of how vital the counsel of Ahithophel is, and thus he prays, and formulates a ruse to counter this 'transfer of allegiance' of one adviser with the feigned transfer of another one.[7] Ahithophel now has an adversary: Hushai, a friend of David who has remained loyal to the king. As Alter notes,

> This crucial moment in the story is an especially deft manifestation of the system of double causation that Gerhard von Rad and others after him have attributed to the David narrative: everything in the story is determined by its human actors, according to the stringent dictates of political realism; yet simultaneously, everything is determined by God, according to a divine plan in history. David, informed that his own shrewd political advisor Ahitophel is part of Absalom's conspiracy, urgently and breathlessly invokes God, 'Thwart, pray, the counsel of Ahitophel, O LORD'. Then he reaches a holy site, an altar on the crest of the Mount of Olives ('where one would bow down to God'), and here he sees Hushai, his loyalty betokened by the trappings of mourning he has assumed, coming toward him. Theologically, Hushai is the immediate answer to David's prayer. Politically, David seizes upon Hushai as the perfect instrument to thwart Ahitophel's counsel, so from a certain point of view David is really answering his own prayer through his human initiative. Yet the encounter with Hushai at a place of worship leaves the lingering intimation that Hushai has been sent by God to David.[8]

3. *Extreme Measures*

The scene is now set for the central episode in Ahithophel's characterization, with Absalom entering Jerusalem and requesting his counsel in 2 Sam. 16.20. But immediately before this, Hushai the Archite, who is recorded in 15.37 as arriving in the city at the same time as Absalom, approaches him in 16.15 pledging his support. After hearing Hushai's reply to his rather sarcastic query, Absalom turns to Ahithophel in 16.20, saying, 'Give your counsel, what should we do?' Thus Ahithophel is now asked to display his renowned sagacity, and for the first time in the narrative he is given the opportunity for direct speech:

> Ahithophel said to Absalom, 'Go in to your father's concubines, the ones he has left to look after the house; and all Israel will hear that you have made yourself odious to your father, and the hands of all who are with you will be strengthened'. (2 Sam. 16.21 NRSV)

---

7. Fokkelman, *King David*, p. 194.
8. Alter, *The David Story*, p. 289. Cf. the remarks of Halpern and Levenson, 'The Political Import of David's Marriages', p. 514: 'What is remarkable…is the allusionary stratigraphy of the text. It is plain to see, for example, that David's voyeurism in 2 Sam. 11.2 and Nathan's curse in 12.11 foreshadow Absalom's rooftop orgy (16.20-22). The narrator is sufficiently subtle (or guileless) to have Bathsheba's grandfather (2 Sam. 11.3; 23.34—the Eliam here is again the only one in the Hebrew Bible) instigate the exaction of YHWH's pound of flesh (16.20-21).'

The first word of Ahithophel's discourse is an imperative, and the absence of any kind of elevated or deferential language indicates that he is used to providing counsel and expecting that it will be heeded. Ahithophel's advice involves Absalom's expropriating his father's concubines, 'an irreversible act of the utmost provocation comparable even to rape'.[9] In 15.16 the narrator describes how David left 'ten concubines to watch the palace'; Ahithophel is clearly aware of this, and acts on it. Consider Hertzberg's remark: 'the fact he [Ahithophel] does not set out from Jerusalem with Absalom but is summoned from his home at Giloh suggests that this "counselor" of the king no longer functioned as such'.[10] This is an interesting proposal, although Ahithophel's introductory epithet 'the counselor of David' seems to indicate that he still occupies this office at the time of the rebellion. At any rate, Ahithophel is pictured as having his finger on the pulse of events within the city, and his precise knowledge about the concubines remaining in the palace illustrates that he is in touch with all that is happening.

The result of this contemptuous act of sleeping with the concubines, Ahithophel assures Absalom, will be that 'when all Israel hears that you have made yourself odious to your father, the hands of all who are with you will be strengthened'. Such ruthless counsel reveals a number of things about Ahithophel. He seems to know David's malleability when it comes to dealing with Absalom. It is not inconceivable, then, that this rebellion could end in reconciliation, with David forgiving Absalom, but dealing severely with his confederate allies. Therefore Ahithophel's counsel is of a 'bridge-burning' nature: it transcends mere embarrassment for David and will cause an unbreachable gap between David and Absalom.[11] As McCarter discusses, to appropriate a royal wife, concubine, or harem was tantamount to making a claim for the throne, as other instances in 2 Samuel 3 (Abner) and 1 Kings 1 (Adonijah) imply.[12] With no chance of reconciliation for Absalom, the rebellion is entrenched.[13]

In addition, this advice portrays Ahithophel as the consummate political strategist, with acute perception of how Absalom is to secure the kingdom. He is clearly aware of how crucial it is to influence public opinion, and this ability to read the 'national mood' indicates that he has considerable aptitude

---

9. Fokkelman, *King David*, p. 209.
10. Hertzberg, *1 & 2 Samuel*, p. 338.
11. Hertzberg, *1 & 2 Samuel*, p. 350.
12. McCarter, *II Samuel*, p. 384.
13. See Halpern, *David's Secret Demons*, p. 46: 'At this juncture, Ahitophel instructs Absalom to sleep with his father's concubines so as to demonstrate *his* commitment to the uprising' (emphasis added). The above analysis assumes that Ahithophel's purpose is to strengthen the resolve of the rebels, whereas Halpern makes the interesting suggestion that Ahithophel may in fact be doubting Absalom's resolve.

in his role as a counselor. At the same time, he is not the least bit cautious of severing the bond between father and son, and it is at this point where a reader might begin to sense something 'personal' emerging in his directive to Absalom. Robert Bergen comments:

> For Ahithophel personally, the scheme must have seemed like a particularly satisfying application of the Torah's *lex talionis*...David had had unlawful sexual relations with Ahithophel's granddaughter at the royal palace in Jerusalem, though she was married to another; so now, unlawful sexual relations with David's harem would take place at the same palace—only in this case the retributive act would be ten times greater than the original offense, and in public![14]

This motive becomes clearer if his imperative is compared with the ingratiating words of Hushai immediately preceding. Consequently, the conflict between the two 'counselors' emerges here as a prelude to the forthcoming confrontation. Their opening speeches to Absalom are qualitatively different, and underscore the different motives. J.P. Fokkelman observes,

> One...is a screening, the other is advice, and yet they have one important point in common: Hushai and Ahithophel both speak of the Absalom–David relationship, although their views are mutually exclusive. Hushai doubly states that the David/Absalom change of throne is a natural and smooth transition. Against this false suggestion of continuity there is Ahithophel's hard and matter-of-fact approach, and his single spoken advice for a complete break is based on reality...one speaker making use of the pleasure principle by playing on Absalom's vanity and pride, while the other represents the reality principle. Ahithophel is unequivocal and sees duality, Hushai ignores this and is equivocal.[15]

Hushai, as revealed in 2 Sam. 15.32-37, is commissioned by David to 'frustrate' the counsel of Ahithophel, and his first words reflect the tone which he will also take in his next (and far more pivotal) speech to Absalom. Hence, Hushai's speech is to be heard in the context of his loyalty to David and his subterfuge here. In contrast, the discourse of Ahithophel has a much more vindictive accent, and in his first portion of counsel it is evident that he is pushing for David's complete and irrevocable displacement. While the motive for Hushai's rhetoric lies in his fidelity to David, Ahithophel's motive, as suggested earlier, seems to lie in a more personal vendetta against the king. As H.W. Hertzberg remarks, the reader 'may not exclude the possibility that Ahithophel, the grandfather of Bathsheba, enjoys a belated revenge for what David has done to his family in the same context'.[16] It seems reasonable to argue, therefore, that the source of Ahithophel's resentment

---

14. Bergen, *1, 2 Samuel*, p. 411.
15. Fokkelman, *King David*, p. 211.
16. Hertzberg, *1 & 2 Samuel*, p. 350.

toward David stems from the king's actions in 2 Samuel 11, and that Absalom's rebellion provides opportunity for retribution. As is apparent in 16.22, allusions to the Bathsheba affair ironically continue to surface, subtly enhancing the connection between those events and Ahithophel's defection.

At the conclusion of Ahithophel's opening discourse, no other counsel is sought, and no one else speaks out. This demonstrates that he has a singular authority, and indeed his characterization to this point configures him as a man of influence and command. Immediately following his advice, in 16.22 the narrator reports: 'and they pitched the tent upon the roof (על־הגג)'. More than just verifying that Ahithophel's counsel is heeded, this action activates an intertextual allusion with ch. 11, where David walks upon the same roof and observes Bathsheba, the daughter of Eliam, bathing. 'The roof from which David had seen Bathsheba and where desire overpowered him is the same roof [על־גג בית־המלך] where now a tent is set up for Absalom, so that he can insult his father "in the sight of all Israel"—words from the prophecy.'[17] Absalom's action reverberates to the prophecy of Nathan in 12.11-12, and makes an association between this episode and that of ch. 11. The connection between these two episodes is important: because my assumption is that the events of 2 Samuel 11 precipitate Ahithophel's alienation, now the prophetic indictment is gradually being realized in the narrative.

It is at this point in 2 Sam. 16.23, after Absalom lies with David's concubines, that the narrator inserts a crucial piece of information, fraught with implication for the characterization of Ahithophel. In biblical narrative, generally speaking, a simile or metaphor is not often given through narration. Thus, when a figure of speech such as this does occur, it provides a unique insight into a character:

> Now in those days the counsel that Ahithophel gave was as if one consulted the oracle of God; so all the counsel of Ahithophel was esteemed, both by David and by Absalom. (2 Sam. 16.23 NRSV)

While one may have expected a detail such as this to have been provided in 2 Sam. 15.12, its disclosure at this moment has a considerable effect. Ahithophel's ability and renown as a counselor is confirmed by the narrator *directly* following the description of his advice to Absalom being carried out. This narrational delay, then, has the function of vividly emphasizing that his counsel has an 'oracular' nature to it, and adds a depth to his characterization as one who has an uncanny adroitness in dispensing instruction. In light of this dramatic statement of 16.23, the subsequent expectation is that in the future his sage advice will certainly be observed, and his counsel will

---

17. Fokkelman, *King David*, p. 210. Cf. R.N. Whybray *The Succession Narrative: A Study of II Samuel 9–20 and I Kings 1–2* (London: SCM Press, 1968), p. 24; Brueggemann, *First and Second Samuel*, p. 310.

be implemented with the same efficiency with which the tent is erected on the roof for Absalom. This insertion also communicates that Ahithophel himself must be accustomed to having his advice heeded, and thus it appears to be proleptic at every level. The audience is made to anticipate that Ahithophel's counsel will be followed. If Ahithophel himself has been used to having his counsel heeded, then conversely it also seems that he would not be accustomed to having his opinion rejected or his perspicuity challenged. Furthermore, through this line the narrator establishes a connection between David and Absalom, indicating 'how infallible Ahithophel's counsel is held to be at court', and that his weighty reputation is such that both the king and his rebellious son regard his words as endued with prescience.[18] The only other person in the narrative to 'breach the gap' between David and Absalom, is, in a pointed irony, Hushai the Archite, the antipode of Ahithophel.[19] Thus the setting is now in place for the escalation of this multi-layered conflict.

> Moreover Ahithophel said to Absalom, 'Let me choose twelve thousand men, and I will set out and pursue David tonight. I will come upon him while he is weary and discouraged, and throw him into a panic; and all the people who are with him will flee. I will strike down only the king... (2 Sam. 17.1-2 NRSV)

After the narrator's insertion concerning the oracular nature of his advice, Ahithophel unveils his next proposal to Absalom. This comment creates an expectation that Ahithophel's new counsel will be expeditiously implemented just like his counsel regarding the concubines. With the situation in Jerusalem now under control, he advises Absalom to advance without delay and eliminate David. Ahithophel's language, though, is framed in the first person, commencing with a verb that can be translated 'I will choose' (אבחרה נא). This verbal construction can be understood as a *cohortative of resolve*, which expresses the speaker's intended course of action.[20] A similar example is provided in Gen. 18.21, 'I *will go down* and see'. Note the translation choices of John Mauchline, '[If I were you] I would choose',[21] and McCarter, 'Let me choose'.[22] These translations bring out the idea of 'request', as though Ahithophel is seeking permission. The sense that is understood in my interpretation here is a *resolution*, rather than a recommendation or a request for authorization. One recalls that in 16.20 he is *asked* for advice; here he seems to speak *before* his counsel is sought, and this may be a glimpse of the 'personal' element overshadowing the 'professional'.

---

18. Hertzberg, *1 & 2 Samuel*, p. 350.
19. Fokkelman, *King David*, p. 211.
20. Waltke and O'Connor, *An Introduction to Biblical Hebrew Syntax*, p. 579.
21. Mauchline, *1 and 2 Samuel*, p. 279.
22. McCarter, *II Samuel*, p. 378.

So, rather than a request, this cohortative has the effect of *announcing* what Ahithophel plans to do. When compared with his previous instructions to Absalom in 16.21, there are some crucial differences in the form of counsel in the two sets of direct speech. Previously, he issues an imperative to Absalom to 'go' (בוא) to the concubines. Now Ahithophel is outlining a different kind of plan. To adopt the parlance of speech-act theory, Ahithophel's counsel in this instance does not contain a 'directive' locution (as in the previous advice), but instead is a 'commissive' statement, committing *himself* to undertake a program.[23] While an imperative would have been appropriate for his counseling role here, this commissive statement suggests that he is offering more than just 'advice' here, and is executing an individually minded agenda.

After pledging that he will choose twelve thousand men, Ahithophel's plan involves his arising and pursuing 'tonight' (הלילה), with a sense of immediacy and purpose. His strategic initiative has a three-fold thrust, involving 'advance–encounter–return', and the cohortatives reflect a fast-paced movement of seek and destroy.[24] Further, Ahithophel declares that *he* will 'come upon' David while the king is 'weary and disheartened', and *he* will thus cause a panic among David's followers that will allow him a clear shot at David: 'I will strike the king alone' (והכיתי את־המלך לבדו). This is virulent language, and certainly adds an element of malignancy to Ahithophel's character. Another contrast with his previous instruction is the absence of Absalom actually doing anything; here it is the presence of Ahithophel which dominates, most noticeably through the six occurrences of the first-person singular in these two verses. Mauchline comments, 'That Ahithophel should have proposed to lead such an army for Absalom...is most unlikely; a wise man's responsibility is to give advice, not to lead troops into battle'.[25] The paradox is that this comment seems accurate—Ahithophel is renowned as a counselor, not a soldier—yet it is clear that he is intending to transcend his office and also assume personal leadership of the army. This plan depicts him as one who is overreaching public duty in favor of a private plan. Hertzberg notes the 'impression that he is concerned to satisfy personal feelings of hatred'; the argument here is that Ahithophel is clearly being portrayed not only as a counselor, but as a would-be *assassin* as well:[26]

> and I will bring all the people back to you as a bride comes home to her husband. You seek the life of only one man, and all the people will be at peace'. The advice pleased Absalom and all the elders of Israel. (2 Sam. 17.3-4 NRSV)

---

23. E. Traugott and M. Pratt, *Linguistics for Students of Literature* (New York: Harcourt, Brace, Jovanovich, 1980), p. 229.
24. Fokkelman, *King David*, p. 211.
25. Mauchline, *1 and 2 Samuel*, p. 279.
26. Hertzberg, *1 & 2 Samuel*, p. 351.

10. *Motives for Defection*

To be sure, Ahithophel's stratagem advocates a minimum of bloodshed, and emphasizes that he intends to target 'one man' rather than engage in mass combat. This undoubtedly has political currency, as 'the return of the people' without extended conflict must appeal to revolutionary ears. 'One attractive feature of his proposal was that the loss of life would be minimal. It would be a quick, crisp operation, with the sole purpose of eliminating David, whose supporters could then be counted on to switch their allegiance to Absalom without further resistance.'[27] The political side of Ahithophel's machination is counterbalanced with the personal side of his scheme: he bears a grudge against David alone, and therefore the king alone is his main target. As Hertzberg implies, he is sure of success and these words evince a rancorous confidence: he knows David, and knows how and when to deliver the lethal strike.[28]

4. *Spy Games*

In 2 Sam. 17.4 the word of Ahithophel is met with manifold approval, as would be expected especially in light of the narrator's insertion about the oracular nature of his counsel. Not only does Absalom find this counsel 'agreeable' (ישׁר), but also it is favorable 'in the eyes of all the elders of Israel'. It is at this moment, though, that Absalom inexplicably summons Hushai the Archite, in order that: 'we may hear what is in his mouth' (ונשׁמעה מה־בפיו). After Hushai is briefed on the counsel of Ahithophel, he then commences his own advice. Hushai's rhetoric is a masterpiece in the use of persuasion and figurative language.

Shimon Bar-Efrat has undertaken a lengthy analysis of Hushai's speech that is not repeated here, but there are several cogent points which unquestionably have bearing on this present study of Ahithophel.[29] First, the manner in which Hushai commences his speech in 17.7 is to qualify what has been said by his adversary: 'It is not good, the counsel which Ahithophel has counseled *this time*'. He starts by planting a seed of doubt by insisting that this is a unique occasion where the impeccable counsel of Ahithophel *should* be questioned. Hushai is implying that normally the advice of Ahithophel is above censure, only 'this time' (בפעם הזאת) it needs to be audited. Moreover, Hushai continues with a decisive change in subject for the verbs; whereas Ahithophel uses a proliferation of the first-person 'I', Hushai abundantly employs the second-person 'you'. 'You yourself know...', he cautions, making Absalom himself the explicit subject and focus of the

---

27. Gordon, *1 & 2 Samuel*, p. 280.
28. Hertzberg, *1 & 2 Samuel*, p. 350.
29. Shimon Bar-Efrat, *Narrative Art in the Bible* (JSOTSup, 70; Sheffield: Almond Press, 1989), pp. 223-37.

discourse. Ahithophel's own strategy places him at the head of the campaign for the reasons discussed above. Hushai, in contrast, makes Absalom the focal point, and the reader can infer that this is a calculated appeal to the young man's vanity.[30] This change of subject represents a critical moment in the narrative, as the fire of Ahithophel's personal agenda for incinerating David is slowly extinguished by Hushai's dissembling oration.

> Absalom and all the men of Israel said, 'The counsel of Hushai the Archite is better than the counsel of Ahithophel'. For the LORD had ordained to defeat the good counsel of Ahithophel, so that the LORD might bring ruin on Absalom. (2 Sam. 17.14 NRSV)

At the conclusion of Hushai's speech, Absalom and the men of Israel declare, 'The counsel of Hushai the Archite is better than the counsel of Ahithophel'. This is a stunning reversal of previous court policy, as hitherto the counsel of Ahithophel has been held in the highest esteem. But at this point, the narrator makes a key disclosure: 'For the LORD had ordained to frustrate the good counsel of Ahithophel in order that the LORD might bring disaster to Absalom'. This revelation is a nexus for a host of thematic forces in the narrative, as the narrator confirms that the advice of Ahithophel is 'good' (הטובה), yet it is frustrated by divine overrule. Ahithophel's counsel, notwithstanding the personal motivation, is acknowledged to be the superior plan, and its implementation would surely have meant calamity for David.

---

30. On Absalom's egotism, see the narrator's comment at 14.25-26: 'And like Absalom there was not a man in Israel to be as highly praised for handsomeness; from the sole of his foot to his crown there was not a blemish on him. And at the end of many days when he would shave (for it would become heavy upon him, and he would cut it), he would weigh the hair of his head: two hundred shekels by the weight of the king.' There is an irony, then, as Josipovici (*The Book of God*, p. 207) notes, when Absalom 'is caught by his beautiful hair in a tree and, as he hangs there helpless, is stabbed to death by Joab. "Absalom gloried in his hair", comments the Mishnah laconically, "therefore he was hanged by his hair".' With a strange twist, both Ahithophel and Absalom die while suspended from the earth. Cf. Ackerman, 'Knowing Good and Evil', p. 51: 'Ironically, the very description of Absalom as the "lamb" without blemish, who proudly weighed his hair annually, gives us insight into the character flaw that led him to choose Hushai's subversive advice over Ahitophel's wise counsel. Ahitophel had been direct and to the point, whereas Hushai had flattered Absalom's vanity. In this story the narrator has created a profound vision of a preordained divine judgment, ironically pronounced by David in response to Nathan's parable, working itself out in the lives of characters who act freely and thus deserve their fate. 2 Samuel 18.9 describes Absalom as being "placed between the heavens and between the earth"; and this emblematizes his fate. The judgment that falls on him and his brothers derives ultimately from both heaven and earth.' For a different slant on this passage from a wider ancient Near East viewpoint, see S.A. Wiggins, 'Between Heaven and Earth: Absalom's Dilemma', *JNSL* 23 (1997), pp. 73-81.

In all probability there is an intertextual reflex here to 2 Sam. 15.31, when David is told of his senior advisor's defection, and he prays, 'Make foolish the counsel of Ahithophel, O LORD'. Upon meeting Hushai the Archite after this, David explains to him that he can be of great assistance, 'And you can frustrate (והפרתה) for me the counsel of Ahithophel'. That the same verb is used here, but with the LORD as the subject (ויהוה צוה להפר) indicates that these two scenes, 15.31-37 and 17.14, have a causal connection. For Ahithophel, 17.14 would indicate that he has *another* adversary in addition to Hushai. As McCarter notes, 'This parenthesis is the last of three theologically explicit passages (11.27; 12.24; and 17.14) stressed by von Rad…as crucial to the interpretation of the succession narrative'.[31]

More will be said below on the thematic significance of the narrator's insertion here at 17.14, but it is now apparent that the rejection of Ahithophel's advice does not augur well for Absalom and the conspiracy. Along with other commentators, Anderson inquires 'Was it rejected?'[32] The argument is nicely summarized by Gunn, presenting the view that Absalom must have pursued David without delay, 'in which case Hushai's advice of general mobilization has been strangely disregarded'.[33] However, as Gunn concludes, Hushai's communication with his allies and the warning sent to David indicates that Hushai has been made aware that time is a factor: 'Ahithophel advises immediate pursuit that night. Hushai's advice delays the pursuit sufficiently for David to be warned and for him to press on.'[34] For this analysis of Ahithophel, the important point is that he *perceives* his advice to have been rejected (and he does not lead the rebel troops into battle), which leads to the final drama of 17.23.

5. *Suspended Sentence*

> When Ahithophel saw that his counsel was not followed, he saddled his donkey and went off home to his own city. He set his house in order, and hanged himself; he died and was buried in the tomb of his father. (2 Sam. 17.23 NRSV)

Ahithophel's final scene occurs immediately after the description of David setting out with all his company in 2 Sam. 17.22, 'and by daybreak not one remained who had not crossed the Jordan'. Perhaps this crossing symbolizes a turning point in the narrative, and carries a portent that the situation is now

---

31. McCarter, *II Samuel*, p. 387; cf. J. Baldwin, *I and II Samuel: An Introduction and Commentary* (Downers Grove, IL: InterVarsity Press, 1988), p. 266.
32. Anderson, *2 Samuel*, p. 216.
33. Gunn, *The Story of King David*, pp. 115-16.
34. Gunn, *The Story of King David*, p. 116.

irretrievable for the rebels. It is at this juncture in the text that the narrator provides a definitive moment in Ahithophel's characterization: the situation filtered through his perspective. The issue for my analysis is: How does the placement of Ahithophel's last scene here in 17.23 influence his characterization? For one, that Ahithophel's final appearance should come *before* the revolution is over allows us to consider that the success of the coup is not his main concern. Most commentators would suggest that the placement of this scene at this point in the narrative indicates that he sees the end in sight, and, rather than be executed for treason, he takes matters into his own hands. This is surely accurate, but it also indicates the importance which he attaches to his own agenda of pursuing David. Moreover, because the scene occurs here in 17.23, the narrative shift in point of view becomes even more pronounced in the wake of David's crossing; immediately after David is safely across the river, Ahithophel's perspective is given.

To emphasize, the narrative point of view shifts the reader's attention to the perspective of the counselor's mind, 'and Ahithophel *saw* that his counsel was not followed'. This shift of focus provides an interior view of his response to rejected counsel for possibly the first time in his career. Despite some exegetes contending that several aspects of his counsel *are* followed,[35] from Ahithophel's point of view, his plan is *not* implemented. His plan involved him leading the rebel troops to crush the king, and because this action is not allowed to happen, his counsel is certainly rejected, and his private ambition to destroy David is thwarted. It is possible to argue that because he is not empowered to 'strike the king alone', his purpose in joining the conspiracy is reduced to vacuity. If his motivation in supporting the *coup d'état* has been to exact vengeance on David, it is the frustration of this motive which leads to his final string of actions in the narrative.

After shifting the point of view to Ahithophel—'when he saw that his counsel was not followed'—the narrator unfolds the advisor's dramatic exit from the story with a touch of pathos. First, the detail 'and he saddled the donkey' has an effect similar to that in the narrative of Abraham in Gen. 22.3 (ויחבש את־חמרו). This detail provides a slight pause in the storytelling, and adds a fateful ambiance to Ahithophel's last journey home. As Fokkelman observes, there is a slower pace to the narrative here (achieved through the verb chain ויקם וילך), reflecting the narrator's unhurried approach in describing Ahithophel's deliberate movements.[36] Further, the phrase 'And he arose, and he went to his house, to his city (אל־עירו)', illustrates an envelope structure in the organization of Ahithophel's narrative portrait, as initially in 15.12 he is summoned by Absalom 'from his city' (מעירו). Thus his entry to

---

35. Gunn, *The Story of King David*, pp. 115-16; McCarter, *II Samuel*, pp. 387-88.
36. Fokkelman, *King David*, p. 230.

and exit from the narrative involve traveling from and returning to 'his city'. The detail 'he gave commands concerning his house' (ויצו אל־ביתו) has an ironic connection with 17.14, where the same verb is used for the LORD's 'ordaining' (צוה) to frustrate Ahithophel's *good* counsel. Finally comes the moment of his death, uniquely recorded as 'he strangled himself' or 'he hanged himself', one of the few suicides in biblical literature.[37] As has been implied here, he descends to the grave as a bitter man, with his desire for revenge unfulfilled.

6. *Conclusion*

To conclude, there are two literary features of Ahithophel's characterization which merit brief reflection. Ahithophel's vocation is 'the counselor of David', and with such a vocation one might expect his character to have a high proportion of direct speech. But this is not strictly the case with Ahithophel, and in fact the salient aspects of his characterization are primarily achieved through narration. First, the sequential unfolding of events in the narrative transpire in such a way that Ahithophel only enters the stage in connection with the rebellion. The contours of his characterization follow the contours of the plot: he is introduced near the outset of the coup (the high point of 2 Sam. 15), and exits the narrative just prior to the death of Absalom (the low point of 2 Sam. 18). Ahithophel's character, then, is presented only in the context of the rebellion, and he cannot be understood apart from his role in this unsuccessful attempt to destroy David. In other words, the rise and fall of events in the rebellion mirrors the rise and fall of events in Ahithophel's narrative world, as his only appearances in the story occur during the fleeting moments of the coup. Second, a significant element of his presentation is through his actions, and the final scene is surely a triumph of characterization through the narration of action and movement. Alter gives a thoughtful assessment:

---

37. For the verb חנק, cf. the standard Hebrew dictionaries: BDB, p. 338, and KB, p. 336 (with the implication that 'he strangled himself by means of hanging'). Hertzberg (*1 & 2 Samuel*, p. 353) lists another 'suicidal' text as 1 Kgs 16.18, which recounts the grim fate of the enigmatic usurper Zimri: 'And when Zimri saw (כראות) that the city was captured, he entered the citadel of the palace and set it on fire around him, and he died'. Hertzberg also refers to the demise of Abimelech (Judg. 9.54) and Saul (1 Sam. 31.4) at the hands of their respective armor-bearers as other (though not of the same degree) examples of this rare action in the Hebrew Bible. One might also consider the 'self-destruction' of Samson in this context. Many commentators note various similarities between Judas 'hanging himself' in Mt. 27.5, and the intertextual allusions of betrayal, 'the son of David', and the ascent of the Mount of Olives (see McCarter, *II Samuel*, p. 389) which makes for an interesting intertextual comparison in this stretch of the David narrative.

This haunting notice of Ahitophel's suicide shows him a deliberate, practical man to the very end, making all the necessary arrangements for his family and being sure to do away with himself in his hometown, where he knows he will be readily buried in the ancestral tomb. Ahitophel kills himself not only because, in quasi-Japanese fashion, he has lost face, but also out of sober calculation: he realizes that Hushai's counsel will enable David to defeat Absalom, and with the old king returned to the throne, an archtraitor like Ahitophel will surely face death. Thus, in tying the noose around his own neck, he anticipates the executioner's sword.[38]

The character of Ahithophel also has a structural role in the narrative, and attending to the details of his characterization yields dividends in terms of understanding the larger narrative in which he participates as a 'player in the drama'.[39] Returning to the von Rad footnote cited at the outset of this chapter, it is suggested that taking seriously the connection of Ahithophel with Bathsheba generates a rich study in character and motive, and contributes to the structural and thematic tensions in the larger narrative sequence. David's sin in 2 Samuel 11 has stratified consequences, and, according to Nathan's prophecy in 2 Samuel 12, is directly responsible for the strife which follows. The Ahithophel–Bathsheba connection is further evidence that 2 Samuel 11 cannot be separated from the political events in which it is interwoven. Absalom's rebellion can be seen as part of the larger pattern of reprisals which reverberate from David's sin: the upheaval in the life of the nation originates from what may have been thought of as 'private events', but of course what happens in secret is soon repeated in 'broad daylight'. Ahithophel is perhaps embittered by the events of 2 Samuel 11, and, as argued here, this is what motivates his defection, which has near-fatal implications for David. But the tension lies in the fact that 'the LORD had ordained to frustrate the good counsel of Ahithophel to bring disaster on Absalom' (17.14). Ahithophel's desire for personal vengeance is doomed to fail. Hence the proleptic anticipation of 16.23—where the narrator describes the 'oracular' nature of Ahithophel's counsel—is ironically never fulfilled.[40] At the end of his brief season in the narrative, Ahithophel is unwilling to reconcile with David, and, unlike Shimei (19.16-23), does not come crawling through the same dust he previously threw at the king pleading for mercy.[41] The events of ch. 11 and the repercussions extend beyond David's own house. That Bathsheba is formally introduced in the narrative as 'the daughter of Eliam' (and therefore the granddaughter of David's senior counselor)

---

38. Alter, *The David Story*, p. 301.
39. Von Rad, *Problem of the Hexateuch*, p. 190.
40. On this larger theological issue within 2 Sam. 15–17, see Polzin, *David and the Deuteronomist*, pp. 149-78, and Polak, 'David's Kingship'.
41. Fokkelman, *King David*, p. 229.

makes this liaison that much more scandalous, and causes an incorrigible acidity in Ahithophel.

Thematically, then, the character of Ahithophel has a most extraordinary conclusion. His characterization is configured, on balance, more through narration than direct speech, and his final scene emphasizes this. While one can ultimately reject the 'Bathsheba' correlation and arrive at the same conclusion about the method of his characterization in 2 Samuel 15–17, the study of character invariably involves an overall interpretation of the broader narrative. Hertzberg concludes his discussion of the counselor as follows: 'Ahithophel does not decide on the step of suicide…because of wounded pride, but because he rightly recognizes that Absalom's cause is lost and that he can only expect a cruel death after David's victory'.[42] The suggestion here is that it is *more* a matter of wounded pride than dedication to Absalom's cause that results in his hanging, as he is unable personally to exact a measure of revenge on David for the Bathsheba affair. In my view, the narrator's patient delineation of Ahithophel's final actions in 17.23 makes the best sense when understood in terms of his foiled purpose of revenge, as he resolutely saddles his donkey and journeys to the grave—a tragic fusion of complex personal, political, and theological factors that permeate the David narrative.

42. Hertzberg, *1 & 2 Samuel*, p. 353.

11

SOLOMON'S SUCCESSION AND JACOB'S KNAVERY: CONNECTIONS BETWEEN GENESIS 27 AND 1 KINGS 1

1. *Introduction*

A legion of readers over the years have reflected at length on the high drama that occupies center stage during the opening episodes of 1 Kings 1. The aged King David himself is the object of several competing interest groups hoping, it would seem, to fill the leadership vacuum created by his infirmity and impending death. As 1 Kings 1 moves toward a climax Solomon is placed on the throne of Israel, yet he himself appears entirely passive until after his coronation. A crucial player in the bid for succession is Bathsheba, whose timely (verbal) intercourse with the king proves decisive for Solomon's candidacy. However, this kind of creative maternal intervention is not entirely without precedent in the Hebrew Bible. In this chapter I will argue that exploring an intertextual relationship with Genesis 27 can help the reader to make sense of the curious maneuverings that eventually result in Solomon being proclaimed as the king of Israel. The contention here is that Bathsheba's negotiating with David on Solomon's behalf activates an allusion to the antecedent episode of Rebekah's negotiations regarding the blessing of Isaac. After a brief survey of previous scholarship, several compelling similarities between Genesis 27 and 1 Kings 1 are considered, and the chapter concludes with a brief reflection on the possible significance of the accession of Solomon sharing language and motifs with the 'stolen blessing' of Jacob.

Scholars have noted a series of literary connections between texts in Genesis and the David narrative in Samuel–Kings. For example, in a useful study that synthesizes earlier scholarship, Gary Rendsburg notes that 'much of Genesis mirrors the events of the United Monarchy of David and Solomon. This is borne out by similar story lines, allusions, and shared language.'[1] In particular, Rendsburg is interested in connections between Genesis 38 and aspects of David's family and career, and he posits:

---

1. G.A. Rendsburg, 'David and his Circle in Genesis xxxviii', *VT* 36 (1986), pp. 438-46 (438).

regardless of the episode's historicity, that we should understand it to refer more to David and his family than it does to Judah and his... But its main purpose was to adumbrate for us events from the life of Israel's greatest king. The author of this chapter realized this goal by matching the characters of Gen. xxxviii with personalities from David's circle.[2]

Rendsburg then proceeds to delineate seven points of correspondence which he observes between these episodes, concluding that the writer of Genesis was a 'commentator who sought to entertain his audience', and he is certain that early readers of Genesis 38, 'at least the educated ones, would have deduced the author's technique, would have realized the true intention of the chapter, and would have derived considerable enjoyment from its reading'.[3] Building on this work, C.Y.S. Ho 'attempts to strengthen the literary correlation between the Judah story and the David story as has been observed by Rendsburg and many other scholars', although he notes that 'issues of date or historicity do not affect the validity of a theory of literary interdependence'.[4] Ho also compiles an impressive list of parallels, and argues that Genesis 38 becomes 'a statement of David's Judahite and Israelite (i.e. Jewish) identity, written probably a little earlier than the Book of Ruth. Ruth links David to the genealogy of Perez via Boaz, and Gen. xxxviii provides an earlier link between Judah and David via Perez.'[5]

---

2. Rendsburg, 'David and his Circle in Genesis xxxviii', p. 441. There is also some brief discussion of allusions to Genesis in the 1 Samuel narrative by Jobling, *1 Samuel*, p. 190. Cf. Alter, *The Art of Biblical Narrative*, p. 120. Also see Rendsburg's article, 'Reading David in Genesis: How We Know the Torah Was Written in the Tenth Century B.C.E.', *BR* 17.1 (2001), pp. 20-33, 46. Cf. the comparable studies of D. Rudman, 'The Patriarchal Narratives in the Book of Samuel', *VT* 54 (2004), pp. 239-49; J. Blenkinsopp, 'Structure, Theme, and Motif in the Succession Narrative (2 Samuel 11–20; 1 Kings 1–2) and the History of Human Origins (Genesis 1–11)', in his *Treasures Old and New: Essays in the Theology of the Pentateuch* (Grand Rapids: Eerdmans, 2004), pp. 102-19.

3. Rendsburg, 'David and his Circle in Genesis xxxviii', pp. 444-46.

4. C.Y.S. Ho, 'The Stories of the Family Troubles of Judah and David: A Study of their Literary Links', *VT* 49 (1999), pp. 514-31 (515).

5. Ho, 'The Stories of the Family Troubles of Judah and David', p. 529. Both Ho and Rendsburg have a number of diachronic concerns in their articles, and both are interested in arguing for various degrees of literary priority in Genesis and Samuel. Even if one is inclined to agree with Rendsburg's diachronic arguments, recent work on intertextuality within biblical studies stresses the importance of a reciprocal flow between texts (from the vantage point of the reader). See further Tull, 'Intertextuality and the Hebrew Scriptures'. In his discussion of literary allusion in the Sodom and Gibeah narratives, Alter (*The World of Biblical Literature* [London: SPCK, 1992], p. 112) notes, 'Allusion, of course, presupposes the temporal priority of one text to another. To contemplate for a moment an extreme possibility, do we know that Judges was written later than Genesis, or that its author was really familiar with Genesis? Might Genesis even be alluding to Judges, and not the other way around? Such a hypothesis is extremely unlikely first because the language of the story of Judges gives evidence of being an elaboration of

In light of these convincing proposals regarding correlations between the David narrative and the ancestral stories, there are reasonable grounds for suggesting other points of correspondence between Genesis and Samuel–Kings. Indeed, in his monograph *The Redaction of Genesis*, Rendsburg writes, 'Further research, it is hoped, will garner even more evidence and point out still other similarities, literary historical, and otherwise, between Genesis and the United Kingdom'.[6] I would like to further this discussion on intertextual connections by exploring a confluence of allusions between Jacob's 'theft' of the blessing in Genesis 27 and Solomon's accession to the throne of Israel in 1 Kings 1. When these two episodes are read as intertexts, a configuration of parallels emerge that invite the reader to consider them in relation to one another. First, in each of these episodes there is an 'aged husband' reclined on his deathbed (it would seem), with the issue of 'succession' looming in the background. Second, both of these narratives feature an 'enterprising mother' who discharges a scheme of deception on the respective husband. As the reader reflects on Bathsheba's actions in 1 Kings 1, there are some striking similarities with the actions of Rebekah in Genesis 27. Third, each mother's stratagem is engineered to support the cause of a younger son over and against the father's more naturally favored older one. Fourth, both mothers use the sacred name (יהוה) to enhance their respective arguments and persuade their interlocutors. Each of these four points will now be elaborated in turn.

2. *Aged Husbands*

Perhaps the most obvious point of similarity is that both the Genesis 27 narrative and 1 Kings 1 are careful to emphasize that the respective husbands—Isaac and David—are old (זקן). In the case of Isaac, the most visible sign of age is his inability to see. This is precisely a quality that will be exploited in the ensuing narrative, as Isaac's blindness earmarks him as a candidate for

---

the language in Genesis 19, going beyond the classical terseness of the Sodom narrative through the addition of little phrases that make the moral judgment of the events more explicit. If, moreover, there were no actual allusion to Sodom in Gibeah, the whole conspicuous function of Sodom as moral paradigm would be lost. In biblical literature, Sodom, not Gibeah, is the proverbial model of a wholly depraved society that condemns itself to destruction; the Hebrew writers repeatedly want to trouble Israel with the grim possibility that it may turn into Sodom, its supposed antitype.' Note the discussion of the Sodom–Judges connection in M.Z. Brettler, 'The Book of Judges: Literature as Politics', *JBL* 108 (1989), pp. 395-418. For a useful comparison of Gen. 38 with the book of Ruth, see E. van Wolde, 'Texts in Dialogue with Texts: Intertextuality in the Ruth and Tamar Narratives', *BibInt* 5 (1997), pp. 1-28.

6. G.A. Rendsburg, *The Redaction of Genesis* (Winona Lake, IN: Eisenbrauns, 1986), p. 120.

deception.⁷ In David's case, his inability to generate 'body heat' is the initial sign in the narrative that things have changed.⁸ The verb 'to warm' used here can convey the notion of physical proximity, and, as Mordechai Cogan notes, the verbal aspect of this phrase 'but he could not get warm' (ולא יחם לו) in the imperfective aspect 'indicates repeated attempts that failed'.⁹ If there is a sexual nuance in this verbal root (as in 'breeding-heat'), then it is surely ironic that a word-play emerges with Gen. 30.39, 'and the flocks mated/ became hot (ויחמו) before the rods [of Jacob]'. Such heat, though, is not a factor with David in this advanced state of years. His virility has clearly declined; the same king who appropriates Bathsheba in 2 Samuel 11 is now an impotent potentate who is unable to be warmed by a young Shunammite maiden.¹⁰

In terms of status, both Isaac and David undeniably are significant figures in the history of the nation. At each of these narrative junctures, the aged father is approaching death (or perhaps, at least, that terminal possibility is raised), and both have a history of favoritism toward an older son. David has evidently not named a successor to the throne of Israel, although he has been casual in his discipline of his handsome son Adonijah. Notably, in Genesis 27 it is Isaac who takes the initiative and seeks to bestow a blessing on the favored son. This is something of a deviation for Isaac—having a much lower profile than either his father or son in Genesis—as he is rarely the author of any plan in the narrative, with the memorable exception of lying about his genealogical relation to his wife in Genesis 26. Finally, in both narratives the term 'clothing' (בגדים) occurs in relation to the aged father. King David is covered in 'clothes' (בגדים) while Isaac gropes the 'clothes' (בגדים) of Esau worn by Jacob. The *double entendre* of 'clothing' (בגדים) with 'deal treacherously' (בגד) functions as a signal to the reader that the aged fathers in Genesis 27 and 1 Kings 1 may be ripe for manipulation.¹¹

---

7. See Sternberg, *The Poetics of Biblical Narrative*, pp. 321-41.

8. In 1 Kgs 1.1, the narrator informs the audience, 'King David had become old, very advanced in days' (והמלך דוד זקן בא בימים). The same phrase (albeit a common one, cf. Josh. 13.1; 23.1; 1 Sam. 17.12) of 'aging' is found in Gen. 24.1: 'Abraham had become old, very advanced in days' (ואברהם זקן בא בימים). Since Gen. 24 presents the narrative of 'Rebekah being secured for Isaac', it is clear that the issue of his son's future seems uppermost in the mind of Abraham. This in turn produces a contrast with David, who is comparatively inactive in terms of securing the future of any of his sons, or for that matter the throne of Israel. In light of the allusions to Rebekah as this narrative in 1 Kgs 1 unfolds, the connection should be noted.

9. M. Cogan, *I Kings* (AB, 10; New York: Doubleday, 2001), p. 156.

10. Consequently, the sight of Bathsheba in 1 Kgs 1.15-16 may rekindle memories in the king's mind of days of old when his potency was not at issue. Cf. Fokkelman, *King David*, pp. 355-56; M.J. Mulder, *1 Kings* (HCOT; Leuven: Peeters, 1998), pp. 55-56.

11. See O.H. Prouser, 'Suited to the Throne: The Symbolic Use of Clothing in the David and Saul Narratives', *JSOT* 71 (1996), pp. 27-37 (30). Standard lexicons (e.g.

3. *Enterprising Mothers*

A second point of similarity is the fact that both Genesis 27 and 1 Kings 1 feature 'enterprising mothers' who are involved in bold machinations against their aged husbands. In contrast to Isaac, Rebekah (since her introduction to the larger narrative in Gen. 24) has appeared assertive and enterprising, perhaps with the exception of the 'lying' affair in Genesis 26, where she is comparatively passive. Bathsheba, it could be argued, is portrayed with a certain ambiguity in 2 Samuel 11.[12] Her only direct speech occurs when she sends a message to David—two Hebrew words, 'I am pregnant' (הרה אנכי) —and it is difficult for the reader to determine if this is a threat, a demand, or an expression of disappointment.[13] In 1 Kings 1 Bathsheba becomes an indispensable participant in the deception promulgated by Nathan the prophet, surrounding the alleged oath purportedly sworn by the king. Numerous scholars have opined that there are grounds for suspecting the oath is a 'pious fraud', and hence Bathsheba's cooperation is requested by the prophet to secure the throne for Solomon.[14] Likewise, Rebekah needs Jacob himself to participate in the plan.

BDB, p. 93; *HALOT*, p. 108; *DCH*, II, pp. 90-93) list the root meaning for בנד as 'treachery' (noun) and 'to deal deceitfully' (verb), in addition to 'covering, garment'.

12. In her analysis of Bathsheba's various appearances in the David narrative, N. Aschkenasy (*Woman at the Window: Biblical Tales of Oppression and Escape* [Detroit: Wayne State University Press, 1998]) takes issue with the reading of Bal (*Lethal Love*, pp. 17-36). After considering all of Bathsheba's scenes, Aschkenasy summarizes as follows: 'In every scene where she appears Bathsheba is at first blush the guileless and naïve female, but it seems that her dangerous and ill-advised acts turn out to be beneficial to her. A reading that assumes that Bathsheba aspired to be the king's wife and to bear the heir to the Davidic throne may also shed a new light on the opening verses [of 2 Sam. 11]. Since we have already learned that nothing about Bathsheba is accidental or casual, why should the first scene in which we see her be a mere accident? It is true that the storyteller never accuses the woman of putting herself in a position where she could be seen by David, on the roof of her home which happened to be right below David's roof, or in a room at her home where the open window was right under David's roof.' The debate is interesting as it serves to underscore the complexity of Bathsheba's presentation through the most economic literary means. See also Yee, 'Fraught with Background', pp. 240-41; cf. Garsiel, 'The Story of David and Bathsheba', pp. 256-59; L.R. Klein, 'Bathsheba Revealed', in A. Brenner (ed.), *Samuel and Kings* (A Feminist Companion to the Bible, Second Series; Sheffield: Sheffield Academic Press, 2000), pp. 47-64.

13. Cf. Brueggemann, *First and Second Samuel*, p. 274: 'Notice "the woman" makes no demand or threat. Her words say enough and say it all.' A more overtly political understanding of Bathsheba's actions is presented by Bailey, *David in Love and War*.

14. Alter, *The Art of Biblical Narrative*, p. 98. Cf. Wesselius, 'Joab's Death and the Central Theme of the Succession Narrative', pp. 345-49. See also the insightful comment of A. Bach, *Women, Seduction, and Betrayal in Biblical Narrative* (Cambridge:

11. *Solomon's Succession and Jacob's Knavery* 145

It is interesting that both Rebekah in Genesis 25 and Bathsheba in 2 Samuel 11 and 12 are portrayed 'with child' in the narrative, and in both episodes their pregnancies are significant parts of the wider story. In the contexts of the respective deceptions that each practice, it is noticeable that Bathsheba and Rebekah each intentionally 'modify quotations' in their direct speech. As will be discussed in a moment, Bathsheba makes a number of key alterations from Nathan's instructions to suit her own rhetorical purposes. Both of these resourceful mothers emerge from their particular episodes as proficient orators. In the case of Rebekah, she is equally selective in recounting to Jacob the words and instruction of Isaac to Esau. Savran notes that Rebekah's 'hopes of gaining Isaac's blessing for Jacob depend entirely upon Jacob's willing participation in a scheme of deception. In order to gain his cooperation she must spark his jealousy and desire without arousing too many of his fears'.[15] As well, Bathsheba's discourse seems calculated to arouse certain emotions in David (resentment and anger among them) with judicious word choice and timing. Rebekah deflects attention away from the matter of 'hunting' which Isaac recounts at length to Esau, and instead focuses on the 'culinary' aspect of Isaac's speech.[16] The characterizations of both Rebekah and Bathsheba, therefore, exhibit similar patterns of literary configuration.

Cambridge University Press, 1997), p. 144: 'One would assume that if Bathsheba had been given assurance of her son's ascendancy to the throne, she would not have needed Nathan to encourage her to remind the king of his promise'.

15. G.W. Savran, *Telling and Retelling: Quotation in Biblical Narrative* (Bloomington: Indiana University Press, 1988), p. 41. Cf. G.J. Wenham, *Genesis 16–50* (WBC, 2; Dallas: Word Books, 1994), pp. 208-209; L.A. Turner, *Genesis* (Readings: A New Biblical Commentary; Sheffield: Sheffield Academic Press, 2000), pp. 115-18.

16. Isaac instructs Esau, 'Now then, lift up your implements, your quiver and your bow, and go out to the open country and hunt game for me. Then make for me tasty dishes just as I love, and bring to me, that I may eat' (Gen. 27.3-4). In 27.7, Rebekah omits this hunting aspect—perhaps mindful of Jacob's tent-dwelling proclivities (cf. 25.27)—curtailing the quotation to 'Bring game to me, and make for me tasty dishes' (הביאה לי ציד ועשׂה־לי מטעמים). Cf. Savran, *Telling and Retelling*, p. 42: 'As a verb, the root [צוד] always refers to hunting, but the noun [צַיִד] standing alone can have a more general connotation of prepared food, as in Josh. 9.5, 14. In the scenes between Esau and Isaac verbal forms of [צוד] are conspicuous (27.3, 5, 30, 32), but in the encounter between Jacob and Isaac in vv. 18-30, only the nominal form appears. When Jacob refers to [צֵידִי] in v. 19, he means simply the food he brought with him. This is not to say that he is unaware of the double meaning of the word in vv. 19 and 25, or to deny that he is deliberately lying to his father. But Rebecca's reformulation of v. 3 has shifted the focus of Jacob's concern away from hunting (which he is not prepared to do). His initial objection to his mother in vv. 11-12 makes no mention of his inability to hunt, centering instead on his fear of being unmasked in this deception, a fear more easily calmed by his mother's promise to assume responsibility if the scheme backfires. In this sense, Rebecca's quotation also reorganizes the "plot", or sequence of events, of Isaac's words to fit her plan for Jacob.'

4. *Younger Sons*

The third similarity is that both Genesis 27 and 1 Kings 1 feature a sibling rivalry where the younger son triumphs over the older. In both episodes, the older son is favored by the father. It is entirely clear that Isaac prefers Esau, as the narrator informs the audience in Gen. 25.28, 'because hunting was in his mouth' (כי־ציד בפיו). While the motives for this favor may be somewhat self-serving, it is certainly without ambiguity. At the same time, 25.28 also imparts the information 'but Rebekah loved Jacob', yet with no motivation disclosed. The rivalry between the brothers that commences with the 'crushing' in the womb is revisited later in the same chapter as Jacob barters the birthright from his older brother. Similarly, in 1 Kings 1 it is possible to argue that David favors Adonijah, as v. 7 reads, 'his father had never grieved him at any time by asking, "Why have you done so?" And he was also a very handsome man, and he was born after Absalom.' Adonijah may in fact view Solomon as a rival, since 1 Kgs 1.9-10 reveal that all of Adonijah's brothers and the sons of the king are invited to En-rogel, but 'his brother Solomon' is not included on the guest list.

Further, one of the most subtle parallels between Genesis 27 and 1 Kings 1 involves the literary technique of 'synchroneity' as delineated by Shemaryahu Talmon. Bernon Lee summarizes Talmon's position thus:

> According to Talmon, authors faced with the task of presenting two or more simultaneous, mutually significant events often have recourse to one method, among others, that fragments the reader's focus, abruptly alternating between one narrative strand involving one set of characters and another involving others. Authors suspend the action in one narrative strand, and later return to it repeating an element (a word, phrase, or clause) from the point where they left off in order to resume the sequence of action.[17]

In Genesis 27 Esau is presented as hunting in the field in order to prepare a feast *at the same time* that Jacob is playing charades inside the tent, and impersonating Esau before his father.[18] Likewise, Adonijah is feasting with his allies while *simultaneously* Bathsheba is 'reminding' King David that he

---

17. B. Lee, 'Fragmentation of Reader Focus in the Preamble to Battle in Judges 6.1–7.14', *JSOT* 97 (2002), pp. 65-86 (66), citing Talmon, 'The Presentation of Synchroneity and Simultaneity in Biblical Narrative'. As Lee (p. 67) further notes, 'The choice to entwine a series of separate developments as opposed to, for example, the maintenance of two distinct, lexically consecutive accounts with a temporal phrase at the beginning of the latter to denote its concurrence ensures that specific correspondences between the parallel sequences are not lost'.

18. With Esau hunting in the field while Jacob 'sits' in the tent, the twin brothers evoke a reflex to their epithets of Gen. 25.27. Turner (*Genesis*, p. 119) lists several other connections between Gen. 25 and 27.

swore an oath concerning Solomon. So, it is conspicuous that while the older brothers are engaged in banqueting of one sort or another, their firstborn privileges are being subverted in favor of a younger son by means of the wiles and skills of an assertive and innovative mother.[19]

5. *The Sacred Name*

The fourth similarity is that Bathsheba and Rebekah both use the sacred name 'LORD' (יהוה) in an apparent deception of an aged husband to further the various interests of a younger son. Notably, the divine name does not occur in any of the 'sources' that the mothers are quoting: Nathan certainly does not use the divine name when reciting his instructions to Bathsheba (he simply tells her to ask the king, 'did you not swear?'), nor does Isaac use the divine name when instructing Esau to go hunting for the 'blessing' meal. Yet Bathsheba transforms and enhances Nathan's instructions by stating to David 'You yourself swore *by the LORD* (ביהוה) *your God*',[20] and Rebekah in like manner recounts to Jacob that his father said, 'Bring game to me, and make for me tasty dishes, that I may bless you *before the LORD* (לפני יהוה) before I die'.

It would appear that both mothers are using the divine name to amplify their case, since in both 'sources' (Nathan and Isaac) the sacred name is not used.[21] What is most striking here, besides the creative innovation, is that at

---

19. Cf. Cogan, *1 Kings*, p. 167: 'it ought to be pointed out that previous readings of 1 Kgs have given insufficient consideration to a characteristic of biblical storytelling that was not adverse to describing the wily ways of heroes, showing how, against the odds, they outsmarted the competition; cf., e.g., Jacob's behavior in securing the birthright from Esau and the blessing of his aged and sightless father (Gen. 25.29-34; 27.1-40)'. During the course of the narratives, Esau is described as 'older' (גדל) in Gen. 27.1, just as Adonijah is described as 'older' (גדול) by Solomon in 1 Kgs 2.22.

20. This is made emphatic through the use of an independent personal pronoun in addition to the verb, 'you indeed swore' (אתה נשבעת). Bathsheba here modifies Nathan's syntax (הלא־אתה אדני המלך נשבעת) of 1.13, a rendering that conceivably is more assertive. My central point here is that just as Rebekah changes Isaac's words to suit her audience, so Bathsheba adopts a similar tactic before her interlocutor.

21. Savran (*Telling and Retelling: Quotation in Biblical Narrative*, p. 64) summarizes the 'quotation' issue in 1 Kings 1 as follows: 'Toward the end of David's career, in 1 Kings 1, an extraordinary example of deceptive quotation is directed at David by Nathan and Bathsheba in their efforts to get the declining king to ensure the succession of Solomon over Adonijah. In vv. 13 and 17 a quotation is ascribed to David in which he vows that Solomon will succeed him. The quote is unverifiable and quite possibly wholly invented by Nathan, for nowhere in 2 Samuel does David make such a promise to Bathsheba. Moreover, the emphasis on David's age and impotence in 1 Kg. 1.1, 4, 15 adds to the impression that he can be manipulated by those around him. The question need not be resolved...the literary quality of the story only benefits from this ambiguity. Because of

prior points in the narrative both mothers have received a divine oracle intimating the 'promise' of their particular younger son. In Gen. 25.23, Rebekah is pregnant with twins (although she is unaware of the reasons for the 'crushing' in her womb), and 'inquires of the LORD' concerning her situation: 'And the LORD said to her, "Two nations are in your womb, and two peoples will be separated from your body. One people will be stronger than the other; and the older will serve the younger."' In 2 Sam. 12.25, Solomon receives a different name (delivered by Nathan) as a sign, it would seem, of divine favor: 'The LORD loved him, and sent by the hand of Nathan the prophet, and he called his name Jedidiah, on account of the LORD'.[22] Therefore, both Rebekah and Bathsheba have an 'oracle' which they could interpret as supporting the claims of their younger sons. This may help to explain why both mothers are not hesitant to include the divine name in their respective speeches, because it is possible that from both of their perspectives there is a degree of legitimacy to their deceptions. The mothers seem to share a common motivation, and both are the recipients of an enigmatic oracle around the time of the birth of their sons.[23] Incidentally, both sons, Jacob and Solomon, receive 'new names' at some point in their lives, perhaps as signs of their electoral status and a foreshadowing of their elevation over their elder sibling.

6. Conclusions

By way of conclusion, I would submit that Bathsheba's actions in 1 Kings 1 are illuminated when compared with Rebekah's similar conduct in Genesis

---

the "reminding" function inherent in some quotations from earlier points in time, we should understand David's "forgetfulness", whether real or contrived, to be the target of their ploy. David must be convinced that he swore this oath and, more important, that he must act immediately to fulfill its conditions. Given the king's overwhelming passivity in 1 Kg. 1.1-10, this will be no mean feat, even if the oath is genuine.'

22. There is an obvious word-play between Jedidiah (ידידיה) and David (דויד/דוד), which may suggest that Jedidiah/Solomon is anticipated as David's successor. Nathan's understanding of this name could be construed as a motivation for installing Solomon on Israel's throne. Cf. Ho, 'The Stories of the Family Troubles of Judah and David', p. 527; Polak, 'David's Kingship'.

23. Of course, in both narratives there is a measure of ambiguity as to whether the husband is aware of the oracle; the actions of both David and Isaac in this regard are equally (and perhaps intentionally) unclear. For further reflection on David and Jacob as fathers, and links between Genesis and Samuel, see D.N. Freedman, 'Dinah and Shechem, Tamar and Amnon', in J.R. Huddlestun (ed.), *Divine Commitment and Human Obligation: Selected Writings of David Noel Freedman* (Grand Rapids: Eerdmans, 1997), pp. 485-95. Freedman (p. 490) concludes: 'Thus the experiences of Jacob foreshadow those of David, while the exploits of the latter fulfill the promises inherent or implicit in the former'.

27, and a number of details that would otherwise remain partially obscure are endowed with heightened significance. To reiterate on the matter of definition discussed earlier, if the notion of intertextual relationship is understood 'metaphorically as a form of citation in which a fragment of discourse is accommodated or assimilated by the focused text', then it is incumbent upon the interpreter to establish 'a relationship between the focused text and its intertext', and forge 'its intertextual identity'.[24] One interpretive dividend for the reader is in the realm of characterization, as the images of Bathsheba in 1 Kings 1 have a higher resolution because of the intertextual relationship with Rebekah in Genesis 27. On the one hand, the parallel roles they play in deceiving their aged husbands invites comparison, since both so plainly know the areas to exploit: Rebekah targets her husband's appetite for culinary delights and his condition of blindness, while Solomon's mother Bathsheba capitalizes on David's sense of authority ('the eyes of all Israel are upon you!') and his contempt for Joab. So, there are similar rhetorical strategies at work in both narratives. On the other hand, though, it may seem that Bathsheba's situation is more desperate, because of the perceived threat of Adonijah, and the maternal rivalries represented by Haggith and Abishag.[25] The role of Nathan the prophet also serves to complicate matters in 1 Kings 1, and this is certainly a divergence from Genesis 27. Yet, both mothers are actively involved in the promotion of younger sons' interests over the socially prescribed firstborn rights of the older, and consequently, Bathsheba is now seen to participate in the reversal of primogeniture so vital

---

24. O. Miller, 'Intertextual Identity', in M.J. Valdes and O. Miller (eds.), *Identity of the Literary Text* (Toronto: University of Toronto Press, 1985), pp. 19-40 (21), cited in J.J. Granowski, 'Jehoiachin at the King's Table: A Reading of the Ending of the Second Book of Kings', in D.N. Fewell (ed.), *Reading between Texts: Intertextuality and the Hebrew Bible* (Louisville, KY: Westminster/John Knox Press, 1992), pp. 173-88 (182). Cf. L. Eslinger, 'Inner-Biblical Exegesis and Inner-Biblical Allusion: The Question of Category', *VT* 42 (1992), pp. 47-58. Note also the theoretical discussion of Rosenberg (*King and Kin*, pp. xi-xii), where intertextuality is described in terms of its 'perennially centrifugal gestures toward other stories, other texts, other uses of a word, its Heraclitean dynamism, its horizontal flux from one signifier to the next, its hauntedness by the conflicting claims of texts, its key moments and junctures, its silences and obscurities, its incommensurate themes and preoccupations, its repetitions and obsessions'. Also note the overview of intertextuality in J.M. O'Brien, *Nahum* (Readings; London: Sheffield Academic Press, 2002), pp. 26-27.

25. Cf. Nicol, 'The Death of Joab', p. 139: 'There is a savage irony in the case Bathsheba presents to David. She contends that, if Adonijah has indeed succeeded him as king, once he is dead she and Solomon will be treated as criminals. The unspoken obverse is that should Solomon succeed his father, Adonijah's life will not be worth living. That is an issue which David prefers to ignore.' Similarly, the Genesis narrative features the threat of Esau toward Jacob, often filtered through Rebekah's perspective (e.g. Gen. 27.41-46).

to the plot of Genesis.²⁶ Not only does this serve to anticipate Bathsheba's prominence as 'queen mother' during the reign of her son (e.g. 1 Kgs 2.19), but such intertextual positioning also locates Bathsheba within a larger tradition of enterprising mothers in Genesis.²⁷

Moreover, this configuration of parallels has implications for the characterization of Solomon that gradually unfolds as 1 Kings continues. Solomon has been referred to as 'a shadowy figure' in the stretch of discourse preceding his coronation.²⁸ But by means of the narrative analogy to the Jacob story, Solomon is actually introduced to the narrative before he even utters a word of direct speech. Hence, the intertextual connection with Genesis 27 functions as a means of indirect characterization. Not only is all the dramatic tension of Jacob's 'theft' of the blessing imported into 1 Kings 1, but through the literary technique of allusion there is an intersection of *character zones* between Solomon and Jacob. R.S. Hendel has described Jacob as, among other things, 'quick-witted and devious'.²⁹ On the heels of these intertextual links with Genesis, a reader may infer that Solomon could have a number of shared characteristics with Jacob; perhaps the latter will be as deceptive as the former. J.T. Walsh comments on the narrative strategy involving Solomon: 'on the surface he will be presented generally in a positive light; beneath the surface the narrator will strew gaps and ambiguities that invite a much more critical appraisal of Solomon'.³⁰ The narrator is

26. For a historical study that affirms the literary currency of this motif, see G.K. Knoppers, 'The Preferential Status of the Eldest Son Revoked?', in S. L. McKenzie and T. Römer (eds.), in collaboration with H.H. Schmid, *Rethinking the Foundations: Historiography in the Ancient World and in the Bible., Essays in Honour of John Van Seters* (BZAW; Berlin: W. de Gruyter, 2000), pp. 115-26.

27. As Rendsburg ('David and his Circle in Genesis xxxviii', p. 441) notes, there are other examples of intertextuality between Genesis and the David narrative. For example, there is a network of correspondences between Gen. 31 (Jacob fleeing from Laban, and Rachel stealing the *teraphim*) and 1 Sam. 19 (David fleeing from Saul, and Michal aiding his escape through *teraphim*). Both of these episodes feature *deceptive father-in-laws* (Saul and Laban), *younger daughters* (Michal and Rachel), *fugitive husbands* (David and Jacob) and *hidden idols* (Michal hides the *teraphim* in the bed to fool Saul's agents, and Rachel hides her father's *teraphim* under her camel's saddle). Cf. Alter, *The David Story*, p. 120.

28. I.W. Provan, 'On "Seeing" the Trees While Missing the Forest: The Wisdom of Characters and Readers in 2 Samuel and 1 Kings', in E. Ball (ed.), *In Search of True Wisdom: Essays in Old Testament Interpretation in Honour of Ronald E. Clements* (JSOTSup, 300; Sheffield: Sheffield Academic Press, 2000), pp. 153-73 (156). Cf. J.T. Walsh, 'The Character of Solomon in 1 Kings 1–5', *CBQ* 57 (1995), pp. 471-93; Provan, 'Why Barzillai of Gilead?'.

29. R.S. Hendel, 'Jacob', in D.N. Freedman (ed.), *Eerdmans Dictionary of the Bible* (Grand Rapids: Eerdmans, 2000), pp. 666-67 (666). Cf. the analysis of Jacob by Heard, *Dynamics of Diselection*, pp. 112-17.

30. Walsh, *1 Kings*, p. 34.

signaling that the character of Solomon may contain many of the ambiguities and complexities of Jacob.

This naturally leads to the theological problem of Solomon's accession. The use of the sacred name by both Rebekah and Bathsheba ironically interweaves the theme of divine election over and against other human schemes. It is undoubtedly significant that in Genesis 27 and 1 Kings 1 the crown and the blessing are secured 'not by hard bargaining but by shrewd misrepresentation'.[31] In Jacob's case, whatever underhanded means are deployed to secure the blessing of Isaac, there is nonetheless a symmetry with the earlier prophetic word of Genesis 25. Similarly, there is no doubt a measure of dubiety surrounding Solomon's accession, yet there seems to be a mysterious dovetail with the divine will in light of 2 Sam. 12.24-25. Iain Provan is surely right in pointing out that 1 Kings 1 'provides no clear signal to the reader of his legitimacy', and S.J. DeVries rather wearily notes, 'There have been all sorts of pro and con arguments whether the throne-succession narrator actually wrote his history to legitimize Solomon in the place of his older brother, or wrote it disparagingly, to show how ruthless Solomon and his party had been in seizing what properly belonged to another'.[32] Perhaps a further implication of this intertextual relationship is that the author is conveying that Solomon's accession, however unsavory, is just as legitimate as Jacob's inheritance of the blessing. Contained in this 're-accentuation of images' (as Bakhtin would refer to it) is a theological freight of meaning, and many of the salient ideological points about God's election in the Jacob narratives are thus transposed onto the David story.[33] It should not be surprising, therefore, that Bathsheba and Rebekah share a measure of duplicity with respect to their husbands, yet both have the weight of a divine oracle hovering in the background. My contention is that an intertextual reading of these two episodes is a useful hermeneutical move. In light of these allusions

---

31. W. Brueggemann, *Genesis* (Atlanta: John Knox Press, 1982), p. 230.

32. Provan, 'On "Seeing" the Trees While Missing the Forest', p. 156; DeVries, *1 Kings*, p. 11. Cf. the perceptive literary study of B.O. Long, 'A Darkness between Brothers: Solomon and Adonijah', *JSOT* 19 (1981), pp. 79-94.

33. Bakhtin, *The Dialogic Imagination*, pp. 419-22. Alter (*The World of Biblical Literature*, p. 121) suggests that intertextuality can have an overt theological function, and can operate as 'a preeminent illustration of the biblical notion that historical events exhibit patterned repetition, in a sense dramatically recur as a manifestation of providential design'. If one assumes with V.P. Hamilton (*The Book of Genesis, Chapters 18–20* [NICOT; Grand Rapids: Eerdmans, 1995], p. 707) that a central theme of the Jacob narrative is 'a beneficent divine plan at work through calamity and confusion', then by extension a theological point in the opening episodes of 1 Kings might be that despite the threat of social and political chaos that broods over the entire monarchical history, the same divine providence at work in Genesis will remain consistent throughout the era of Solomon and beyond.

to Genesis 27 in 1 Kings 1, the reader has a host of expectations about character, motive, and the unpredictable nexus between divine will and human volition.[34]

---

34. Reflecting on ideological connections between Genesis and the books of Samuel, Halpern (*David's Secret Demons*, p. 360) notes: 'Jacob gives preferment to Rachel's son, because of Jacob's love for Rachel, which has led earlier to Jacob's being fooled by Laban. Unwittingly, each human actor in the drama plays a part for perfectly venal reasons. The principle of double or complementary causation is at work here: causation at the divine level as well as at a human level; but no superhuman agency is invoked for the day-to-day operation of the relations in question. To reverse the old proverb, God proposes, Man disposes. Yahweh sets the pieces in place and the drama plays itself out as foreordained, yet with each agent in the drama acting volitionally. And it is the dream itself which causes the brothers to act in such a way as to bring about its fulfillment. The dream is a self-working prophecy.' Halpern further comments, 'In the Joseph and Absalom stories, good things happen to bad people, bad things turn out to be good things by misadventure. It is no coincidence that just after the sale of Joseph into slavery, Judah, David's putative ancestor, enters into ambiguous sexual relations with a Canaanite daughter-in-law, Tamar (Gen. 38). This is a comment on events in Samuel transposed onto the Joseph story, but indirectly.'

12

THE SWEARING ISSUE:
A CURSORY SURVEY OF OATHS IN 1 KINGS 1–2

The opening episodes of 1 Kings, as is well documented, abound with collusion and intrigue.[1] A variety of agendas—political and theological—intersect in a network of power struggles, court factions, equivocal language, and bureaucratic schemes.

In terms of the broader Deuteronomistic History, the opening chapters of 1 Kings feature an unusually high concentration of oaths or dialogue surrounding oaths, such as: Nathan's instructions to Bathsheba surrounding an alleged oath (1.13), Bathsheba's subsequent declaration to David about this same purported oath (1.17), David's 'oath within an oath' concerning the accession of Solomon (1.29), Adonijah's request for an oath and Solomon's noncompliance (1.51-52), David's oath involving Shimei the Benjaminite (2.8) and its sequel (2.42), and the rare instance of a 'double oath' sworn by Solomon with respect to Adonijah (2.23-24). This final chapter explores the 'swearing issue' in 1 Kings 1–2, underscoring the point that the *character zone* of Solomon is encompassed by the language of oaths. Moreover, I am arguing that the use of oaths is part of the larger structure of the narrative of transition from the reign of David to the era of Solomon: just as Solomon ascends to the throne of Israel by means of a creative use of oaths in 1 Kings 1, I contend that in 1 Kings 2 Solomon's hold on power is consolidated through an equally creative and dubious use of oaths. In what follows, I will

---

1. For example, see P. K. McCarter, 'Plots, True and False: The Succession Narrative as Court Apologetic', *Int* 35 (1981), pp. 355-67; L. Eslinger, *Into the Hands of the Living God* (JSOTSup, 84; Sheffield: Almond Press, 1989), pp. 123-82; G.N. Knoppers, *Two Nations under God: The Deuteronomistic History of Solomon and the Dual Monarchies*. I. *The Reign of Solomon and the Rise of Jeroboam* (HSM, 52; Atlanta: Scholars Press 1993), pp. 157-76; Long, *1 Kings*, pp. 36-57; Mulder, *1 Kings*, pp. 32-129; C.L. Seow, '1 & 2 Kings', in *NIB*, II, pp. 3-295 (13-36); W. Brueggemann, *1 & 2 Kings* (Macon, GA: Smyth & Helwys, 2000), pp. 11-42; Halpern, *David's Secret Demons*, pp. 391-400; V. Fritz, *1 & 2 Kings* (trans. A. Hagedorn; Continental Commentary; Minneapolis: Fortress Press, 2003), pp. 13-32.

briefly consider seven scenes in 1 Kings 1–2 involving oaths, and conclude with several observations about the characterization of Solomon that subsequently emerges.[2]

1. *Oath 1: Nathan's 'Reminder' to Bathsheba of David's (Purported) Oath Regarding the Succession of Solomon (1 Kings 1.5-10)*

By way of background, 1 Kgs 1.5-10 presents a power-seeking Adonijah, the son of Haggith ('feast-lady'), feasting with his allies and imitating the pretensions of Absalom (cf. 2 Sam. 15.1).[3] In the midst of such emerging factionalism, Nathan the prophet approaches Bathsheba with *his* rendition of these current events and a plan of how she can save her life. He counsels her in v. 13:

> 'Go with haste to King David, and say to him, "Did you not, O my lord the king, swear an oath to your maid-servant, saying, 'Solomon your son will reign after me, and he will sit upon my throne'? Why then is Adonijah reigning?" Look!, while you are still speaking with the king, I also will come in after you and fill up your words'. (1 Kgs 1.13)

I have earlier analyzed this scene from the point of view of Nathan's role, but several points merit reiteration and expansion for the present argument. First, the mention of 'the son of Haggith' to Bathsheba intensifies the 'maternal rivalry' that simmers in the substratum of these opening episodes. There is more at stake than just a son being crowned king: there is also the office of the queen mother hinted at.[4] Nathan reminds or informs Bathsheba

---

2. The reader will notice a triangular word-play on Bathsheba's name (בת־שבע), the number 'seven' (שבע), and the verbal root 'swear an oath' (שבע).

3. I.W. Provan, *1 and 2 Kings* (NIBC, 7; Peabody, MA: Hendrickson, 1995), p. 30: 'While the son of the feast-lady eats, the daughter-of-the-oath reminds the king of what he has sworn and so ensures that Adonijah is dependent for his life upon Solomon's own oath. The story is constructed quite deliberately so as to make these connections between the mothers and their sons clear and to invest the characters with a sense of predestination.' See further M. Garsiel, 'Puns upon Names as a Literary Device in 1 Kings 1–2', *Bib* 72 (1991), pp. 379-86.

4. J.T. Walsh, *1 Kings* (Berit Olam; Collegeville, MN: Liturgical Press, 1996), p. 7. See also Z. Ben-Barak, 'The Status and Right of the *Gĕbîrâ*', *JBL* 110 (1991), pp. 23-34; S. Ackerman, 'The Queen Mother and the Cult in Ancient Israel', *JBL* 112 (1993), pp. 385-401. Commenting on the actions of 1 Kgs 2.19, Cogan (*1 Kings*, p. 176) remarks: 'The title *gĕbîrâ*, "Queen Mother" (cf. 1 Kings 15.13 and Note there) is not used here; it is rather the personal relationship between mother and son, not her (purported) position at court, that is signaled here (as it is in the response "Ask, my mother" in v. 20)'. For a comparative study, see E. Fuchs, 'The Literary Characterization of Mothers and Sexual Politics in the Hebrew Bible', in A. Bach (ed.), *Women in the Hebrew Bible: A Reader* (New York: Routledge, 1999), pp. 127-39.

12. The Swearing Issue

of this contest, revealing his intent to persuade by rhetoric. Second, several commentators have noted that Adonijah has *not* become king at this point in the narrative, but this dramatic elaboration by the prophet heightens the efficacy of his speech to Bathsheba.[5] Again this depicts the prophet as one who is willing to use a little bit of hyperbole to further his point. These two matters need to be kept in mind as the reader reflects on the 'oath' which is the centerpiece of Nathan's plan. As most every recent scholar agrees, there is an ambiguity surrounding this oath because the narrative does not explicitly record such an oath sworn by King David.[6] Even in the place where it might well be expected, 2 Sam. 12.25, it is distinctly lacking.[7]

The ambiguity surrounding the oath may of course be a deliberate narrative device. The oath cannot indisputably be verified in any antecedent text and its equivocal nature seems to be highly developed as this episode moves toward a climax.[8] I would argue that this is a *prelude* to how various figures will 'do things with oaths' in 1 Kings 1–2.[9] As mentioned, the oath in question is not presented at any point in the narrative hitherto; furthermore, David is not previously presented as speaking directly to Bathsheba, either before or after their marriage. In the biblical material of 2 Samuel, the king never speaks to this particular queen, and does not swear any oath. Nathan's strategy, therefore, may revolve around the psychology of *auto-suggestion*: he asks David 'did you not swear an oath…?' Such a question may cause the aged father to conclude that he must have. Nathan provides detailed instructions to Bathsheba, instructing her to speak such words to the king,

---

5. Walsh, *1 Kings*, p. 10: 'We hear only Nathan's part of the conversation, but it is enough to reveal his political agenda and his verbal deftness. His claim that Adonijah "has become" king is a double distortion: it changes Adonijah's words in verse 5 from the future to the past tense, transforming them from an innocent assertion into an act of treason; and it implies that Adonijah intends his feast at En-Rogel to be his inauguration as king.' The reader further notes that En-rogel is mentioned in 2 Sam. 17.17, and it is a place where the royal ambitions of Absalom take a turn for the worse. The topographical notice of En-rogel in 1 Kgs 1, therefore, may arouse a similar expectation.

6. Alter, *The Art of Biblical Narrative*, p. 98; Provan, *1 and 2 Kings*, p. 26.

7. See Savran, *Telling and Retelling*, p. 64, for an efficient summary of the 'quotation' issue.

8. Cf. Halpern, *David's Secret Demons*, p. 396: 'The text's most important silence concerns David's promise to Bathsheba: the text does not claim that he designated Solomon before Nathan and Bathsheba insist that he had sworn to do so… There is no assertion that Bathsheba and Nathan were telling the truth.' See also Exum, *Tragedy and Biblical Narrative*, p. 140: 'Although Bathsheba and Nathan claim David had promised the throne to Solomon, we have only their word for it; the text does not record such an important act on David's part'.

9. I am playfully appropriating the title of the important linguistic study of speech-act theory by J.L. Austin, *How to Do Things with Words* (Cambridge, MA: Harvard University Press, 1962).

and assures her that he will appear to 'fill up her words'. According to a basic principle in biblical narrative that is referred to as 'command and compliance', when one figure (usually a superior) gives another figure (often an underling) a set of instructions, a reader expects conformity to those instructions.[10] If there is any divergence or 'artistic enhancement', it should be duly noted, for it can be an important aspect of the narrative consecution. The reader may expect, therefore, that Bathsheba will 'comply' with Nathan's instructions.

2. *Oath 2: Bathsheba's 'Quotation' of David's (Supposed) Oath Regarding the Succession of her 'Issue', Solomon (1 Kings 1.17-18)*

Before Bathsheba speaks a word in this scene, 1.15 provides a dramatic tableau. As Bathsheba enters the inner chamber of King David, she is confronted with Abishag the Shunammite. Abishag is somewhat humorously described as 'ministering' (משרת) to the king, since the reader is fully aware that David has not been physically intimate with her. Bathsheba *herself*, therefore, provides a moment of contrast, a flashback to the days of David's virility, and an implicit reminder of the point where his career decisively changes (2 Sam. 11). The two women, who are understood to be *opponents* (in perhaps the same implicit vein as Bathsheba and Haggith), must perceive one another as Bathsheba enters the room. Brueggemann notes, 'the meeting is perhaps a grating one for Bathsheba, to see the virgin now occupying her place'.[11] The struggle for succession is foregrounded here in the royal chamber, and hence the narrative focus in 1.15 functions as a spatial setting and preface to the speech of Bathsheba.[12] If this is 'grating' to Bathsheba, then it

10. Walsh, *1 Kings*, p. xvi. For theoretical discussions of repetition in Biblical Hebrew prose, see Alter, *The Art of Biblical Narrative*, pp. 88-113; Sternberg, *The Poetics of Biblical Narrative*, pp. 365-436.

11. Brueggemann, *1 & 2 Kings*, p. 14. See also A. Bach, 'The Pleasure of her Text', in A. Brenner (ed.), *A Feminist Companion to Samuel and Kings* (A Feminist Companion to the Bible, 5; Sheffield: Sheffield Academic Press, 1994), pp. 106-28.

12. In terms of the *narrative perspective* of 1.15, Walsh (*1 Kings*, p. xvi) argues that Bathsheba's point of view is refracted here: 'A subtle signal that the narrator is showing us something from a character's point of view is when the narrator appears to repeat information he has already given to us. Since we already know about David's age (1.1) and Abishag's attendance on the king (1.4), the repetition of this information in 1.15 is meant to show us David's age and Abishag's presence at his side through the eyes of Bathsheba as she enters the king's chamber. The effects of manipulating the reader's point of view include evoking (or preventing) identification with or sympathy for a character, giving (or withholding) from the reader information available only to some characters or to the narrator, and endowing (or not) particular information or judgments with the authority of the narrator.'

might be reflected in the perceived tone of her speech, that as B.O. Long speculates, is perhaps forceful and harsh.[13] In light of Nathan's instructions above, the reader expects Bathsheba to go in and 'inquire' of the king: 'Did you not, my lord the king, swear an oath to your servant, saying: "Your son Solomon shall succeed me as king, and he shall sit on my throne"? Why then is Adonijah king?' Bathsheba's actual speech to David, however, contains rather different oath language:

> 'My lord, you yourself swore an oath by the LORD your God to your maidservant, "Surely Solomon your son will reign after me and he will sit upon my throne". But now, behold, Adonijah is reigning, and my lord the king you don't know!' (1 Kgs 1.17-18)

It is significant, as several scholars have pointed out, that Bathsheba transforms Nathan's question ('did you not swear…?') into an outright statement of fact ('*you yourself* swore an oath'), and also adds the crucial phrase 'by the LORD your God', presumably invoking the sacred name to add the highest degree of solemnity to the supposed oath. In my view, Bathsheba's 'mis-quotation' of Nathan's instruction lends support to the idea that the oath is suspicious. Not only does this buttress the notion that the oath is fabricated, but it enhances my previous contention that Bathsheba is 'creative' with quotations and oaths when necessary. This, I will suggest below, is an important component in the characterization of her son, Solomon: the son will manifest the attributes of the mother as the narrative continues.

Furthermore, when Nathan eventually enters the royal bedchamber, he makes no mention of this oath. Of course, Nathan has a history of arriving on the scene at major moments in David's life, so one may expect a momentous speech. The reader is entitled to think that Nathan, as he instructs Bathsheba, will extrapolate on the 'oath' sworn by David concerning Solomon. However, his strategy is rather different, as he addresses David in 1.24-25:

> 'O my lord the king, you must have said (אתה אמרת) "Adonijah shall be king after me, and he will sit on my throne". For he has gone down today and has sacrificed a multitude of oxen, fatlings and sheep, and summoned all the king's sons and captains of the army and Abiathar the priest, and behold (even now) they are eating and drinking before him, and they have said, "May King Adonijah live!"'

At least two problems arise here. First, Nathan 'quotes' the supposed direct speech of Adonijah's supporters, claiming '…they have said, "May King Adonijah live!"'[14] The dilemma is that Nathan's utterance is not a 'verifiable quotation', and since nowhere in the preceding narrative is such a speech uttered, the reader is inclined to suspect that Nathan has concocted

---

13. Long, *1 Kings*, p. 37.
14. See also Savran, *Telling and Retelling*, p. 65.

this quotation. This matter needs to be raised because it would indicate that Nathan is 'creative' with quotations, just as he may be 'creative' with the inquiry concerning the oath. Second, not only does Nathan avoid the so-called 'oath of Solomon', but he seems to imply that David has previously uttered another quasi-oath, to the effect that Adonijah is to be the king's successor.[15] Of course, the fact that the 'oath of Solomon' is not even mentioned surely casts a further air of skepticism around it; one would presume that if it were authentic, this would be a convenient moment for the prophet to remind the aged monarch.

3. *Oath 3: David's Oath Concerning Solomon, Which Includes a 'Self-Quotation' of his (Apparent) Earlier Oath (1 Kings 1.29-31)*

Nathan's discourse evidently produces its intended effect, since this elaborate scene continues as Bathsheba is called forth in 1.28: 'King David answered and said, "Summon Bathsheba to me". And she came before the king and she stood before the king.' It would seem plausible that Bathsheba's posture of 'standing' is an indication of her confidence before David and represents a moment of ascendancy over her rival Abishag.[16] Her confidence is well

---

15. On this point, note the interpretation offered by Lasine, *Knowing Kings*, p. 113: 'According to his own words, Nathan is the only personage in chapter 1 besides David who has not been informed of actions that allegedly involve Adonijah's accession to the throne. When he breaks in on Bathsheba's audience with the king, Nathan does not act as an informer making his king aware of a political danger. On the contrary, he speaks as though David knows everything and he, Nathan, knows nothing, because David has not informed *him*.'

16. DeVries (*1 Kings*, p. 15) observes Bathsheba's change in posture: she no longer bows low and prostrate as a supplicant before the sovereign, but stands. Some commentators have struggled with v. 28b ('And she came before the king and stood before the king'), and a number of critics have deleted part of it or modified it. Cogan helpfully summarizes the issue: 'Many find the second "before the king" tautologous (e.g. Gray: "an ugly repetition"); the versions show much variation and some translations follow LXX[BA], Vulg., "she stood before him" (e.g. NEB, NAB). Others concur with Montgomery and Gehman that "Semitic rhetoric is repetitive"' (Cogan, *I Kings*, p. 160, citing J. Gray, *I & II Kings* [OTL; Philadelphia: Westminster Press, 1963]; J.A. Montgomery and H.S. Gehman, *A Critical and Exegetical Commentary on the Books of Kings* [ICC; Edinburgh: T. & T. Clark, 1951]). I would suggest that this posture is very important to the *contest* with Abishag, and the repetition underscores the victory of Bathsheba: she is now the sole subject of the verb 'to stand' (עמד; cf. 1.2 and 15). As Walsh (*1 Kings*, p. 19) maintains, now Bathsheba 'is a summoned subject; she therefore does not bow but "stands before the king"—the standard Hebrew phrase for being at his service. Ironically, this was the position for which Abishag was sought'. Walsh (p. 19) continues, 'Bathsheba's implied victory over her beautiful rival foreshadows David's decision to support

placed, moreover, since David swears an oath (invoking the earlier oath he now claims to have sworn) just as Bathsheba suggests:

> And the king swore an oath, and he said, 'As the LORD lives who has ransomed my life from every disaster, surely just as I swore an oath to you by the LORD God of Israel, saying, "Surely Solomon your son will reign after me and he will sit upon my throne in place of me", thus I will surely do this day'. And Bathsheba bowed low, face to the ground, and she was prostrate to the king, and she said, 'May my lord King David live forever'. (1 Kgs 1.29-31)

Ultimately, whether David ever swore such an oath cannot be determined. The oath has incrementally gathered momentum as this narrative progresses, and Bathsheba emerges as one of the most important players in the succession of Solomon, if not the entire David story. The contours of the oath have been successively modified in several stages: it starts off as a question by Nathan, it is transformed into an emphatic statement by Bathsheba (with 'the LORD your God' added), and David himself further intensifies the oath language in 1.29-30. As Alter observes, the king's oath 'raises Bathsheba's language to still another level of politically efficacious resonance: Nathan had made no mention of the vow; Bathsheba had said "you...swore by the LORD your God"; David now encompasses the whole national realm in declaring, "as I swore to you by the LORD God of Israel"' (כאשר נשבעתי לך ביהוה אלהי ישראל)[17]. Bathsheba's role in this particular episode comes to a formal conclusion with her deferential language addressed to David—'May my lord King David live forever' (יחי אדני המלך דוד לעלם)—an ironic contrast to the alleged words of Adonijah's party who, according to Nathan's testimony in 1.25, merely say 'May King Adonijah live!' (יחי המלך אדניהו). This incidental detail, one might add, is yet another intriguing aspect of the collusion between Nathan and Bathsheba: it provides a fitting conclusion to her portrayal in this episode since it is *her* syntactic construction that ends up on David's lips. The triumph of this collusion is all the more extraordinary since neither Nathan nor Bathsheba seem to be in the king's chamber at the same time, but their words dovetail perfectly.[18] My argument here is that just as oaths (and the various suspicions aroused by them) are a major factor in

---

Solomon over the handsome Adonijah'. It would seem that Bathsheba's contest with Haggith parallels Solomon's contest with his antagonist, Adonijah: as Adonijah's hopes are fading, Solomon's star is rising.

17. Alter, *The David Story*, p. 369.

18. As Savran (*Telling and Retelling*, p. 107) concludes, 'we are left in doubt about the accuracy of David's memory and the degree to which he (and we) have been manipulated by Nathan and Bathsheba. In spite of the divine promise in 2 Sam. 7, one sees the extent to which human interests control the choice of the king. As David's power declines following Nathan's condemnation in 2 Sam. 12.7-14, it is fitting that Nathan figures strongly in the choice of his successor as well.'

Solomon's coronation, so the role of oaths continues to be prominent as he makes a series of moves to secure his throne.

4. *Oath 4: Adonijah's Request for an Oath of Amnesty and Solomon's Noncompliance (1 Kings 1.50-53)*

> Now Adonijah was afraid of Solomon's face, and he arose and went and clutched the horns of the altar. And it was reported to Solomon, 'Look! Adonijah is afraid of King Solomon, and behold, he has seized the horns of the altar, saying, "Let King Solomon swear an oath to me today that he will not put his servant to death with the sword"'. Solomon said, 'If he will be a man of worth, then not one of his hairs will fall to the earth. But if evil is found in him, then he will die.' And King Solomon sent, and they brought him down from the altar. And he came and he was prostrate before King Solomon, and Solomon said to him, 'Go to your house'. (1 Kgs 1.50-53)

In light of the fact that Solomon is crowned *instead of* Adonijah by means of some dubious work with oaths, it is surely ironic that Adonijah here asks for an 'oath', since it is precisely by this means that he has been outmaneuvered for the throne! Also, there is a structural irony in that Adonijah commences his career in 1 Kings 1 by 'lifting himself up' (נשא), and he ends this long chapter, rather ingloriously, by being 'brought down' (ירד).[19] By 'seizing the horns of the altar', perhaps Adonijah invokes the principle of Exod. 21.12, and hopes for clemency on the grounds of his brother's compassion.[20] The situation in the narrative is one of gunboat diplomacy: Adonijah clinging to the altar, Solomon sitting on his throne, with mediators sailing back and forth.

Jerome T. Walsh reflects on the nature of Adonijah's conduct: since the reader has 'not yet seen Solomon in action and knows very little about his

---

19. Cf. Long, *1 Kings*, p. 38. Long outlines a chiastic structure to the narrative: (A) Adonijah's aggrandizement (B) Appeals to David (C) David's oath (B′) Actions leading to coronation (A′) Adonijah's fall.

20. See Cogan, *1 Kings*, p. 164: 'Asylum at YHWH's altar was the accepted procedure by which a person suspected of manslaughter might save his life (until trial?; cf. Exod. 21.14). The law of the cities of refuge offered permanent asylum; cf. Deut. 19.1-10. In Adonijah's case, the altar offered him political asylum.' For background on the 'horns of the altar', see G.H. Jones, *1 and 2 Kings*. I. *1 Kings 1–16:34* (NCBC; Grand Rapids: Eerdmans, 1984), p. 105: 'Because they were used to sprinkle blood, the horns were exceptionally sacred (cf. Am. 3.14)'. In terms of the mechanics of the oath-language, see Gray, *I & II Kings*, p. 94: '"To swear" in Hebrew means "to lay oneself under seven (oaths)". Note the expression of a negative in Hebrew after the oath formula, expressed or understood, lit. "if he slays", which is actually affirmative, the phrase being the protasis of a conditional sentence, the apodosis understood, and often expressed, being "So may Yahweh do to me and more also..." Conversely, a strong asseverative is expressed by the apodosis in the negative.'

12. *The Swearing Issue*   161

character; Adonijah presumably knows him better than we do. Is Adonijah's fear of bloody reprisals from Solomon an accurate reading of Solomon's character? Or is it perhaps a projection of how Adonijah himself would have acted had he been victorious?'[21] Further, when Adonijah asks his younger brother for an oath of amnesty, a reader may ask if this is 'naïve complacency', or wonder if Adonijah has more sinister motives? After all, such traits may well be manifested again in Adonijah, and this is not the last occasion where he will present a request to 'King Solomon' (see 1 Kgs 2.17).

Meanwhile, this scene features the inaugural direct speech of Solomon. According to another basic principle of Hebrew narrative, often a character's first words can provide a defining moment of characterization.[22] Solomon's response to Adonijah, as several assiduous commentators have pointed out, is legally evasive. While on the surface Solomon appears to comply with Adonijah's request, 'he does not swear an oath, and the amnesty he grants is conditional rather than absolute. Moreover, the conditions are couched in vague generalities that offer Adonijah nothing in the way of real security.'[23] Solomon states clearly enough that if 'evil' is found in Adonijah, he will die; but 'who defines "wickedness", and who will do the finding? The answer is clear: Solomon will decide, as and when he wishes, whether the conditions have been fulfilled.'[24]

A multitude of questions present themselves about Solomon and his character at the end of 1 Kings 1. How is Solomon presented, on the whole, in this episode? Is it positive, negative, or are there gaps and ambiguities that are not fully resolved at this early point in the narrative? What should readers expect in the future? What kind of king is Solomon going to be? Should a reader be surprised to encounter the 'fall' of Solomon in 1 Kings 11, ostensibly because of a divided heart? Burke Long's discussion merits careful reflection. Despite Solomon's apparent passivity before he is crowned, after the ceremony the fledgling monarch 'emerges as a presence in his own right. He is decisive, aloof, somewhat noncommittal, very cautious.'[25] Solomon's dealings with his older brother Adonijah are especially intriguing. 'The narrator offers no comment, as though we are meant to suppose the reconciliation were less than total, or the wound between brothers not quite, or perhaps never to be, healed. In this moment of understatement, one feels that the narrative finds a resting point, but the matter is not at its end.'[26]

---

21. Walsh, *1 Kings*, p. 31.
22. Alter, *The David Story*, p. 105.
23. Walsh, *1 Kings*, p. 32.
24. Walsh, *1 Kings*, p. 32.
25. Long, *1 Kings*, p. 39.
26. Long, *1 Kings*, p. 39.

On balance, 1 Kings 1 is a narrative that looks backward and forward. 'The story is about Solomon becoming king, but also about a darkness between brothers that we have heard before (2 Sam. 13–14), and about a grasping for the throne that we have known before (2 Sam. 15–18).'[27] Long convincingly outlines these numerous connections with preceding themes and events. I would add that the narrative also looks forward, especially in light of the fact that oaths (and their various modifications) are such a prominent feature of 1 Kings 2 (e.g. vv. 8, 11, 43). Adonijah's 'request for an oath' thus functions as something of a pivot for the various oaths which envelope Solomon's *character zone*. Given the frequency of oaths (ambivalent or otherwise) in 1 Kings 1 (vv. 13, 17, 51), and pre-eminently the doubt surrounding David's recollection of his otherwise dormant oath concerning the succession (1 Kgs 1.29-30: 'Then the king swore an oath, "As the LORD lives, who has delivered me from all adversity, just as I swore an oath to you by the LORD God of Israel, that your son Solomon should be king after me and take my place on my throne, so I shall bring it about this very day"'), it turns out that equivocal oaths are a hallmark of Solomon's early reign. This pattern continues as the narrative unfolds.

5. *Oath 5: David's 'Self-Quotation' of his Oath concerning Shimei to Solomon (1 Kings 2.8-9)*

The context of this scene is David's deathbed instructions to Solomon. The instructions themselves are a mixed bag, as one scholar explains: 'David's speech has long troubled commentators. It is an uneasy combination of religious platitudes and unscrupulous violence. The juxtaposition of verses 2-4 and 5-9 is jarring, and many scholars have suggested that verses 2-4 are an insertion by a later deuteronomistic editor.'[28] By any measure, the speech readily divides in two halves: the speech opens with a 'Deuteronomic' theological injunction to 'keep the charge of the LORD your God' (-את ושמרת משמרת יהוה אלהיך), while the second part outlines practical and political problems with individuals that Solomon needs to address.

Without eschewing the assured results of source-critical analysis, there are some other issues besides 'deuteronomistic' additions that are at stake here; specifically: How does this speech integrate with what has come before in the narrative, and what is to come? In the first instance, consider David's comments on the divine word of promise. He implores Solomon carefully to adhere to the Torah, and in so doing guarantee success, as in 2.4, 'Then the LORD will establish his word that he spoke concerning me: "If your heirs

---

27. Long, *1 Kings*, p. 40.
28. Walsh, *1 Kings*, p. 37.

take heed to their way, to walk before me in faithfulness with all their heart and with all their soul, there shall not fail you a successor on the throne of Israel"'. A host of commentators point to 2 Samuel 7 as the 'source' of this quotation, which is surely the most natural intertext.[29] The only difficulty, however, is that the exact wording of this 'quotation' of direct divine speech is not found in 2 Samuel 7. While the oracle delivered by Nathan certainly contains promise, it does so in *unconditional terms*, whereas David's 'quote' to Solomon is laced with *conditional language*.[30] Since David's changes to the wording of the divine promise may be perceived as minimal, some would demur that such changes are inconsequential, or the fault of a clumsy redactor. However, I would prefer to argue that this very act provides a reflex back to his 'recollection' of the earlier oath in 1.29-30, and anticipates his 'selective memory' in what follows (that is, in the second part of the speech). It must be stressed that if David is open to playing fast and loose with divine quotations, how will he treat his own 'words from the past' when he quotes *himself* in the Shimei affair? This is precisely the issue in the second part of the speech, as attention turns to pressing matters of settling old scores. After discussing the respective cases of Joab (Solomon is told to 'use wisdom') and Barzillai ('let them be among those who eat at your table'), attention turns to Shimei:

> Behold, there is also with you Shimei son of Gera the Benjaminite from Bahurim, the one who cursed me with a sickening curse on the day I walked to Mahanaim. Now, he came down to meet me at the Jordan and I swore to him by the LORD, saying, 'I will not cause you to die by the sword'. But now do not reckon him innocent, for you are a wise man and you know what you should do to him, and you will bring down his gray head in blood to Sheol. (1 Kgs 2.8-9)

The king's discourse here clearly presupposes and refers to the background episodes of Shimei in 2 Sam. 16.5-14 (where he curses while hurling

---

29. See J.G. McConville, 'The Old Testament Historical Books in Modern Scholarship', *Themelios* 22.3 (1997), pp. 3-13 (9); cf. Knoppers, *Two Nations Under God*, pp. 70-71.

30. According to Walsh (*1 Kings*, p. 39) the divine word 'of which David speaks is not found elsewhere in these exact terms, but the reference is almost certainly to Yahweh's promise to David in 2 Samuel 7.12-16'. Walsh further notes that Nathan's oracle has no mention of a condition. See further the discussions of W.M. Schniedewind, *Society and the Promise to David: The Reception History of 2 Samuel 7.1-17* (New York: Oxford University Press, 1999), pp. 28-39; D. Vanderhooft, 'Dwelling beneath the Sacred Place: A Proposal for Reading 2 Samuel 7.10', *JBL* 118 (1999), pp. 625-33; D.F. Murray, *Divine Prerogative and Royal Pretension: Pragmatics, Poetics and Polemics in a Narrative Sequence about David (2 Samuel 5.17–7.29)* (JSOTSup, 264; Sheffield: Sheffield Academic Press, 1998). Note Exum's discussion (*Tragedy and Biblical Narrative*, p. 141) of the 'changing' affirmation between 2 Sam. 7 and David's expression in 1 Kgs 2.

rocks) and 19.18-23 (where he apologizes while falling prostrate).³¹ In response to this humble repentance of Shimei and the grossly *impolitic* cries of Abishai for death of the offender, David replies in 2 Sam. 19.23-24, '"What have I to do with you, you sons of Zeruiah, that you should today become an adversary to me?"... The king said to Shimei, "You shall not die". And the king swore an oath to him (וישבע לו המלך).' In his Anchor Bible volume, Mordechai Cogan appears to be far more alert to the intricacies of David's imperial hermeneutic than the genetically vicious Abishai. Cogan mentions in passing the possibility that David's rhetorical question ('Shall anyone be put to death in Israel today?') may have had something to do with the fact that Shimei is accompanied by one thousand of his Benjaminite colleagues.³² If such a hypothesis has even a fraction of plausibility (which, one guesses, it does), then David's 'famous last words' in 1 Kgs 2.8-9 should be read accordingly. Martin J. Mulder, for instance, thinks that David's stress on 'today' has a shifty nuance that points to a future revision of this policy: 'What is striking is that in the preceding verse the sons of Zeruiah, who wanted to kill Shimei on the spot, are told twice that *today* (היום) this was David's decision, a subtle way of alluding to "a delayed execution" (cf. also vs. 21)'.³³

J.P. Fokkelman is convinced that David's stress on 'place names' anticipates the 'topographical aspects' of Solomon's measure in the sequel— 'Shimei will be cut off from his place and tribal area', so clearly David's use of place names is political: Shimei is dangerous *because of* these geographical vicinities.³⁴ Iain Provan questions not only David's reminiscences about the Shimei affair, but also David's recasting of his oath.³⁵ Similarly, consider Walsh's assessment:

> David's account of his dealings with Shimei is selective. He leaves out his earlier assertion that Shimei cursed him at Yahweh's bidding; he leaves out Shimei's apology; and he leaves out the thousand Benjaminites whose presence compromised the freedom and sincerity of the royal pardon. In this way he portrays Shimei's crime of *lèse majesté* in the worst possible light, and his own leniency in the best. Even more deceptive is the way David rewords his oath. His promise to Shimei in 2 Samuel 19.23 was without loopholes: 'You shall not die'. When he recounts this to Solomon, he rephrases it to 'I shall not put you to death by the sword', leaving open the possibility that someone else, such as Solomon, could do so, or even that David himself could do so by

---

31. Cf. R. Polzin, 'Curses and Kings: A New Reading of 2 Samuel 15–16', in Exum and Clines (eds.), *The New Literary Criticism*, pp. 201-26.
32. Cogan, *I Kings*, p. 174.
33. Mulder, *1 Kings*, p. 101.
34. Fokkelman, *King David*, p. 389.
35. Provan, 'Why Barzillai of Gilead (1 Kings 2.7)?'

some other means. David's instruction for dealing with Shimei is as roundabout as his directive about Joab and uses very similar language. Solomon is to use his wisdom again, and Shimei is to die a bloody death.[36]

There are a number of important issues that arise here for Solomon's unfolding characterization. In the first instance, this deathbed scene adds to the rather malodorous fog that has clouded the use of oaths to this point in 1 Kings. The irony of the final words of David to his son is palpable: Solomon mounts the throne of Israel due to David's recollection of an earlier oath; now he is instructed to circumvent a bothersome oath 'through wisdom'. Further, this seems to set the tone for Solomon's use of oath(s) with Shimei, and foreshadows much of what Solomon will do in the sequel to this episode as 1 Kings 2 proceeds. David's instruction seems to provide Solomon with the necessary license to be liberal with oaths. As DeVries observes, the king's 'static formula leaves plenty of room for maneuvering; the killing may be done by some other means, or some other person may do it'.[37] It is striking that David is arguably manipulated by an oath earlier in 1 Kings; now *he* does the manipulating with respect to an oath! In contrast to commentators who accuse the king of senility in 1 Kings 1, David certainly seems in full control of some of his faculties as he outlines his orders for the elimination of various rivals.[38]

Considerable scholarly energy has been expended in classifying various layers of redaction, sifting what is original from what is deuteronomistic elaboration. No doubt this is diachronically helpful in its own way, but what should not be overlooked is the role of this speech for the narrative presentation of Solomon. There appears to be, one could infer, a measure of continuity between David's characterization, and the gradually unfolding portrait of Solomon. Notwithstanding the reputed 'deuteronomistic coloring of some verses' that so many commentators digress on at length,[39] there may be a more subtle aspect of characterization here, as Solomon receives a strong

---

36. Walsh, *1 Kings*, p. 42. Cf. Savran, *Telling and Retelling*, p. 80: 'At the very end of David's life, in his final speech to Solomon in 1 Kg. 2.2-9, he instructs his son how to consolidate his power and settle some old scores at the same time. When, in 2.8, he quotes his oath of clemency to Shimei ben Gera (2 Sam. 19.24), he changes the emphasis from a general promise—[לֹא תָמוּת] (You will not die)—to a more specific limitation on David's personal behavior—(*I* will not put you to death by the sword) [אִם־אֲמִיתְךָ בֶּחָרֶב]. The implication is that once David is dead, Solomon will be free to act against Shimei.'

37. DeVries, *1 Kings*, p. 36.

38. On David's 'sound mind', see P.R. House, *1, 2 Kings* (New American Commentary, 8; Nashville: Broadman & Holman, 1995), pp. 88-89, 93. Cf. Provan, *1 & 2 Kings*, p. 26.

39. See the discussion in Mulder, *1 Kings*, p. 86. Cf. S. Isser, *The Sword of Goliath: David in Heroic Literature* (Atlanta: Society of Biblical Literature, 2003), p. 167.

prompt from his father to 'do things with oaths'. One could almost argue that David is encouraging Solomon to adopt a 'deconstructive' stance toward any inconvenient oath; that is, read 'between the lines' and against the grain, looking for fissures in the 'text' that will 'divide it against itself'.[40] As Walsh reflects on the developing characterization of Solomon, he suggests that the new sovereign

> is always attentive to the niceties of legal observance, yet he is not above twisting evidence, and, if need be, falsifying it in order to gain what he wants. The ambivalence in David's speech between pious obedience to the law and ruthless expediency aptly foreshadows the ambiguity we will find in the narrator's characterization of Solomon.[41]

I certainly agree that Solomon becomes an increasingly ambiguous character as this narrative sequence continues to unfold. Building on Walsh's observation, my contention is that Solomon's indifference toward oaths is a key component of the writer's strategy in the opening chapters of 1 Kings.

6. *Oath 6: Solomon's Vitriolic and Oath-laden Reaction to Adonijah's Bridal Request (through Bathsheba) for Abishag (1 Kings 2.23-25)*

When Adonijah submits his solicitation in 1 Kgs 1.51-53, he unsuccessfully attempts to procure an oath of amnesty from his brother Solomon. Instead of the requested oath, Adonijah merely receives an imperative from the newly crowned king, 'Go to your house' (לך לביתך), a domicile that is presumably located outside the boundaries of the royal palace. In his next (and final) scene of the narrative, Adonijah presents a request for Abishag to be given to him as a wife. It is not insignificant that he initially approaches Bathsheba, the new queen mother, with his petition.[42] Adonijah's initiative in approaching Bathsheba certainly reminds one of Nathan's actions in the previous chapter. In this scene, Adonijah is asking Bathsheba to mediate his request, and commentators proffer a number of opinions on the precise motives of both Adonijah's request for Abishag and his request of Bathsheba for

---

40. Miscall, *1 Samuel*, pp. xx-xxv. Cf. the theoretical discussion of D.N. Fewell, 'Deconstructive Criticism: Achsah and the (E)razed City of Writing', in G.A Yee (ed.), *Judges and Method: New Approaches in Biblical Studies* (Minneapolis: Fortress Press, 1995), pp. 119-45.

41. Walsh, *1 Kings*, p. 38.

42. Scholars are divided over Adonijah's *motives* in asking for Abishag as a wife: is it a step closer to the throne (as Solomon declares), or a simple request for a lovely bride? The emphasis in my analysis is that Adonijah's motives are not the central issue that is foregrounded here; rather, it is the king's interpretation that matters, and the fact that Solomon chooses to view this request as a (tacit) claim to the throne.

assistance.⁴³ I would contend that the dialogue between Bathsheba and Adonijah anticipates both the larger storyline of 1 Kings 2 and the resolution of this particular scene.

After his long assertion about the great expectations surrounding his bid for the kingdom and the subsequent deflation of those hopes, Adonijah then presents his request for Abishag the Shunammite. Bathsheba's response is telling: 'Good (טוב), I will speak about you (עליך) to the king'. On the surface, it is difficult to ascertain exactly what Bathsheba's affirmation 'good' (טוב) means in the context of the dialogue. At this point, Eric Siebert's analysis is instructive:

> Does Bathsheba think that Abishag will make a nice bride for Adonijah or does she think the request is 'good' since she knows it will give Solomon the pretext he needs to be rid of his older brother once and for all? DeVries recognizes this as 'another of our narrator's enigmatic touches, hinting that Bathsheba's seeming good-natured compliance may have disguised her design to get rid of Adonijah'.⁴⁴

Siebert further notes the irony surrounding the preposition על, as Bathsheba claims that she will 'speak about you (עליך) to the king'. Since this preposition can often be translated in an adversative sense ('I will speak *against* you'), the reader is left wonder 'whether Bathsheba intended to speak for or against Adonijah'.⁴⁵ This ambiguous language serves to foreshadow the resolution of this affair, as Bathsheba's equivocation is a preview of the license that Solomon will take when presented with the request.

As this episode in 1 Kgs 2.13-25 moves toward a climax, Bathsheba's role as the mediator of Adonijah's request is of particular interest, since there are parallels to the earlier scene with Nathan. When transmitting Adonijah's request to Solomon, Bathsheba makes one minor alteration: 'She said, "A

---

43. Cf. the summary of Seow, '1 & 2 Kings', pp. 32-33: 'The narrator leaves many questions unanswered in this story. Is Adonijah a hopeless "romantic", who naively believes that Abishag is legitimately available to him because her relationship with David was never consummated? Or has he really been exposed as a desperate and deceitful manipulator, trying to use two women (Abishag and Bathsheba) to achieve his political ambition? Is Adonijah's concession of defeat (v. 15b) merely a sinister ploy verbalized only to get what he really wants? Or does his action reflect a genuine, if bitter, recognition that the kingdom is truly beyond him now and only a consolation prize is possible? Is Bathsheba merely a nice old woman who is easily manipulated? Or is she coldly calculating and shrewder than she seems at first blush? Does she, in fact, know her son so well that she could anticipate his reaction and the dire consequences for Adonijah and, possibly, also for young and lovely Abishag?'

44. E.A. Seibert, 'Propaganda and Subversion in the Solomonic Narrative: Scribes, Historiography, and the Rhetoric of Persuasion' (PhD dissertation, Drew University, 2002), p. 150, citing DeVries, *1 Kings*, p. 37.

45. Seibert, 'Propaganda and Subversion in the Solomonic Narrative', p. 150.

request, a small one (אחת קטנה), I am making of you. Do not refuse me"' (2.20). As Alter observes, this is far from an innocuous mode of delivery: 'In accordance with the established convention of biblical narrative, she uses the very same words Adonijah has spoken to her, adding only the adjective 'small'. This is just a tiny request, she appears to say, full knowing that Solomon is likely to see it, on the contrary, as a huge thing—a device that could be turned into a ladder to the throne on which Solomon sits'.[46] Granted, Bathsheba's change in the wording is a 'small' one, but it serves to reinforce her subtle use of language—perhaps further drawing attention to the idea that the 'oath of Solomon' in 1 Kings 1 is contrived—and continues her characterization as a shrewd player in the royal court.[47] Although the portrait of Bathsheba in this scene is open to divergent readings, in light of the previous episode (1 Kgs 1.11-21) the balance would shift toward a more calculating figure.[48] Moreover, when Bathsheba delivers her report to Solomon, he responds with ballistic fury, taking this 'argumentation as proof of Adonijah's refusal to relinquish his pretensions to the throne'.[49] The crescendo of Solomon's imprecatory speech contains uncommon oath language:

> Then King Solomon swore an oath by the LORD, 'So may God do to me, and more also, for Adonijah has spoken this word against his own life! Now therefore as the LORD lives, who has established me and placed me on the throne of my father David, and who has made me a house as he promised, today Adonijah shall be put to death.' So King Solomon sent Benaiah son of Jehoiada; he struck him down, and he died. (1 Kgs 2.23-25)

In contrast to the cloud of ambiguity that envelops the purported oath by which Solomon is installed on the throne of Israel, there is no questioning this oath that he swears to Adonijah, replete with the divine name. Indeed,

---

46. Alter, *The David Story*, p. 379.

47. Contrast Whybray, *The Succession Narrative*, p. 40: 'We thus have a consistent and thoroughly credible picture of Bathsheba as a good-natured, rather stupid woman who was a natural prey both to more passionate and to cleverer men'. For a recent and compelling study of Bathsheba as a more 'round' character, see Aschkenasy, *Woman at the Window*, pp. 109-17.

48. Walsh, *1 Kings*, p. 54: 'The character of Bathsheba in the episode, then, like that of Adonijah, is open to very divergent readings. She may be exactly what she appears to be: a woman trying to reconcile estranged brothers by arranging a marriage. Against this reading is the difficulty of harmonizing such a Bathsheba with the shrewd conniver of chapter 1. Or she may be knowingly and gleefully bringing her son what he wants most: an excuse for disposing of a dangerous rival. The narrator leaves us free to choose.' The imaginative dimension of Bathsheba's characterization is attested in a range of studies, including: Exum, *Fragmented Women*, pp. 198-200; G.G. Nicol, 'The Alleged Rape of Bathsheba: Some Observations on Ambiguity in Biblical Narrative', *JSOT* 73 (1997), pp. 43-54; Klein, 'Bathsheba Revealed'.

49. Fokkelman, *King David*, p. 396.

Walsh labels it a rare 'double oath', and Fokkelman describes it as follows: 'Solomon first enunciates the negative formula of self-cursing (v. 23b) plus its content and then repeats it all ponderously with the positive oath formula of v. 24ab plus content. In commemorating God's most recent deeds in the second instance, Solomon once more links the necessity of Adonijah's execution with his own succession.'[50] The irony of Adonijah's situation is not lost on the reader: Adonijah does not receive an oath of reprieve from his younger brother when he asks for it in 1 Kgs 1.51, yet now he gets a 'double oath' when asking for Abishag. If Solomon is hesitant to swear an oath to Adonijah previously, he is suddenly very loquacious with oath language here. This naturally has implications for Solomon's characterization. Brueggemann notes, 'Solomon's speech in v. 24 voices, for the first time, his claim that he is king by Yahweh's action. And since Adonijah has not only threatened Solomon but has failed to accept Yahweh's will, he must die. The self-righteous, self-serving decree of vv. 23-24 is promptly enacted (2.25).'[51] Moreover, this would illustrate that in his unwillingness to swear an oath earlier to Adonijah, Solomon may well be awaiting the opportune moment to seal his older brother's fate. In other words, these oaths (and the lack thereof in 1 Kgs 1.51-53) seem to indicate that Solomon is plotting Adonijah's downfall at the outset of his reign, despite his reassuring words, 'If he proves to be a worthy man, not one of his hairs shall fall to the ground'.[52]

7. Oath 7: Circumlocutions around David's Awkward Oath to Shimei, and the Resolution of This 'Cursed' Affair (1 Kings 2.42-43)

After the successive banishment of Abiathar and liquidation of Joab in 1 Kgs 2.26-35, the narrative returns to the Shimei affair, concerning whom David claims to have sworn an oath—'You will not die by the sword'—in 1 Kgs 2.8. Solomon, though, is instructed by David to 'use his wisdom' with

---

50. Fokkelman, *King David*, p. 397; cf. Walsh, *1 Kings*, p. 53.
51. Brueggemann, *1 & 2 Kings*, p. 34. Cf. Gunn, *The Story of King David*, p. 106: 'Just as David clothed his deceitful involvement in Uriah's death with public expressions of righteous indignation at the manner of his death, so now we see his son putting a public face on the forthcoming murder, with highsounding phrases of moral rectitude'.
52. This reminds one of David's earlier oath concerning a son, ironically Absalom whom Adonijah is later compared with. A number of scholars note that this oath is 'literally fulfilled' as Absalom is suspended between heaven and earth! The uncanniness of this connection, then, is that three brothers and David the father are momentarily connected by this oath. S.W. Hahn argues that events such as 'oaths' of this magnitude are part of a larger 'theo-drama' that spans the Hebrew Bible and the New Testament (see S.W. Hahn, 'Kinship by Covenant: A Biblical Theological Analysis of Covenant Types and Texts in the Old and New Testaments' [PhD dissertation, Marquette University, 1995]).

respect to this oath, and the denouement of this sordid business is now at hand. Solomon tells Shimei in 2.36-37: 'Build yourself a house in Jerusalem, and live there, and do not go out from there to any place whatsoever. For on the day you go out, and cross the Wadi Kidron, know for certain that you shall die; your blood shall be on your own head.' Shimei's response then follows, 'The sentence is fair; as my lord the king has said, so will your servant do'. There is an absence, the reader notices, of any oath language here. A grave complication arises, however, when Shimei journeys westward to Gath to search for two runaway servants.

> When Solomon was told that Shimei had gone from Jerusalem to Gath and returned, the king sent and summoned Shimei, and said to him, 'Did I not make you swear an oath by the LORD, and solemnly adjure you, saying, "Know for certain that on the day you go out and go to any place whatever, you shall die"? And you said to me, "The sentence is fair; I accept". Why then have you not kept your oath to the LORD and the commandment with which I charged you?' The king also said to Shimei, 'You know in your own heart all the evil that you did to my father David; so the LORD will bring back your evil on your own head. But King Solomon shall be blessed, and the throne of David shall be established before the LORD forever.' Then the king commanded Benaiah son of Jehoiada; and he went out and struck him down, and he died. So the kingdom was established in the hand of Solomon. (1 Kgs 2.41-46)

'There is no suggestion in the narrative', as Brueggemann observes, 'that Shimei's departure from Jerusalem was anything but innocent. There is no hint that he was engaged in subversion against the king. More likely, he was compelled, as we often are, by economic risk, in this case the loss of slaves.'[53] Solomon's instructions are 'do not cross the Kidron Valley', that is, 'do not go east'. In the event, Shimei goes west to Gath, and the king launches his strike. DeVries is surely correct when he notes: 'Here we clearly see that Shimei's transgression of his parole is only the pretext by which Solomon shall carry out his father's order in vv 8-9'.[54] Furthermore, a number of commentators have observed that Solomon further changes his earlier ruling. In 2.37 the king says: 'For on the day you go out, and cross the Wadi Kidron, know for certain that you shall die'; yet in 2.42 he 'quotes himself' as having said: 'Did I not make you swear an oath by the LORD, and solemnly adjure you [הלוא השבעתיך ביהוה ואעד בך], saying, "Know for certain that on the day you go out and go to any place whatever, you shall die"? And you said to me, "The sentence is fair; I will obey".' In the midst of these various modifications there is some wry humor for the reader (but not, in all likelihood, for Shimei) in the royal rephrasing of the Benjaminite's

---

53. Brueggemann, *1 & 2 Kings*, p. 36.
54. DeVries, *1 Kings*, p. 33.

pledge: when Solomon puts the words 'I will obey' (שמעתי) in Shimei's mouth, it is a word-play on his name (שמעי).[55]

It is all the more intriguing that Solomon's language is so full of 'swearing' when he and Shimei are again face-to-face. Twice he refers to 'an oath' *that is not recorded in narrative*, that is, in 2.42 when the king says ('Did I not make you swear by the LORD'), and 2.43 ('Why then have you not kept your oath to the LORD'). Walsh's appraisal merits reflection:

> Solomon claims that he made Shimei swear by Yahweh. If this were true, Shimei would be guilty not only of disobeying Solomon's order but of violating a sacred oath as well—a serious crime in itself. But there is no evidence in the earlier dialogue that Shimei bound himself by oath to obey the king. He agreed to do the king's bidding, but without any oath formula or invocation of the divine name.[56]

Further, Joel Rosenberg regards the circumstances surrounding Shimei's demise as having a foul fragrance:

> The details of I Kgs 2.36-46, especially 39-41, suggest that Shimei's violation of the ban on his activities was rigged: anonymous informants guide Shimei, in search of his runaway slaves, to a spot, the Philistine town of Gath, where the local royalty has had a long-standing relationship to Jerusalem, and where other anonymous informants spot Shimei's illegal presence and report it to Solomon.[57]

At this important narrative juncture—the end of David's long reign and the outset of the new era of Solomon's kingdom—why does the Deuteronomist characterize Solomon in this manner? Why is this literary strategy used? By any measure, in light of this indifferent demeanor with regard to oaths, the reader will not be altogether surprised when Solomon makes a marriage alliance with the king of Egypt in 1 Kgs 3.1 ('And Solomon made himself a son-in-law with Pharaoh', ויתחתן שלמה את־פרעה), and his later amassing of gold and imported horses (1 Kgs 10.14, 26-28) in contravention of the Deuteronomic code (see Deut. 17.16-17).[58] Regardless of whether one completely agrees with the suggestion about the 'rigged' nature of Shimei's liquidation, Rosenberg has to be commended for pointing out minute details in the language of the story: by means of the very architecture of the narrative, the

---

55. See Garsiel, 'Puns upon Names as a Literary Device in 1 Kings 1–2', p. 385. Cf. Fokkelman, *King David*, p. 406.
56. Walsh, *1 Kings*, pp. 62-63.
57. Rosenberg, *King and Kin*, p. 187.
58. Cf. J.G. McConville, *Deuteronomy* (Apollos Old Testament Commentary, 5; Downers Grove, IL: InterVarsity Press, 2002), pp. 294-95. See further G.N. Knoppers, 'The Deuteronomist and the Deuteronomic Law of the King: A Reexamination of a Relationship', *ZAW* 108 (1996), pp. 329-46.

reader is confronted with what amounts to a subtle narrative indictment of the new king's conduct.[59]

In his earlier deathbed speech, David advises Solomon to 'use wisdom' in dealing with the rather awkward oath of Shimei—as one might paraphrase it, David commissions Solomon to deploy his forensic imagination and find a 'legal loophole'.[60] This is precisely what Solomon does: he circumvents the oath David swore to Shimei by means of the ingenious use of another oath! Thus, the father's execution order is carried out.[61] During the speech of 1 Kgs 2.2-9, David seems to appeal to Solomon as a 'faithful son'; the resolution of the Shimei affair, however ghastly, serves to illustrate that Solomon has the capacity for obedience to the commands of a superior. This is striking contrast to the later disobedience for which Solomon is condemned in 1 Kings 11, although the one is obviously a corollary of the other in light of the larger narrative. Finally, as Brueggemann observes: 'It may be worth noting that Solomon's phrase, "the Lord will bring back your evil" (2.44), is closely paralleled to David's earlier statement, "The Lord will repay me with good" (2 Sam. 16.12)'.[62] Based on this shared language, Brueggemann concludes: 'The verbs "bring back/repay" both attest that the outcome is not a human determination, but is an enactment of God's governance. Moreover, as in v. 33 when Joab's condemnation is matched by a dynastic affirmation, so here Shimei's condemnation is matched by another sweeping dynastic affirmation (2.45).'[63]

---

59. Although commenting on 1 Kgs 3, contrast the position of Cogan, *1 Kings*, p. 189: 'Some recent commentators have suggested that even in 3.1-3, Dtr characterizes Solomon as bearing "the seeds of his own destruction", in his alliance with Egypt and his order of priorities, completing his own house before the Temple (Provan, 44-46; see also Walsh 70, 85). Such readings, however, may be over-reading, inasmuch as Dtr describes Solomon, and only him of the kings of the Davidic dynasty, as "loving YHWH" (v. 3), so that his marriage to the Egyptian princess and his sacrifice outside Jerusalem are both understood and excused. Together they serve as the counter to the decadence of the king's later years.'

60. Alter, *The David Story*, p. 376. Cf. Nelson's summary (*First and Second Kings*, p. 28) of the Shimei affair and his view of Solomon's wisdom: 'The narrator may intend the reader to realize that Solomon had a political motive for keeping Shimei on the Jerusalem side of the Kidron (v. 37) away from his pro-Saul kinfolk in nearby Bahurim (v. 8). Yet Shimei's violation occurs in the opposite direction and for an innocent reason. There is no political danger in his action. He transgresses only the letter (v. 37), not the spirit, of the prohibition. Solomon is a "wise man" (v. 9), however, and takes this as an opportunity to eliminate Shimei's "grievous curse" (v. 8).'

61. For a recent study of the David story as a broader cultural intertext, see W.H.U. Anderson, 'David as a Biblical "Goodfella" and "The Godfather": Cultural-Social Analogies with Monarchy and *La Cosa Nostra*', *SJOT* 18 (2004), pp. 60-76.

62. Brueggemann, *1 & 2 Kings*, p. 36.

63. Brueggemann, *1 & 2 Kings*, p. 36.

8. Conclusions

This chapter has endeavored to explore some literary implications of the language of oaths that abound in the opening chapters of 1 Kings. I will now conclude by suggesting three ways in which such *swearing* provides something of an index to the characterization of Solomon that is beginning to unfold in this highly intricate narrative.

The atmosphere of equivocal language that accompanies Solomon to the throne of Israel actually serves to complicate the lofty royal claims he often proffers (e.g. to Adonijah in 1 Kgs 2.24; to Joab in 2.33; and to Shimei in 2.45). The problem with equivocal language and oaths, in these various scenes, is that they tend to destabilize the accession of Solomon in the reader's mind rather than build it up, as the new king claims to his miscellaneous captive audiences. Of course the same reader may well conclude that there is a hidden providence at work here, just as when Jacob secures the blessing through rather furtive means in Genesis 27, as I have previously argued.[64] But here my point is that the dubious oaths actually serve to undermine Solomon's own utterances about divine election, and render problematic his own rhetorical claims. Lyle Eslinger has argued that the later speeches of Solomon need to be heard in light of the larger story, and I would suggest that the manner in which Solomon treats 'oath-language' would enhance this contention.[65] In his *Theology of the Old Testament*, Walter Brueggemann states 'Solomon is devastatingly critiqued as a king who proceeded autonomously'; consequently, this narrative stretch may function as a built-in piece of judgment against Solomon as one who uses insincere oaths (see Lev. 5.4).[66] J.P. Fokkelman mentions the 'sinister undertone' which accompanies the first mention of Solomon and 'wisdom' surely enhanced by Solomon's deployment of oaths.[67] Hugh Pyper has expressed that there 'has been remarkably little discussion of the oath forms of the Old Testament and what there has been concentrates...on philology and com-

---

64. Reflecting on some of the sordid details of the early chapters of 1 Kings, Seow ('1 & 2 Kings', p. 23) reflects: 'Yet there is a subtle, even subliminal, message throughout the story. Quietly conveyed in this very entertaining story is a conviction that the will of God is somehow being worked out behind all the scandals and human schemes.' Seow refers to the work of S.E. McEvenue, 'The Basis of Empire: A Study of the Succession Narrative', *Ex auditu* 2 (1986), pp. 34-45.

65. Eslinger, *Into the Hands of the Living God*, pp. 123-82.

66. Brueggemann, *Theology of the Old Testament*, p. 608.

67. Fokkelman, *King David*, p. 389. Solomon's wisdom seems to resemble that of Jonadab in 2 Sam. 13.3, an observation in line with Provan's discussion of the 'hermeneutics of suspicion' which this narrative invites; see Provan, 'Why Barzillai of Gilead (1 Kings 2.7)?'.

parative linguistics rather than on the narratological functions of the oath'.[68] I would submit that one of the central functions of oaths in 1 Kings 1–2 is to characterize Solomon and provide a frame of reference for his own speech to be measured.

Second, Solomon's problem with swearing, in my view, serves to unsettle the notion that his career is divided into two parts: a glorious start and powerful reign in the first part, that in the second part finishes poorly with apostasy and the guarantee of a divided kingdom. 'The root of Solomon's downfall', argues Cogan, 'was his many foreign wives, the very danger of which Israel was warned by Moses in Deut. 7.1-4'.[69] Cogan of course has a host of commentators on his side, and, no doubt, Solomon's foreign wives do not assist him in retaining his orthodoxy. But the problem seems deeper than this, and I am tempted to resist the position that Cogan adumbrates. By contrast, I would prefer to argue that the ways in which Solomon 'does things with oaths' lends credence to the idea that despite the appearance that all is well on the surface, there is a negative subtext that flows underneath Solomon's presentation from the earliest parts of the narrative.[70] These opening chapters thus fire a 'warning shot' that sends a signal about Solomon's equivocal language and willingness to bend the rules for himself.

The reader may wonder if Solomon's 'fall' is anticipated, not least because *from the outset* there is a cavalier treatment of oaths. It is conspicuous that Solomon himself does not formally appear in the lengthy opening chapter of 1 Kings until close to the end—yet it would seem that so much of what takes place (especially in the realm of oaths) actually serves a purpose as an intentional component of his characterization. Solomon is indirectly introduced and indeed hovers in the shadows at a far earlier point in the narrative than his first formal appearance. All the earlier language of oaths in 1 Kings 1 is reactivated once Solomon is crowned. The pattern of 'oath creativity' that is manifested before his reign is then revisited afterwards. As has been argued above, Solomon accedes the throne by means of 'creativity' with oaths, and consolidates his power through an equally artistic policy with oaths. The subtle variations in wordings and quotations that infuse the narratives of 1 Kings 1–2 mirror the liberty that is taken with oaths and reflect negatively on David's promised successor.

68. Pyper, *David as Reader*, p. 131.
69. Cogan, *1 Kings*, p. 329.
70. Walsh, *1 Kings*, p. 34: 'on the surface he [Solomon] will be presented generally in a positive light; beneath the surface the narrator will strew gaps and ambiguities that invite a much more critical appraisal of Solomon'. See also Walsh's article, 'The Characterization of Solomon in First Kings 1–5', for a discussion of the wider narrative, M.A. Sweeney, 'The Critique of Solomon in the Josianic Edition of the Deuteronomistic History', *JBL* 114 (1995), pp. 607-22.

As a further example, Solomon's royal claims and dynastic affirmations provide an interesting point of comparison with David, especially with respect to the use of the divine name. James Linville has observed that David tends to use (or is quoted as using) the title 'God of Israel' in 1 Kgs 1.30, 48, whereas Solomon does not:

> The simpler divine name put in Solomon's mouth makes him appear less aware than David of the national or ethnic focus of Yahweh's dealing with the monarchs. A similar impression is gained in comparing David's labeling of Abner and Amasa as the commanders of the forces of Israel in 1 Kgs 2.5 with Solomon's later words on the subject.[71]

Linville then notes that in 1 Kgs 2.32, Solomon changes this wording: 'Abner son of Ner, commander of the army of Israel, and Amasa son of Jether, commander of the army of Judah'. Accordingly, Linville remarks that such use of language has a role in later events in the story: 'Solomon seems not to care about healing the old division, and fittingly, he shall be responsible for the ultimate collapse of the United Monarchy'.[72]

Third, the various things that Solomon 'does' with oaths serves to characterize *him* as 'the swearing issue'. Just as David and Bathsheba 'do things with oaths', so their 'issue' Solomon continues this questionable family tradition. So, on the one hand, he is very much 'his father's son'; that is, Solomon continues the complexity of characterization that is seen in David. Indeed, the narrative seems to overlap these portraits such that the mystery of David (with all the accumulated freight of meaning) is then transposed to his son. Just as David has shown an exceptional capacity for political survival—often resorting to underhanded means—so (the reader is led to believe) Solomon will demonstrate the same resourcefulness. The Shimei affair must be a case in point. David's political sensibilities are manifested in his treatment of Shimei in 2 Samuel 19, and his foresight in 1 Kgs 2.8 is in a similar vein. Solomon is thus encouraged to be politically savvy, just as his father. When Solomon is urged to 'use your wisdom' (with respect to the awkward oath of Shimei) there is a highly effective overlap of *character zones* here between David and Solomon.[73]

---

71. J.R. Linville, *Israel in the Book of Kings: The Past as a Project of Social Identity* (JSOTSup, 272; Sheffield: Sheffield Academic Press, 1998), p. 124.

72. Linville, *Israel in the Book of Kings*, p. 124.

73. Perdue ('"Is there Anyone Left of the House of Saul...?"') outlines two readings of David, the second of which is not particularly flattering. Purdue notes (p. 79): 'In this second reading, David is consistently deceitful, ruthless, and treacherous, with self-interest the driving force behind his speeches and actions. His final oration to Solomon then is not surprising. This speech corresponds to David's statements and actions throughout the narrative. And now Solomon, like his father before him, initiates his reign with the same callous deceit, treachery, and brutality. Indeed, a new David sits on the throne of Israel.'

Yet, on the other hand, Solomon is very much 'his mother's son', and this narrative provides a useful instance of reciprocal characterization: mother and son are both skilled at political posturing, and they both have some aptitude for exercising 'poetic license' when it comes to oaths. A poignant example would be the role Bathsheba played in the 'Adonijah request' of 1 Kgs 2.13-25, an event that shares an important point of similarity with her conduct in 1.17-21.[74] In both scenes Bathsheba approaches a king and elicits an oath that favors (ironically enough) her boy. In the first case the king is David, in the second case the king is her son Solomon. Of course, that Bathsheba should be able to procure such a vociferous 'double oath' from her son, and the fact that Solomon himself later displays such creativity with oaths, should not be all that surprising: Solomon is, after all, the son of Bathsheba, whose name evidently means something like 'daughter of swear-an-oath'!

---

74. See Garsiel, 'Puns upon Names as a Literary Device in 1 Kings 1–2', p. 381.

BIBLIOGRAPHY

Abrams, M.H., *A Glossary of Literary Terms* (New York: Holt, Rinehart & Winston, 1993).
Ackerman, J.S., 'Knowing Good and Evil: A Literary Analysis of the Court History in 2 Samuel 9–20 and 1 Kings 1–2', *JBL* 109 (1990), pp. 41-60.
—'Who Can Stand before YHWH, This Holy God? A Reading of 1 Samuel 1–15', *Prooftexts* 11 (1991), pp. 1-24.
Ackerman, S., 'The Queen Mother and the Cult in Ancient Israel', *JBL* 112 (1993), pp. 385-401.
Ackroyd, P.R., *The First Book of Samuel: Commentary* (New York: Cambridge University Press, 1971).
—*The Second Book of Samuel* (New York: Cambridge University Press, 1977).
Albrektson, B., 'Difficilior lectio probabilior: A Rule of Textual Criticism and its Use in Old Testament Studies', in A.S. van der Woude (ed.), *Remembering All the Way* (OTS, 21; Leiden: E.J. Brill, 1981), pp. 5-18.
Alter, R., *The Art of Biblical Narrative* (New York: Basic Books, 1981).
—*The David Story: A Translation with Commentary of 1 & 2 Samuel* (New York: Norton, 1999).
—*The World of Biblical Literature* (London: SPCK, 1992).
Amit, Y., *Reading Biblical Narratives: Literary Criticism and the Hebrew Bible* (trans. Yael Lotan; Minneapolis: Fortress Press, 2001).
Anderson, A.A., *2 Samuel* (Dallas: Word Books, 1989).
Anderson, W.H.U., 'David as a Biblical "Goodfella" and "The Godfather": Cultural-Social Analogies with Monarchy and *La Cosa Nostra*', *SJOT* 18 (2004), pp. 60-76.
Armerding, C.E., 'Were David's Sons Really Priests?', in G.F. Hawthorne (ed.), *Current Issues in Biblical and Patristic Interpretation: Studies in Honor of Merrill C. Tenney* (Grand Rapids: Eerdmans, 1975), pp. 75-86.
Arnold, B.T., *1 & 2 Samuel* (NIVAC; Grand Rapids: Zondervan, 2003).
—'The Amalekite's Report of Saul's Death: Political Intrigue or Incompatible Sources?', *JETS* 32 (1989), pp. 289-98.
Aschkenasy, N., *Woman at the Window: Biblical Tales of Oppression and Escape* (Detroit: Wayne State University Press, 1998).
Aster, S.Z., 'What was Doeg the Edomite's Title? Textual Emendation versus a Comparative Approach to 1 Samuel 21:8', *JBL* 122 (2003), pp. 353-61.
Auerbach, E., *Mimesis: The Representation of Reality in Western Literature* (trans. W.R. Trask; Princeton, NJ: Princeton University Press, 1953).
Auld, A.G., '1 and 2 Samuel', in J.D.G. Dunn and J.W. Rogerson (eds.), *Eerdmans Commentary on the Bible* (Grand Rapids: Eerdmans, 2003).

—'From King to Prophet in Samuel and Kings', in J.C. de Moor (ed.), *The Elusive Prophet: The Prophet as a Historical Person, Literary Character, and Anonymous Artist* (OTS, 45; Leiden: E.J. Brill, 2001), pp. 31-44.

Auld, A.G., and C.Y.S. Ho, 'The Making of David and Goliath' *JSOT* 56 (1992), pp. 19-39.

Austin, J.L., *How to Do Things with Words* (Cambridge, MA: Harvard University Press, 1962).

Bach, A., 'The Pleasure of her Text', in A. Brenner (ed.), *A Feminist Companion to Samuel and Kings* (A Feminist Companion to the Bible, 5; Sheffield: Sheffield Academic Press, 1994), pp. 106-28.

—*Women, Seduction, and Betrayal in Biblical Narrative* (Cambridge: Cambridge University Press, 1997).

Bailey, R.C., *David in Love and War: The Pursuit of Power in 2 Samuel 10–12* (JSOTSup, 75; Sheffield: JSOT Press, 1990).

Bakhtin, M.M., *The Dialogic Imagination: Four Essays* (ed. M. Holquist; Austin: University of Texas Press, 1981).

—*Problems of Dostoevsky's Poetics* (ed. and trans. C. Emerson; Minneapolis: University of Minnesota Press, 1984).

Bal, M., 'De-disciplining the Eye', *Critical Inquiry* 16 (1990), pp. 506-31.

—*Lethal Love: Feminist Literary Readings of Biblical Love Stories* (Bloomington: Indiana University Press, 1987).

Baldick, C., *The Concise Dictionary of Literary Terms* (Oxford: Oxford University Press, 1990).

Baldwin, J.G., *I and II Samuel: An Introduction and Commentary* (Downers Grove, IL: InterVarsity Press, 1988).

Bar-Efrat, S., *Narrative Art in the Bible* (JSOTSup, 70; Sheffield: Almond Press, 1989).

Barnard, D.T., *With Skilful Hand: The Story of King David* (Montreal: McGill; Kingston: Queen's University Press, 2004).

Barnet, J.A., *Not the Righteous But Sinners: M.M. Bakhtin's Theory of Aesthetics and Problem of Reader–Character Interaction in Matthew's Gospel* (JSNTSup, 246; London/New York: T. & T. Clark, 2003).

Barrick, W.B., 'Saul's Demise, David's Lament and Custer's Last Stand', *JSOT* 73 (1997), pp. 25-41.

Barthélemy, D. (ed.), *Critique textuelle de l'Ancien Testament. I. Josué, Juges, Ruth, Samuel, Rois, Chroniques, Esdras, Néhémie, Esther* (OBO, 50/1; Freiburg: Universitätsverlag; Göttingen: Vandenhoeck & Ruprecht, 1982).

Barthélemy, D., D.W. Gooding, J. Lust, and E. Tov (eds.), *The Story of David and Goliath: Textual and Literary Criticism* (OBO, 73; Freiburg: Editions Universitaires Fribourg; Göttingen: Vandenhoeck & Ruprecht, 1986).

Barthes, R., 'La lutte avec l'ange: Analyse textuelle de Génèse 32.22-33', in R. Barthes *et al.*, *Analyse structurale et exégèse biblique* (Neuchâtel: Delachaux & Niestlé, 1971), pp. 26-39 (ET in *Image, Music, Text* [trans. S. Heath; New York: Hill & Wang, 1977], pp. 125-41).

Ben-Barak, Z., 'The Status and Right of the *Gĕbîrâ*', *JBL* 110 (1991), pp. 23-34.

Bergen, D.A., 'Bakhtin Revisits Deuteronomy: Narrative Theory and the Dialogical Event of Deut. 31.2 and 34.7', *Journal of Hebrew Scriptures* 2, Article 4 (1999) <http://purl.org/jhs>.

Bergen, R.D., *1, 2 Samuel* (NAC; Nashville: Broadman & Holman, 1996).

Birch, B.C., 'The First and Second Books of Samuel', in *NIB*, II, pp. 947-1383.
Blenkinsopp, J., *Gibeon and Israel: The Role of Gibeon and the Gibeonites in the Political and Religious History of Early Israel* (Cambridge: Cambridge University Press, 1972).
—'Structure, Theme, and Motif in the Succession Narrative (2 Samuel 11–20; 1 Kings 1–2) and the History of Human Origins (Genesis 1–11)', in *Treasures Old and New: Essays in the Theology of the Pentateuch* (Grand Rapids: Eerdmans, 2004), pp. 102-19.
Bodner, K., 'The "Embarrassing Syntax" of Psalm 47,10: A (Pro)vocative Option', *JTS* 54 (2003), pp. 570-75.
—'The Locutions of 1 Kings 22.28: A New Proposal', *JBL* 122 (2003), pp. 533-43.
Bowman, R., 'The Complexity of Character and an Ethics of Complexity: The Case of King David', in W.P. Brown (ed.), *Character Ethics and the Bible* (Grand Rapids: Eerdmans, 2001).
Brettler, M.Z., 'The Book of Judges: Literature as Politics', *JBL* 108 (1989), pp. 395-418.
Bright, J., *A History of Israel* (Philadelphia: Westminster Press, 2nd edn, 1972).
Brooks, P., *Reading for the Plot: Design and Intention in Narrative* (Cambridge, MA: Harvard University Press, 1984).
Brueggemann, W., *1 & 2 Kings* (Macon, GA: Smyth & Helwys, 2000).
—'2 Samuel 21–24: An Appendix of Deconstruction?', *CBQ* 50 (1988), pp. 383-97.
—*The Covenanted Self: Explorations in Law and Covenant* (Minneapolis: Fortress Press, 1999).
—*First and Second Samuel* (Interpretation; Louisville, KY: John Knox Press, 1990).
—*Genesis* (Atlanta: John Knox Press, 1982).
—*Theology of the Old Testament* (Minneapolis: Fortress Press, 1997).
Camp, C.V., 'The Wise Women in 2 Samuel: A Role Model for Women in Early Israel?', *CBQ* 43 (1981), pp. 14-29.
Campbell, A.F., *1 Samuel* (FOTL, 7; Grand Rapids: Eerdmans, 2003).
Campbell, A.F., and M.A. O'Brien, *Unfolding the Deuteronomistic History: Origins, Upgrades, Present Text* (Minneapolis: Fortress Press, 2000).
Caspi, M. M., 'Forgotten Meaning: Dialogized Hermeneutics and the Aqedah Narrative', *SJOT* 18 (2004), pp. 93-107.
Ceresko, A.R., 'A Rhetorical Analysis of David's "Boast" (1 Samuel 17.34-37): Some Reflections on Method', *CBQ* 47 (1985), pp. 58-74.
Childs, B.S., *Introduction to the Old Testament as Scripture* (Philadelphia: Fortress Press, 1979).
Claassens, L.J.M., 'Biblical Theology as Dialogue: Continuing the Conversation on Mikhail Bakhtin and Biblical Theology', *JBL* 122 (2003), pp. 127-44.
Clines, D.J.A., and Tamara C. Eskenazi (eds.), *Telling Queen Michal's Story: An Experiment in Comparative Interpretation* (JSOTSup, 119; Sheffield: Sheffield Academic Press, 1991).
Cogan, M., *I Kings: A New Translation with Introduction and Commentary* (AB, 10; New York: Doubleday, 2001).
Cogan, M., and H. Tadmor, *II Kings: A New Translation with Introduction and Commentary* (AB, 11; New York: Doubleday, 1988).
Conroy, C., *1–2 Samuel, 1–2 Kings, with an Excursus on Davidic Dynasty and Holy City Zion* (Wilmington, DE: Michael Glazier, 1983).

—*Absalom, Absalom! Narrative and Language in 2 Samuel 13–20* (Rome: Biblical Institute Press, 1978).
Cook, J.E., 'Hannah and/or Elkanah on their Way Home (1 Samuel 2.11)? A Witness to the Complexity of the Tradition History of the Samuel Texts', *OTE* 3 (1990), pp. 247-62.
—*Hannah's Desire, God's Design: Early Interpretations of the Story of Hannah* (JSOTSup, 282; Sheffield: Sheffield Academic Press, 1999).
Craig, K.M., Jr, 'Rhetorical Aspects of Questions Answered with Silence in 1 Samuel 14:37 and 28:6', *CBQ* 56 (1994), pp. 221-39.
Cryer, F., 'David's Rise to Power and the Death of Abner: An Analysis of I Samuel xxvi 14-16 and the Redactional-Critical Implications', *VT* 35 (1985), pp. 385-94.
Cuddon, J.A., *A Dictionary of Literary Terms and Literary Theory* (Oxford: Basil Blackwell, 3rd edn, 1991).
Dällenbach, L., *The Mirror in the Text* (trans. J. Whiteley with E. Hughes; Cambridge: Polity Press, 1989).
Daube, D., 'Absalom and the Ideal King', *VT* 48 (1998), pp. 315-25.
DeVries, S.J., *1 Kings* (WBC, 12; Waco, TX: Word Books, 1985).
Driver, S.R., *Notes on the Hebrew Text and the Topography of the Books of Samuel* (Oxford: Clarendon Press, 2nd edn, 1913).
Epp, E.J., 'The Oxyrhynchus New Testament Papyri: "Not without Honor except in their Hometown"?', *JBL* 123 (2004), pp. 5-55.
Eslinger, L.M., 'A Change of Heart: 1 Samuel 16', in L. Eslinger and G. Taylor (eds.), *Ascribe to the Lord: Biblical and Other Studies in Memory of Peter C. Craigie* (JSOTSup, 67; Sheffield: JSOT Press, 1988), pp. 341-61.
—*House of God or House of David: The Rhetoric of 2 Samuel 7* (JSOTSup, 164; Sheffield: JSOT Press, 1994).
—'Inner-Biblical Exegesis and Inner-Biblical Allusion: The Question of Category', *VT* 42 (1992), pp. 47-58.
—*Into the Hands of the Living God* (JSOTSup, 84; Sheffield: Almond Press, 1989).
—*Kingship of God in Crisis: A Close Reading of 1 Samuel 1–12* (Bible and Literature Series, 10; Sheffield: Almond Press, 1985).
Evans, C.A., 'David in the Dead Sea Scrolls', in S. Porter *et al.* (eds.), *The Scrolls and the Scriptures: Qumran Fifty Years After* (JSPSup, 26; Roehampton Institute London Papers, 3; Sheffield: Sheffield Academic Press, 1997), pp. 183-97.
Evans, M.J., *1 and 2 Samuel* (NIBC, 6; Peabody, MA: Hendrikson, 2000).
Exum, J.C., *Fragmented Women: Feminist (Sub)versions of Biblical Narratives* (JSOTSup, 163; Sheffield: Sheffield Academic Press, 1993).
—*Tragedy and Biblical Narrative: Arrows of the Almighty* (Cambridge: Cambridge University Press, 1992).
Exum, J.C., and D.J.A. Clines (eds.), *The New Literary Criticism and the Hebrew Bible* (JSOTSup, 143; Sheffield: JSOT Press, 1993).
Fewell, D.N., 'Deconstructive Criticism: Achsah and the (E)razed City of Writing', in G.A Yee (ed.), *Judges and Method: New Approaches in Biblical Studies* (Minneapolis: Fortress Press, 1995), pp. 119-45.
Fewell, D.N. (ed.), *Reading between Texts: Intertextuality and the Hebrew Bible* (Louisville, KY: Westminster/John Knox Press, 1992).
Fish, S., *Is There a Text in This Class? The Authority of Interpretive Communities* (Cambridge, MA: Harvard University Press, 1980).

Flanagan, J.W., 'Court History or Succession Document? A Study of 2 Samuel 9–20 and 1 Kings 1–2', *JBL* 91 (1972), pp. 172-81.

—'Social Transformation and Ritual in 2 Samuel 6', in C.L. Meyers and M.P. O'Connor (eds.), *The Word of the Lord Shall Go Forth: Essays in Honor of David Noel Freedman in Celebration of his Sixtieth Birthday* (Winona Lake, IN: Eisenbrauns, 1983), pp. 361-72.

Fokkelman, J.P., *Narrative Art and Poetry in the Books of Samuel. I. King David (2 Sam. 9–20 and 1 Kings 1–2)* (Assen: Van Gorcum, 1981).

—*Narrative Art and Poetry in the Books of Samuel. II. The Crossing Fates (1 Sam. 13–31 and 2 Sam. 1)* (Assen: Van Gorcum, 1986).

—*Narrative Art and Poetry in the Books of Samuel. III. Throne and City (2 Sam. 2–8 and 21–24)* (Assen: Van Gorcum, 1990).

—*Narrative Art and Poetry in the Books of Samuel. IV. Vow and Desire (1 Sam. 1–12)* (Assen: Van Gorcum, 1993).

Fontaine, C.R., *Traditional Sayings in the Old Testament: A Contextual Study* (Bible and Literature Series, 5; Sheffield: Almond Press, 1982).

Fox, E., *Give Us a King! Samuel, Saul, and David* (New York: Schocken Books, 1999).

Fox, M.V., 'The Uses of Indeterminacy', *Semeia* 71 (1995), pp. 173-92.

Freedman, D.N., 'Dinah and Shechem, Tamar and Amnon', in J.R. Huddlestun (ed.), *Divine Commitment and Human Obligation: Selected Writings of David Noel Freedman* (Grand Rapids: Eerdmans, 1997), pp. 485-95.

Fretheim, T.E., 'The Book of Genesis', in *NIB*, I, pp. 319-674.

—'Divine Foreknowledge, Divine Constancy, and the Rejection of Saul's Kingship', *CBQ* 47 (1985), pp. 595-602.

Freund, E., *The Return of the Reader: Reader-Response Criticism* (London: Methuen, 1987).

Frisch, Amos, '"And David Perceived" (2 Samuel 5,2): A Direct Insight into David's Soul and its Meaning in Context', *SJOT* 18 (2004), pp. 77-92.

Fritz, V., *1 & 2 Kings* (trans. A. Hagedorn; Continental Commentary; Minneapolis: Fortress Press, 2003).

Frolov, S., 'Succession Narrative: A "Document" or a Phantom?', *JBL* 121 (2002), pp. 81-104.

Fuchs, E., 'The Literary Characterization of Mothers and Sexual Politics in the Hebrew Bible', in Alice Bach (ed.), *Women in the Hebrew Bible: A Reader* (New York: Routledge, 1999), pp. 127-39.

García-Treto, F.O., 'A Reader-Response Approach to Prophetic Conflict: The Case of Amos 7.10-17', in Exum and Clines (eds.), *The New Literary Criticism*, pp. 114-24.

Garsiel, M., *The First Book of Samuel: A Literary Study of Comparative Structures, Analogies, Parallels* (Ramat-Gan, Israel: Revivim, 1985).

—'Puns upon Names as a Literary Device in 1 Kings 1–2', *Bib* 72 (1991), pp. 379-86.

—'The Story of David and Bathsheba: A Different Approach', *CBQ* 55 (1993), pp. 244-62.

Genette, G., *Narrative Discourse: An Essay in Method* (trans. J.E. Lewin; Ithaca, NY: Cornell University Press, 1980).

George, M., 'Constructing Identity in 1 Sam 17', *BibInt* 7 (1998), pp. 389-412.

Glück, J.J., 'Merab or Michal', *ZAW* 77 (1965), pp. 72-81.

Goldingay, J., *Old Testament Theology. I. Israel's Gospel* (Downers Grove, IL: InterVarsity Press, 2003).

Gordon, R.P., *1 & 2 Samuel: A Commentary* (Grand Rapids: Zondervan, 1986).

Granowski, J.J., 'Jehoiachin at the King's Table: A Reading of the Ending of the Second Book of Kings', in Fewell (ed.), *Reading between Texts*, pp. 173-88.
Gray, John, *I & II Kings* (OTL; Philadelphia: Westminster Press, 1963).
Green, B., 'Enacting Imaginatively the Unthinkable: 1 Samuel 25 and the Story of Saul', *BibInt* 11 (2004), pp. 1-23.
—*How Are the Mighty Fallen? A Dialogical Study of King Saul in 1 Samuel* (JSOTSup, 365; Sheffield: Sheffield Academic Press, 2003).
—*King Saul's Asking* (Interfaces; Collegeville, MN: Liturgical Press, 2003).
—*Mikhail Bakhtin and Biblical Scholarship: An Introduction* (Atlanta: Society of Biblical Literature, 2000).
Greenberg, M., 'The Use of Ancient Versions for Interpreting the Hebrew Text', in *Congress Volume: Göttingen, 1977* (VTSup, 29; Leiden: E.J. Brill, 1978), pp. 131-48.
Gressmann, H., 'The Oldest History Writing in Israel', in D.M. Gunn (ed.), *Narrative and Novella in Samuel: Studies by Hugo Gressman and Other Scholars 1906–1923* (trans. David E. Orton; JSOTSup, 116; Sheffield: Almond Press, 1991), pp. 9-58.
Gros Louis, K.R.R. 'The Difficulty of Ruling Well: King David of Israel', *Semeia* 8 (1977), pp. 15-33.
Gunkel, H., *Das Märchen im Alten Testament* (Tübingen: J.C.B. Mohr [Paul Siebeck], 1921).
Gunn, D.M., 'David and the Gift of the Kingdom (2 Sam 2–4, 9–20, 1 Kgs 1–2)', *Semeia* 3 (1975), pp. 14-45.
—*The Fate of King Saul* (JSOTSup, 14; Sheffield: Almond Press, 1985).
—'In Security: The David of Biblical Narrative', in J.C. Exum (ed.), *Signs and Wonders: Biblical Texts in Literary Focus* (Semeia Studies; Atlanta: Scholars Press, 1988), pp. 133-52
—'Reflections on David', in A. Brenner and C. Fontaine (eds.), *A Feminist Companion to Reading the Bible: Approaches, Methods and Strategies* (Sheffield: Sheffield Academic Press, 1997), pp. 548-66.
—*The Story of King David* (JSOTSup, 6; Sheffield: JSOT Press, 1978).
Hafemann, S.J. (ed.), *Biblical Theology: Retrospect and Prospect* (Downers Grove, IL: InterVarsity Press, 2002).
Hahn, S.W., 'Kinship by Covenant: A Biblical Theological Analysis of Covenant Types and Texts in the Old and New Testaments' (PhD dissertation, Marquette University, 1995).
Halpern, B., *David's Secret Demons: Messiah, Murderer, Traitor, King* (Grand Rapids: Eerdmans, 2001).
Halpern, B., and J.D. Levenson, 'The Political Import of David's Marriages', *JBL* 99 (1980), pp. 507-18.
Hamilton, V.P., *The Book of Genesis, Chapters 18–20* (NICOT; Grand Rapids: Eerdmans, 1995).
—*Handbook on the Historical Books* (Grand Rapids: Baker Book House, 2001).
Heard, R.C., *Dynamics of Diselection: Ambiguity in Genesis 12–36 and Boundaries in Post-Exilic Judah* (Atlanta: Society of Biblical Literature, 2001).
Hendel, R.S., 'Jacob', in D.N. Freedman (ed.), *Eerdmans Dictionary of the Bible* (Grand Rapids: Eerdmans, 2000), pp. 666-67.
Herrmann, S., *A History of Israel in Old Testament Times* (trans. J. Bowden; Philadelphia: Fortress Press, 1981).

Hertzberg, H.W., *1 & 2 Samuel* (trans. J.S. Bowden; OTL; Philadelphia: Westminster Press, 1964).
Ho, C.Y.S., 'The Stories of the Family Troubles of Judah and David: A Study of their Literary Links', *VT* 49 (1999), pp. 514-31.
Hobbs, T.R., *2 Kings* (WBC, 13; Waco, TX: Word Books, 1985).
Holloway, S.W., 'Distaff, Crutch, or Chain Gang: The Curse on the House of Joab in 2 Samuel iii 29', *VT* 37 (1987), pp. 370-75.
House, Paul R., *1, 2 Kings* (NAC, 8; Nashville: Broadman & Holman, 1995).
—*Old Testament Theology* (Downers Grove, IL: InterVarsity Press, 1998).
Howard, D.M., Jr, 'The Transfer of Power from Saul to David in 1 Sam 16:13-14', *JETS* 32 (1989), pp. 473-83.
Humphreys, W.L., 'From Tragic Hero to Villain: A Study of the Figure of Saul and the Development of 1 Samuel', *JSOT* 22 (1982), pp. 95-117.
Isser, S., *The Sword of Goliath: David in Heroic Literature* (Studies in Biblical Literature, 6; Atlanta: Society of Biblical Literature, 2003).
James, W., *The Principles of Psychology* (New York: Dover Publications, 1918).
Japhet, S., *I & II Chronicles* (OTL; Louisville, KY: Westminster/John Knox Press, 1993).
Jarick, J., *1 Chronicles* (Readings: A New Biblical Commentary; London: Sheffield Academic Press, 2002).
Jobling, D., *1 Samuel* (Berit Olam; Collegeville, MN: Liturgical Press, 1998).
Johnstone, W., *1 & 2 Chronicles. I. 1 Chronicles–2 Chronicles 9, Israel's Place among the Nations* (JSOTSup, 253; Sheffield: Sheffield Academic Press, 1997).
Jones, G.H., *1 and 2 Kings*, I (NCBC; Grand Rapids: Eerdmans, 1984).
—*The Nathan Narratives* (JSOTSup, 80; Sheffield: JSOT Press, 1990).
Josipovici, G., *The Book of God: A Response to the Bible* (New Haven: Yale University Press, 1988).
Kearney, P.J., 'The Role of the Gibeonites in the Deuteronomic History', *CBQ* 35 (1973), pp. 1-19.
Keil, C.F., and F. Delitzsch, *Biblical Commentary on the Books of Samuel* (trans. J. Martin; Grand Rapids: Eerdmans, 1956).
Kessler, J., 'Sexuality and Politics: The Motif of the Displaced Husband in the Books of Samuel', *CBQ* 62 (2000), pp. 409-23.
Kessler, M., 'Narrative Technique in 1 Sm 16, 1-13', *CBQ* 32 (1970), pp. 543-54.
Kirsch, J., *King David: The Real Life of the Man Who Ruled Israel* (New York: Ballantine, 2000).
Klein, L.R., 'Bathsheba Revealed', in A. Brenner (ed.), *Samuel and Kings* (A Feminist Companion to the Bible, Second Series; Sheffield: Sheffield Academic Press, 2000), pp. 47-64.
Klein, R.W., *1 Samuel* (WBC, 10; Waco, TX: Word Books, 1983).
Knierim, R., 'The Messianic Concept of the First Book of Samuel', in F.T. Trotter (ed.), *Jesus and the Historian* (Philadelphia: Westminster Press, 1978), pp. 20-51.
Knoppers, Gary N., 'The Deuteronomist and the Deuteronomic Law of the King: A Reexamination of a Relationship', *ZAW* 108 (1996), pp. 329-46.
—'The Preferential Status of the Eldest Son Revoked?', in S.L. McKenzie and T. Römer (eds.), in collaboration with H.H. Schmid, *Rethinking the Foundations: Historiography in the Ancient World and in the Bible. Essays in Honour of John Van Seters* (BZAW, 294; Berlin: W. de Gruyter, 2000), pp. 115-26.
—'Rehoboam in Chronicles: Villain or Victim?', *JBL* 109 (1990), pp. 423-40.

—*Two Nations under God: The Deuteronomistic History of Solomon and the Dual Monarchies*. I. *The Reign of Solomon and the Rise of Jeroboam* (HSM, 52; Atlanta: Scholars Press 1993).
Knowles, M.P., 'What was the Victim Wearing? Literary, Economic, and Social Contexts for the Parable of the Good Samaritan', *BibInt* 12 (2004), pp. 145-74.
Lasine, S., 'Indeterminacy and the Bible', *HS* 27 (1986), pp. 48-80.
—*Knowing Kings: Knowledge, Power, and Narcissism in the Hebrew Bible* (Semeia Studies, 40; Atlanta: Society of Biblical Literature, 2001).
Lee, B., 'Fragmentation of Reader Focus in the Preamble to Battle in Judges 6.1–7.14', *JSOT* 97 (2002), pp. 65-86.
Leithart, P.J., 'Nabal and his Wine', *JBL* 120 (2001), pp. 525-27.
Lemche, N.P., 'David's Rise', *JSOT* 10 (1978), pp. 2-25.
Levenson, J.D., '1 Samuel 25 as Literature and History', *CBQ* 40 (1978), pp. 11-28.
—*Sinai and Zion: An Entry into the Jewish Bible* (Minneapolis: Winston Press, 1985).
Linville, J.R., *Israel in the Book of Kings: The Past as a Project of Social Identity* (JSOTSup, 272; Sheffield: Sheffield Academic Press, 1998).
Long, B.O., *1 Kings, with an Introduction to Historical Literature* (FOTL, 9; Grand Rapids: Eerdmans, 1984).
—*2 Kings* (FOTL, 10; Grand Rapids: Eerdmans, 1991).
—'A Darkness between Brothers: Solomon and Adonijah', *JSOT* 19 (1981), pp. 79-94.
Long, V.P., *The Reign and Rejection of King Saul: A Case for Literary and Theological Coherence* (Atlanta: Scholars Press, 1989).
Lust, J., 'The Story of David and Goliath in Hebrew and Greek', *Ephemerides theologicae lovanienses* 59 (1983), pp. 5-25.
Mailloux, S., *Interpretive Conventions: The Reader in the Study of American Fiction* (Ithaca, NY: Cornell University Press, 1982).
Mandolfo, C., *God in the Dock: Dialogic Tension in Psalms of Lament* (JSOTSup, 357; Sheffield: Sheffield Academic Press, 2001).
—'"You Meant Evil Against Me": Dialogic Truth and the Character of Jacob in Joseph's Story', *JSOT* 28 (2004), pp. 449-65.
Marcus, D., 'David the Deceiver and David the Dupe', *Prooftexts* 6 (1986), pp. 163-71.
Mauchline, John, *1 and 2 Samuel* (NCB; London: Oliphants, 1971).
McCann, J.C., Jr, *The Book of Psalms*, in *NIB*, IV, pp. 639-1280.
McCarter, P.K., *1 Samuel: A New Translation with Introduction, Notes, and Commentary* (AB, 8; Garden City, NY: Doubleday, 1980).
—*II Samuel: A New Translation with Introduction, Notes and Commentary* (AB, 9; Garden City, NY: Doubleday, 1984).
—'Plots, True and False: The Succession Narrative as Court Apologetic', *Int* 35 (1981), pp. 355-67.
McCarthy, D.F., 'II Samuel 7 and the Structure of the Deuteronomistic History', *JBL* 84 (1965), pp. 131-38.
McConville, J.G., *Deuteronomy* (Apollos Old Testament Commentary, 5; Downers Grove, IL: InterVarsity Press, 2002).
—'The Old Testament Historical Books in Modern Scholarship', *Themelios* 22.3 (1997), pp. 3-13.
McEvenue, S.E., 'The Basis of Empire, A Study of the Succession Narrative', *Ex auditu* 2 (1986), pp. 34-45.

Miller, Owen, 'Intertextual Identity', in M.J. Valdes and O. Miller (eds.), *Identity of the Literary Text* (Toronto: University of Toronto Press, 1985), pp. 19-40.

Miscall, Peter D., *1 Samuel: A Literary Reading* (Bloomington: Indiana University Press, 1986).

—'Michal and her Sisters', in Clines and Eskenazi (eds.), *Telling Queen Michal's Story*, pp. 246-60.

—*The Workings of Old Testament Narrative* (Semeia Studies; Philadelphia: Fortress Press; Chico, CA: Scholars Press, 1983).

Mitchell, C., 'The Dialogism of Chronicles', in M.P. Graham and S.L. McKenzie (eds.), *The Chronicler as Author: Studies in Text and Texture* (JSOTSup, 263; Sheffield: Sheffield Academic Press, 1999), pp. 311-26.

Montgomery, J.A., and H.S. Gehman, *A Critical and Exegetical Commentary on the Books of Kings* (ICC; Edinburgh: T. & T. Clark, 1951).

Mulder, M.J., *1 Kings* (HCOT; Leuven: Peeters, 1998).

Mullen, E.T., Jr, *Narrative History and Ethnic Boundaries: The Deuteronomistic Historian and the Creation of Israelite National Identity* (Atlanta: Scholars Press, 1993).

Murray, D.F., *Divine Prerogative and Royal Pretension: Pragmatics, Poetics and Polemics in a Narrative Sequence about David (2 Samuel 5.17–7.29)* (JSOTSup, 264; Sheffield: Sheffield Academic Press, 1998).

Nelson, R.D., *First and Second Kings* (Interpretation; Atlanta: John Knox Press, 1987).

Newsom, C.A., 'Bakhtin, the Bible, and Dialogic Truth', *JR* 76 (1996), pp. 290-306.

—*The Book of Job: A Contest of Moral Imaginations* (New York: Oxford University Press, 2003).

—'The Book of Job as Polyphonic Text', *JSOT* 26 (2002), pp. 87-108.

Nicol, G.G., 'The Alleged Rape of Bathsheba: Some Observations on Ambiguity in Biblical Narrative', *JSOT* 73 (1997), pp. 43-54.

—'The Death of Joab and the Accession of Solomon: Some Observations on the Narrative of 1 Kings 1–2', *SJOT* 7 (1993), pp. 135-51.

Niditch, S., *War in the Hebrew Bible* (Oxford: Oxford University Press, 1993).

Noth, M., *The Deuteronomistic History* (JSOTSup, 15; Sheffield: JSOT Press, 1981 [originally published 1943]).

—*The History of Israel* (trans. P.R. Ackroyd; New York: Harper & Row, 1960).

O'Brien, J.M., *Nahum* (Readings: A New Biblical Commentary; London: Sheffield Academic Press, 2002).

Olson, D.T., 'The Book of Judges', in *NIB*, II, pp. 721-888.

—'Biblical Theology as Provisional Monologization: A Dialogue with Childs, Brueggemann, and Bakhtin', *BibInt* 6 (1998), pp. 162-80.

Payne, D.F., '1 & 2 Samuel', in D.A. Carson *et al.* (eds.), *New Bible Commentary, 21st Century Edition* (Downers Grove, IL: InterVarsity Press, 1994), pp. 296-333.

Perdue, L.G., '"Is There Anyone Left of the House of Saul...?" Ambiguity and the Characterization of David in the Succession Narrative', *JSOT* 30 (1984), pp. 67-84.

Person, R.F., 'The Ancient Israelite Scribe as Performer', *JBL* 117 (1998), pp. 601-609.

—*The Deuteronomic School: History, Social Setting, and Literature* (Studies in Biblical Literature, 2; Atlanta: Scholars Press, 2002).

Peterson, E.H., *First and Second Samuel* (Louisville, KY: Westminster/John Knox Press, 1999).

—'Why Did Uzzah Die? Why Did David Dance? 2 Samuel 6–7', *Crux* 26.3 (1995), pp. 3-8.

Pfeiffer, R., *Introduction to the Old Testament* (New York: Harper, 1941).
Pisano, S., *Additions or Omissions in the Books of Samuel: The Significant Pluses and Minuses in the Massoretic, LXX, and Qumran Texts* (OBO, 57; Freiburg: Universitätsverlag; Göttingen: Vandenhoeck & Ruprecht, 1984).
Polak, F., 'David's Kingship—A Precarious Equilibrium', in H.G. Reventlow, Y. Hoffman, and B. Uffenheimer (eds.), *Politics and Theopolitics in the Bible and Postbiblical Literature* (JSOTSup, 171; Sheffield: Sheffield Academic Press, 1994), pp. 119-47.
Polzin, R., 'Curses and Kings: A New Reading of 2 Samuel 15–16', in Exum and Clines (eds.), *The New Literary Criticism*, pp. 201-26.
—*David and the Deuteronomist: A Literary Study of the Deuteronomic History*. III. *2 Samuel* (Bloomington: Indiana University Press, 1993).
—*Moses and the Deuteronomist: A Literary Study of the Deuteronomic History*. I. *Deuteronomy, Joshua, Judges* (Bloomington: Indiana University Press, repr., 1993 [1980]).
—*Samuel and the Deuteronomist: A Literary Study of the Deuteronomic History*. II. *1 Samuel* (Bloomington: Indiana University Press, repr., 1993 [1989]).
Powell, M.A., *What is Narrative Criticism?* (London: SPCK, 1993).
Propp, W.H., 'Kinship in 2 Samuel 13', *CBQ* 55 (1993), pp. 39-53.
Prouser, O.H., 'Suited to the Throne: The Symbolic Use of Clothing in the David and Saul Narratives', *JSOT* 71 (1996), pp. 27-37.
Provan, Iain W., *1 and 2 Kings* (NIBC, 7; Peabody, MA: Hendrickson, 1995).
—'On "Seeing" the Trees While Missing the Forest: The Wisdom of Characters and Readers in 2 Samuel & 1 Kings', in E. Ball (ed.), *In Search of True Wisdom: Essays in Old Testament Interpretation in Honour of Ronald E. Clements* (JSOTSup, 300; Sheffield: Sheffield Academic Press, 1999), pp. 153-73.
—'Why Barzillai of Gilead (1 Kings 2.7)? Narrative Art and the Hermeneutics of Suspicion in 1 Kings 1–2', *TynBul* 46 (1995), pp. 103-16.
Pyper, H.S., *David as Reader: 2 Samuel 12.1-15 and the Poetics of Fatherhood* (Biblical Interpretation Series, 23; Leiden: E.J. Brill, 1996).
—'Reading David's Mind: Inference, Emotion and the Limits of Language', in A.G. Hunter and P.R. Davies (eds.), *Sense and Sensitivity: Essays on Reading the Bible in Memory of Robert Carroll* (JSOTSup, 348; Sheffield: Sheffield Academic Press, 2002), pp. 73-86.
Rad, G. von, 'The Beginning of Historical Writing in Ancient Israel', in *The Problem of the Hexateuch and Other Essays* (trans. E.W.T. Dicken; New York: McGraw-Hill, 1966), pp. 116-204.
—*Old Testament Theology*. I. *The Theology of Israel's Historical Traditions* (trans. D.M.G. Stalker; New York: Harper & Row, 1962).
—*The Problem of the Hexateuch and Other Essays* (trans. E.W. Trueman Dicken; Edinburgh: Oliver & Boyd, 1966).
—*Studies in Deuteronomy* (trans. D. Stalker; London: SCM Press, 1953).
Reis, P.T., 'Collusion at Nob: A New Reading of 1 Samuel 21–22', *JSOT* 61 (1994), pp. 59-73.
—'Cupidity and Stupidity: Woman's Agency and the "Rape" of Tamar', *JANES* 25 (1997), pp. 43-60.
—*Reading the Lines: A Fresh Look at the Hebrew Bible* (Peabody, MA: Hendrickson, 2002).

Rendsburg, G.A., 'Confused Language as a Deliberate Literary Device in Biblical Hebrew Narrative', *Journal of Hebrew Scriptures* 2, Article 6 (1999) <http://www.purl.org/jhs>.
—'David and his Circle in Genesis xxxviii', *VT* 36 (1986), pp. 438-46.
—'Reading David in Genesis: How We Know the Torah Was Written in the Tenth Century B.C.E', *BR* 17.1 (2001), pp. 20-33, 46.
—*The Redaction of Genesis* (Winona Lake, IN: Eisenbrauns, 1986).
Rendtorff, R., 'Samuel the Prophet: A Link between Moses and the Kings', in C.A. Evans and S. Talmon (eds.), *The Quest for Context and Meaning: Studies in Biblical Intertextuality in Honor of James A. Sanders* (Leiden: E.J. Brill, 1997), pp. 27-36.
Ridout, G.P., 'Prose Compositional Techniques in the Succession Narrative (2 Sam. 7, 9-10; 1 Kings 1–2)' (PhD dissertation, Graduate Theological Union; Ann Arbor: University Microfilms, 1971).
Riffaterre, M., *Fictional Truth* (Baltimore: The Johns Hopkins University Press, 1990).
Rimmon-Kenan, S., *Narrative Fiction: Contemporary Poetics* (London: Routledge, 1983).
Roberts, J.M.M., 'The Legal Basis for Saul's Slaughter of the Priests at Nob (1 Samuel 21–22)', *JNSL* 25 (1999), pp. 21-29.
Rofé, A., 'Moses' Mother and her Slave-Girl according to 4QExod^b', *Dead Sea Discoveries* 9 (2002), pp. 38-43.
Rosenberg, Joel, '1 and 2 Samuel', in R. Alter and F. Kermode (eds.), *The Literary Guide to the Bible* (Cambridge, MA: Harvard University Press, 1987), pp. 122-45.
—*King and Kin: Political Allegory in the Hebrew Bible* (Bloomington: Indiana University Press, 1986).
Rost, L., *The Succession to the Throne of David* (trans. M. Rutter and D. Gunn; Historic Texts and Interpreters in Biblical Scholarship, 1; Sheffield: Almond Press, 1982).
Roth, P., *The Human Stain* (New York: Vintage, 2000).
Rudman, D., 'The Patriarchal Narratives in the Book of Samuel', *VT* 54 (2004), pp. 239-49.
Sanders, J.A., 'Stability and Fluidity in Text and Canon', in G.J. Norton and S. Pisano (eds.), *Tradition of the Text: Studies Offered to Dominique Barthélemy in Celebration of his 70th Birthday* (OBO, 109; Freiburg: Universitätsverlag; Göttingen: Vandenhoeck & Ruprecht, 1991), pp. 203-17.
—'The Task of Text Criticism', in H.T.C. Sun and K.L. Eades (eds.), with J.M. Robinson and G.I. Moller, *Problems in Biblical Theology: Essays in Honor of Rolf Knierim* (Grand Rapids: Eerdmans, 1997), pp. 315-27.
Satterthwaite, P.E., 'David in the Books of Samuel: A Messianic Expectation?', in P.E. Satterthwaite, R.S. Hess, and G.J. Wenham (eds.), *The Lord's Anointed: Interpretation of Old Testament Messianic Texts* (Grand Rapids: Baker, 1995), pp. 41-65.
Savran, G.W., *Telling and Retelling: Quotation in Biblical Narrative* (Bloomington: Indiana University Press, 1988).
Schearing, L.S., and S.L. McKenzie (eds.), *Those Elusive Deuteronomists: The Phenomenon of Pan-Deuteronomism* (JSOTSup, 268; Sheffield: Sheffield Academic Press, 1999).
Schipper, J., '"Why do you still speak of your affairs?": Polyphony in Mephibosheth's Exchanges with David in 2 Samuel', *VT* 54 (2004), pp. 344-51.
Schley, D.G., 'Joab', in *ABD*, III, pp. 852-54.
—'Joab and David: Ties of Blood and Power', in M.P. Graham, W.P. Brown, and J.K. Kuan (eds.), *History and Interpretation: Essays in Honour of John H. Hayes* (JSOTSup, 173; Sheffield: JSOT Press, 1993), pp. 90-105.

Schniedewind, W.M., *Society and the Promise to David: The Reception History of 2 Samuel 7.1-17* (New York: Oxford University Press, 1999).
Scholes, R., and R. Kellogg, *The Nature of Narrative* (New York: Oxford University Press, 1966).
Schwartz, R.M., 'Adultery in the House of David: The Metanarrative of Biblical Scholarship and the Narratives of the Bible', *Semeia* 54 (1991), pp. 35-55.
Seibert, E.A., 'Propaganda and Subversion in the Solomonic Narrative: Scribes, Historiography, and the Rhetoric of Persuasion' (PhD dissertation, Drew University, 2002).
Seitz, C.R., *Word without End: The Old Testament as Abiding Theological Witness* (Grand Rapids: Eerdmans, 1998).
Seow, C.L., '1 & 2 Kings', in *NIB*, III, pp. 3-295.
Simon, U., 'Minor Characters in Biblical Narrative', *JSOT* 46 (1990), pp. 11-19.
—*Reading Prophetic Narratives* (Bloomington: Indiana University Press, 1997).
Smith, H.P., *A Critical and Exegetical Commentary on the Books of Samuel* (ICC; Edinburgh: T. & T. Clark, 1899).
Spina, F., 'Eli's Seat: The Transition from Priest to Prophet in 1 Samuel 1–4', *JSOT* 62 (1994), pp. 67-75.
—'A Prophet's "Pregnant Pause": Samuel's Silence in the Ark Narrative (1 Samuel 4.1–7.12)', *Horizons in Biblical Theology* 13 (1991), pp. 59-73.
Sternberg, M., *The Poetics of Biblical Narrative: Ideological Literature and the Drama of Reading* (Bloomington: Indiana University Press, 1985).
Steussy, M.J., *David: Biblical Portraits of Power* (Columbia: University of South Carolina Press, 1999).
Stoebe, H.J., *Das erste Buch Samuelis* (KAT, 8.1; Gütersloh: Gerd Mohn, 1973).
Stone, K., *Sex, Honor and Power in the Deuteronomistic History* (JSOTSup, 234; Sheffield: Sheffield Academic Press, 1996).
Sweeney, M.A., 'The Critique of Solomon in the Josianic Edition of the Deuteronomistic History', *JBL* 114 (1995), pp. 607-22.
—*King Josiah of Judah: The Lost Messiah of Israel* (New York: Oxford University Press, 2001).
Sykes, S., 'Time and Space in Haggai–Zechariah 1–8: A Bakhtinian Analysis of a Prophetic Chronicle', *JSOT* 76 (1997), pp. 97-124.
Talmon, S., 'The Presentation of Synchroneity and Simultaneity in Biblical Narrative', in J. Heinemann and S. Werses (eds.), *Studies in Hebrew Narrative Art throughout the Ages* (Scripta hierosolymitana, 27; Jerusalem: Magnes Press, 1978), pp. 9-26.
Teshima, I., 'Textual Criticism and Early Biblical Interpretation'. in J. Krašovec (ed.), *The Interpretation of the Bible* (JSOTSup, 289; Sheffield: Sheffield Academic Press, 1998), pp. 165-79.
Thiselton, A.C., 'The Supposed Power of Words in the Biblical Writings', *JTS* 25 (1974), pp. 283-99.
Thompson, S., *Motif-Index of Folk Literature* (6 vols.; Copenhagen: Rosenkilde & Bagger, 1955–58).
Toorn, K. vander, and C. Houtman, 'David and the Ark', *JBL* 113 (1994), pp. 209-31.
Tov, E., 'The Composition of 1 Samuel 16–18 in the Light of the Septuagint Version', in J.H. Tisgay (ed.), *Empirical Modes for Biblical Criticism* (Philadelphia: University of Pennsylvania Press, 1985), pp. 97-130.
Traugott, E.C., and M.L. Pratt, *Linguistics for Students of Literature* (New York: Harcourt, Brace, Jovanovich, 1980).

Trible, P., *Texts of Terror: Literary-Feminist Readings of Biblical Narratives* (Philadelphia: Fortress Press, 1984).
Tull, P., 'Intertextuality and the Hebrew Scriptures', *Currents in Research: Biblical Studies* 8 (2000), pp. 59-90.
Turner, L.A., *Genesis* (Readings: A New Biblical Commentary; Sheffield: Sheffield Academic Press, 2000).
Ulrich, E.C., *The Qumran Text of Samuel and Josephus* (HSM, 19; Missoula, MT: Scholars Press, 1978).
Ulrich, E.C. et al., *Qumran Cave 4. VII. Genesis to Numbers* (DJD, 12; Oxford: Clarendon Press, 1994).
Van Seters, J., *In Search of History: Historiography in the Ancient World and the Origins of Biblical History* (New Haven: Yale University Press, 1983).
Vanderhooft, D., 'Dwelling beneath the Sacred Place: A Proposal for Reading 2 Samuel 7:10', *JBL* 118 (1999), pp. 625-33.
VanderKam, J.C., 'Davidic Complicity in the Deaths of Abner and Eshbaal', *JBL* 94 (1980), pp. 521-39.
Walsh, J.T., *1 Kings* (Berit Olam; Collegeville, MN: Liturgical Press, 1996).
—'The Characterization of Solomon in 1 Kings 1–5', *CBQ* 57 (1995), pp. 471-93.
Walters, S.D., 'Hannah and Anna: The Greek and Hebrew Texts of 1 Samuel 1', *JBL* 107 (1988), pp. 385-412.
—'Saul of Gibeon', *JSOT* 52 (1991), pp. 61-76.
Waltke, B.K., and M.P. O'Connor, *An Introduction to Biblical Hebrew Syntax* (Winona Lake, IN: Eisenbrauns, 1990).
Weingreen, J., 'The Rebellion of Absalom', *VT* 19 (1969), pp. 263-66.
Weippert, H., ' "Histories and 'History'": Promise and Fulfillment in the Deuteronomistic Historical Work', in G.N. Knoppers and J.G. McConville (eds.), *Reconsidering Israel and Judah: Recent Studies on the Deuteronomistic History* (trans. P.T. Daniels; Winona Lake, IN: Eisenbrauns, 2000), pp. 47-61 (ET of 'Geschichten und Geschichte: Verheissung und Erfüllung im deuteronomistischen Geschichtswerk', in J.A. Emerton [ed.], *Congress Volume: Leuven, 1989* [VTSup, 43; Leiden: E.J. Brill, 1991], pp. 116-31).
Wenham, G.J., *Genesis 16–50* (WBC, 2; Dallas: Word Books, 1994).
Wesselius, J.W., 'Collapsing the Narrative Bridge', in J.W. Dyk et al. (eds.), *Unless Some One Guide Me: Festschrift for Karel A. Deurloo* (Amsterdamse cahiers voor exegese van de Bijbel en zijn tradities, Supplement Series, 2; Maastricht: Shaker, 2001), pp. 247-55.
—'Joab's Death and the Central Theme of the Succession Narrative (2 Samuel ix–1 Kings ii)', *VT* 40 (1990), pp. 336-51.
Whedbee, J.W., 'On Divine and Human Bonds: The Tragedy of the House of David', in G.M. Tucker, D.L. Petersen, and R.R. Wilson (eds.), *Canon, Theology, and Old Testament Interpretation: Essays in Honor of Brevard S. Childs* (Philadelphia: Fortress Press, 1988), pp. 147-65.
White, H.C., Review of Pyper, *David as Reader*, *CBQ* 60 (1998), pp. 341-42.
—'The Trace of the Author in the Text', *Semeia* 71 (1995), pp. 45-64.
Whybray, R.N., *The Succession Narrative: A Study of II Samuel 9–20 and I Kings 1–2* (London: SCM Press, 1968).
Wiggins, S.A., 'Between Heaven and Earth: Absalom's Dilemma', *JNSL* 23 (1997), pp. 73-81.

Willey, P.W., 'The Importunate Woman of Tekoa and How She Got her Way', in Fewell (ed.), *Reading between Texts*, pp. 115-31.
Willis, J.T., 'An Anti-Elide Narrative Tradition from a Prophetic Circle at the Ramah Sanctuary', *JBL* 90 (1971), pp. 288-308.
Wimmers, I.C., *Poetics of Reading: Approaches to the Novel* (Princeton, NJ: Princeton University Press, 1988).
Wolde, E. van, 'Texts in Dialogue with Texts: Intertextuality in the Ruth and Tamar Narratives', *BibInt* 5 (1997), pp. 1-28.
Wyatt, N., ' "Jedidiah" and Cognate Forms as a Title of Royal Legitimation', *Bib* 66 (1985), pp. 112-25.
Yadin, A., 'Goliath's Armor and Israelite Collective Memory', *VT* 54 (2004), pp. 373-95.
Yee, G.A., ' "Fraught with Background": Literary Ambiguity in 2 Samuel 11', *Int* 42 (1988), pp. 240-53.

INDEXES

INDEX OF REFERENCES

Hebrew Bible		2.3a	89	9.54	96, 137
Genesis		2.3b	89, 97	18.14-20	119
1.15-16	143	2.5	90	21.25	109
17.17	94	21.12	160		
18.21	131	21.14	160	*Ruth*	
19	142	35–40	123	2.7	119
22.3	136			4.1	28
24	143, 144	*Leviticus*			
24.1	143	1.11	116	*1 Samuel*	
25	145, 146, 151	5.4	173	1–2	116
				1	123
25.23	148	*Numbers*		1.17	114
25.27	145, 146	3.29	116	1.23	114, 115, 123
25.28	146	3.35	116		
25.29-34	147	30.13	114	2	37
26	143, 144	32.24	114	2.20	35
27	7, 9, 140, 142-44, 146, 149-52, 173			2.21	35
		Deuteronomy		2.27-36	3, 34
		7.1-4	174	2.31-34	58
		8.3	114	2.33	35
27.1-40	147	13.6	56	3	13, 37
27.1	147	16.18	56, 116	3.25	53, 54
27.3-4	145	17.16-17	171	4–6	54
27.7	145	19.1-10	160	4.11	34
27.41-46	149	21.19	56, 116	8	83
27.41	94	23.24	114	8.20	86
30.39	143	25.7	56, 116	9.5	30
32	42			9.12-13	119
37.28	119	*Joshua*		9.17	36
37.30	119	9.5	145	10	14
38	140, 141, 152	13.1	143	10.2	30
		23.1	143	10.15	4
				13.14	45, 65, 66
Exodus		*Judges*		14	91
1–2	90	9	117, 118, 123	14.7	65
1.15-21	90			14.21	119
2.3	89, 90	9.50-54	106	14.37	33

1 Samuel (cont.)		19	37, 150	2.27	44	
14.52	30	19.17	37	2.31	59	
15.13	114	19.18	27	3	4, 9, 38,	
16	1, 2, 10,	20	37		41, 42, 44-	
	11, 13, 15,	20.1	21, 27		47, 55, 57,	
	16, 20, 77	21–22	25, 34		60, 62, 64,	
16.1-13	13, 22	21	3, 25, 26,		65, 105,	
16.1-11	13		31, 32, 37		115, 116,	
16.1	13	21.1-10	25, 36		128	
16.3	13	21.2-4	26	3.1-5	44, 45	
16.4	27	21.2	27	3.1	45	
16.6-7	10, 22, 23	21.4	28	3.6-11	46	
16.6	13, 23	21.8	27, 28, 32,	3.6	45, 46,	
16.7	2, 14-16,		36		104	
	19, 21	21.9	30	3.7	45, 46,	
16.13	11, 14	21.10-11a	31		105	
16.21	91	21.11	31	3.8	43, 48, 59,	
17	2, 10-12,	22	52		104	
	16, 20, 23,	22.1-4	20	3.9-10	50	
	31, 77	22.6b-10	32	3.12	49	
17.9	11	22.7	32	3.16	51	
17.12	143	22.9-10	31	3.17-21	51	
17.22-23	19	22.14-15	27	3.17-18	51	
17.23-30	10, 22, 23	22.15a	33	3.18b	51	
17.23-29	16	22.20-23	35	3.22-39	103, 104	
17.23-27	17	22.22-23	35	3.22-29	104	
17.23	19	23.6	36	3.22-26	52	
17.25	17	25.44	51	3.24-25	104, 105	
17.26	17	26	57	3.27-30	56	
17.28-30	18	26.14	49	3.27	43, 56, 57,	
17.28-29	11	26.15	4		104, 115	
17.28	2, 10-12,	26.16	55	3.28-39	107	
	18, 22	26.18	21	3.28-29	62	
17.29	1, 12, 18	27	55	3.30	57, 105	
17.32-37	18	29.8	21	3.31-34	59	
17.38	119	30.26	53	3.33	59	
17.54	27	31.4	137	3.35-39	61	
17.55	4			3.36-37	41, 42, 61-	
18	26, 50	*2 Samuel*			63, 65	
18.1	37	1	108, 122	3.37	55, 62	
18.6	59	2	42	4	108, 122	
18.11	94	2.8-9	49	4.12	49	
18.16	84	2.12-32	57	7	4, 5, 51,	
18.17-29	18	2.22	43		65, 67, 69,	
18.20	37	2.23	43, 56		71, 72, 77,	
19–22	3, 26	2.26-27	43		159, 163	

Index of References

7.1-17	68	11.2	23, 91, 127	12.1-4	71
7.1-3	68			12.2	23
7.3-16	70	11.3	5, 7, 20, 84, 90-93, 95-97, 124-27	12.4	23
7.4-8a	68			12.7-14	159
7.4-7	69			12.9	23
7.4	69			12.10	7
7.5-7	69	11.3a	94	12.11-12	130
7.5a	69	11.3b	84, 92-97	12.11	23, 127
7.5b	69	11.4	92	12.12-32	43
7.5c-7	69	11.6	92, 100	12.13-15	71
7.5c-7a	69	11.7	23, 96	12.24-25	70, 72, 151
7.7b	69	11.11	107		
7.11b-17	68	11.12	92	12.24	135
7.12	72	11.14-25	98, 99, 104	12.25	73, 148, 155
7.18	87				
8	80	11.14-15	99-101	12.28	111
8.16	57	11.14	92, 100	13–14	162
9	77	11.15-20	96	13.1-2	91
9.4	43	11.15	116	13.3	173
10–12	80	11.16-24	106	14	71, 107, 111
10	77, 80, 81, 86	11.16-17	101, 117		
		11.17	108	14.25-26	134
10.1-5	83	11.18-22	105	15–18	162
10.1	86	11.18-21	110, 117	15–17	7, 124, 138, 139
10.2	81	11.19-24	108		
10.3	55	11.19-21	91	15	7, 97, 137
10.6	81	11.20	108	15.1	154
10.8	81	11.21	96	15.12	124-26, 130, 136
11	2, 5-7, 9, 22, 23, 64, 77-79, 85-88, 90, 91, 95-100, 102-106, 109, 111, 120, 123, 126, 130, 138, 143-45, 156	11.22-25	6, 112, 113, 116		
				15.16	128
		11.22	108, 112	15.31-37	135
		11.23-25	108	15.31	126, 135
		11.23-24	108	15.32-37	129
		11.23	96, 108, 119	15.34	126
				15.37	127
		11.23a	119	16.5-14	163
		11.24	96	16.12	172
		11.25	23, 96, 109	16.15	127
				16.20-22	127
11.1-4	79	11.27	135	16.20-21	127
11.1-3	91	12	2, 5, 23, 67, 88, 91, 138, 145	16.20	127, 131
11.1	5, 78-85, 88, 92, 100			16.21-22	95
				16.21	127, 132
		12.1-15	70	16.22-23	41
11.1a	80, 81, 86	12.1-7	71	16.22	130

2 Samuel (cont.)		36.37	4	1.25	159	
16.23	124, 125, 130, 138	*1 Kings*		1.27	75	
				1.28	158	
17.1-2	131	1–2	153-55, 174	1.29-31	158, 159	
17.3-4	132			1.29-30	159, 162, 163	
17.4	133	1	5, 7, 9, 22, 67, 72, 128, 140, 142-44, 146-53, 155, 158, 161, 162, 174	1.30	175	
17.7	133			1.48	175	
17.14	134, 135, 137, 138			1.50-53	160	
				1.51-53	166, 169	
17.17	155			1.51-52	8, 153	
17.22	135			1.51	162, 169	
17.23	135, 136, 139			2	1, 64, 162, 163, 165, 167	
17.27-29	43	1.1-31	72			
18	137	1.1-10	148			
18.2-4	82	1.1	143, 147, 156	2.2-9	18, 165, 172	
18.9	134					
18.14	96	1.2-4	162	2.4	162	
18.24	96	1.2	158	2.5	175	
19	64, 175	1.4	147, 156	2.6	111	
19.5-7	111	1.5-10	154	2.8-9	162-64, 170	
19.7	64	1.5-9	162			
19.16-23	138	1.5	155	2.8	8, 153, 162, 165, 169, 172, 175	
19.18-23	164	1.7	146			
19.21	164	1.8	72			
19.23-24	164	1.9-10	146			
19.23	164	1.10	72	2.9	172	
19.24	165	1.11-21	168	2.11	162	
20	64	1.11-18	8	2.13-25	167, 176	
20.10	104	1.11-14	73	2.15b	167	
21.8	46	1.13	8, 147, 153, 154, 162	2.17	161	
21.17	82			2.19	150, 154	
23	93, 102			2.20	154, 168	
23.34	7, 96, 124-27	1.15-21	74	2.22	147	
		1.15	147, 156, 158	2.23-25	166, 168	
23.34b	126			2.23-24	8, 153, 169	
23.37	90	1.16	75			
23.39	102, 121	1.17-21	176	2.23b	169	
27.3	145	1.17-18	156, 157	2.24	173	
27.5	145	1.17	8, 147, 153, 162	2.25	169	
27.11-12	145			2.26-35	169	
27.18-30	145	1.22-27	75	2.27	34	
27.19	145	1.23	75	2.27b	34	
27.25	145	1.24-25	157	2.32	175	
27.30	145	1.24	75	2.33	172, 173	
27.32	145	1.24ab	169	2.34	6	

2.36-46	171	*1 Chronicles*		Talmud		
2.36-37	170	11.39	90	*Sanhedrin*		
2.37	170, 172	19.2	81	69b	125	
2.39-41	171	20.1	80-82	101a	125	
2.41-46	170	27.18	20			
2.42-43	169	29.29	76	Josephus		
2.42	8, 153, 170, 171			*Antiquities*		
2.43	162, 171	*2 Chronicles*		7.7.1	5, 91	
2.45	172, 173	9.29	76	7.131	90	
3	172	36.10	80			
3.1-3	172			Classical		
3.1	171	*Psalms*		Homer		
3.3	172	20.5	65	*Iliad*		
1,29	153			6.168-90	101	
10.14	171	*Isaiah*				
10.26-28	171	44.26	114			
11	161, 172					
12	64	*Jeremiah*				
12.15	114	17.16	114			
12.16	64	33.14	114			
15.13	154	35.16	114			
16.18	137					
20.22	80	*Amos*				
20.26	80	3.14	160			
27	142	7	99			
		New Testament				
2 Kings		*Matthew*				
6.8	28	27.5	137			
20.19	94					
25	63					

INDEX OF AUTHORS

Ackerman, J.S. 23, 124, 125, 134
Ackerman, S. 154
Ackroyd, P.R. 58, 117
Albrektson, B. 82
Alter, R. 1, 13, 17, 19, 28, 30, 36, 44,
    51, 53, 71, 72, 74, 78, 82, 91,
    100-104, 107, 108, 114, 127, 138,
    141, 144, 150, 151, 155, 156,
    159, 161, 168, 172
Anderson, A.A. 67, 69, 80, 90, 94, 103,
    125, 135
Anderson, W.H.U. 172
Arnold, B.T. 25, 34, 43
Aschkenasy, N. 144, 168
Aster, S.Z. 30
Auerbach, E. 104, 124
Auld, A.G. 10, 36, 44, 45, 53
Austin, J.L. 155

Bach, A. 144, 156
Bailey, R.C. 21, 93, 108, 125
Bakhtin, M.M. 3, 11, 15, 39-41, 109,
    110, 151
Bal, M. 78, 100, 106, 107, 117, 123, 144
Baldick, C. 29
Baldwin, J.G. 135
Bar-Efrat, S. 133
Barnet, J.A. 38
Barthélemy, D. 10, 120
Barthes, R. 83
Ben-Barak, Z. 154
Bergen, D.A. 110
Bergen, R.D. 22, 59, 81, 106, 129
Birch, B.C. 10, 26, 31, 33, 35, 37, 49,
    50, 53, 57, 60, 64
Blenkinsopp, J. 141
Brettler, M.Z. 142
Brooks, P. 29
Brueggemann, W. 13, 22, 47, 50, 53,
    59, 60, 62, 66, 69, 79, 86, 88, 91,
    92, 100, 103, 106, 107, 130, 144,
    151, 153, 156, 169, 170, 172, 173

Campbell, A.F. 25, 34, 114
Caspi, M.M. 38
Ceresko, A.R. 60
Childs, B.S. 66
Claassens, L.J.M. 12
Cogan, M. 94, 143, 147, 154, 158, 160,
    164, 172, 174
Conroy, C. 117
Cook, J.E. 114, 115
Cross, F.M. 89
Cryer, F. 105
Cuddon, J.A. 95, 98

Dällenbach, L. 54
Daube, D. 125
Delitzsch, F. 54
DeVries, S.J. 75, 151, 158, 165, 167,
    170
Driver, S.R. 114, 116

Epp, E.J. 113
Eslinger, L.M. 6, 13, 14, 22, 69, 70,
    114, 149, 153, 173
Evans, C.A. 97
Exum, J.C. 1, 49, 50, 52, 54, 57, 58, 60,
    93, 100, 155, 163, 168

Fewell, D.N. 166
Fish, S. 99
Flanagan, J.W. 50
Fokkelman, J.P. 10, 13, 15, 19, 22, 32,
    33, 37, 65, 72, 74-76, 83, 109,
    127-32, 136, 138, 143, 164, 168,
    169, 171, 173
Fontaine, C.R. 14

Fox, E. 77, 78, 83
Fox, M.V. 78
Freedman, D.N. 148
Fretheim, T.E. 42
Freund, E. 98
Fritz, V. 153
Frolov, S. 43, 64
Fuchs, E. 154

García-Treto, F.O. 99
Garsiel, M. 11, 18, 81, 85, 101, 102, 144, 154, 171, 176
Gehman, H.S. 158
Genette, G. 29
George, M. 17
Goldingay, J. 66
Gooding, D.W. 10
Gordon, R.P. 29, 133
Granowski, J.J. 149
Gray, J. 160
Green, B. 16, 25, 33, 36, 38, 110
Greenberg, M. 6
Gressmann, H. 60, 125
Gros Louis, K.R.R. 21
Gunkel, H. 101, 116, 117
Gunn, D.M. 13, 20, 21, 48, 63, 116, 122, 135, 136, 169

Hahn, S.W. 169
Halpern, B. 21, 25, 44, 45, 47, 49, 126-28, 152, 153, 155
Hamilton, V.P. 25, 46, 151
Heard, R.C. 43, 150
Hendel, R.S. 150
Hertzberg, H.W. 10, 29, 54-56, 60, 64, 114, 121, 128, 129, 131-33, 137, 139
Ho, C.Y.S. 10, 141, 148
Hobbs, T.R. 94
Holloway, S.W. 58
House, P.R. 165

Isser, S. 165

James, W. 95
Japhet, S. 20

Jobling, D. 34, 109, 141
Johnstone, W. 20
Jones, G.H. 67, 72, 160
Josipovici, G. 1, 63, 134

Keil, C.F. 54
Kellogg, R. 95
Kessler, J. 13, 44, 45
Klein, L.R. 144, 168
Klein, R.W. 19
Knoppers, G.N. 37, 150, 153, 163, 171
Knowles, M.P. 38

Lasine, S. 55, 158
Lee, B. 146
Lemche, N.P. 105
Levenson, J.D. 44, 45, 127
Linville, J.R. 175
Long, B.O. 75, 94, 151, 153, 157, 160-62
Long, V.P. 13
Lust, J. 10

Mailloux, S. 98, 99
Mandolfo, C. 38
Marcus, D. 21
Mauchline, J. 10, 14, 27, 81, 131, 132
McCarter, P.K. 19, 30, 34, 42, 44, 45, 48, 51, 65-67, 69, 80, 81, 90, 93, 94, 101, 102, 106, 108, 114, 126, 128, 131, 135-37, 153
McConville, J.G. 163, 171
McEvenue, S.E. 173
McKenzie, S.L. 11
Miller, O. 149
Miscall, P.D. 19, 32, 115, 166
Mitchell, C. 38
Montgomery, J.A. 158
Mulder, M.J. 143, 153, 164, 165
Mullen, E.T., Jr 34
Murray, D.F. 163

Nelson, R.D. 34, 73, 172
Newsom, C.A. 12, 38
Nicol, G.G. 104, 105, 149, 168

O'Brien, J.M. 149
O'Brien, M.A. 34
O'Connor, M.P. 46, 131
Olson, D.T. 12, 38

Payne, D.F. 80
Perdue, L.G. 16, 21, 120, 175
Person, R.F. 11, 90
Pisano, S. 112, 116, 119
Polak, F. 21, 90, 91, 96, 138, 148
Polzin, R. 11-16, 18, 26, 34, 38, 43, 44, 49, 57, 59, 61, 62, 69, 71, 77, 82-84, 86, 100, 109, 115, 138, 164
Powell, M.A. 29
Pratt, M.L. 132
Prouser, O.H. 143
Provan, I.W. 103, 150, 151, 154, 155, 164, 165, 172, 173
Pyper, H.S. 15, 63, 71, 101, 102, 174

Rad, G. von 26, 34, 124, 138
Reis, P.T. 25, 27, 28, 30, 32
Rendsburg, G.A. 119, 140-42, 150
Rendtorff, R. 13
Ridout, G.P. 122
Riffaterre, M. 29
Rimmon-Kenan, S. 29
Roberts, J.M.M. 30
Rofé, A. 89, 90, 97
Rosenberg, J. 21, 84, 122, 149, 171
Roth, P. 47
Rudman, D. 141

Sanders, J.A. 113, 116, 123
Savran, G.W. 145, 147, 155, 157, 159, 165
Schearing, L.S 11
Schipper, J. 48
Schley, D.G. 110
Schniedewind, W.M. 163
Scholes, R. 95
Seibert, E.A. 167
Seitz, C.R. 37
Seow, C.L. 153, 167, 173

Simon, U. 80, 82, 87, 90, 97, 119
Smith, H.P. 10, 20, 81, 108, 112
Sternberg, M. 13, 14, 29, 78, 85, 91, 95, 100, 102, 107-109, 122, 123, 143, 156
Steussy, M.L. 20, 82, 86, 108
Stoebe, H.J. 116
Sweeney, M.A. 174
Sykes, S. 12

Tadmor, H. 94
Talmon, S. 42, 146
Teshima, I. 79
Thompson, S. 116, 117
Tov, E. 10
Traugott, E.C. 132
Trible, P. 109
Tull, P. 12
Turner, L.A. 145, 146

Ulrich, E.C. 89, 90, 115

Van Seters, J. 34
Vanderhooft, D. 163
VanderKam, J.C. 58, 105

Walsh, J.T. 75, 150, 154-56, 158, 161-63, 165, 166, 168, 169, 171, 172, 174
Walters, S.D. 114, 115, 131
Waltke, B.K. 46
Weippert, H. 35
Wenham, G.J. 145
Wesselius, J.W. 27, 95, 104, 144
Whedbee, J.W. 21, 85
White, H.C. 12, 101
Whybray, R.N. 130, 168
Wiggins, S.A. 134
Wimmers, I.C. 102
Wolde, E. van 142
Wyatt, N. 72

Yee, G.A. 78, 86-88, 93, 100, 144

www.ingramcontent.com/pod-product-compliance
Lightning Source LLC
Chambersburg PA
CBHW070943230426
43666CB00011B/2538